S0-BSG-011

Khul-Khaal

Contemporary Issues in the Middle East

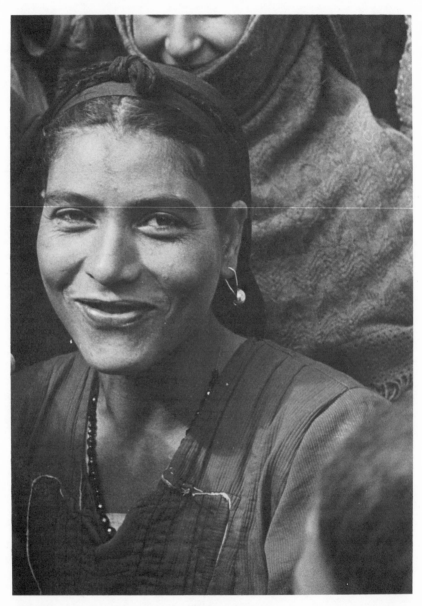

"I woke up one day when I was a youngster and opened my eyes suddenly and found that I was grown up."—Om Gad. Photograph by Asma el-Bakry.

Khul-Khaal

FIVE EGYPTIAN WOMEN TELL THEIR STORIES

Nayra Atiya

SYRACUSE UNIVERSITY PRESS   1982

Copyright © 1982 by Syracuse University Press
Syracuse, New York 13210

All Rights Reserved

First Edition

Atiya, Nayra.
  Khul-Khaal, five Egyptian women tell their stories.
  (Contemporary issues in the Middle East)
  Consists of stories recorded on tape, which were
translated, arranged, and written by Nayra Atiya.
  1. Women—Egypt—Biography.   2. Women, Muslim—
Biography.   3. Fate and fatalism.   I. Title.
II. Series.
HQ1793.A87   305.4'0962   82-5773
ISBN 0-8156-0177-8   AACR
ISBN 0-8156-0181-6 (pbk.)

Manufactured in the United States of America

Contents

74439

NAYRA ATIYA is a writer and painter. She received the M.A. in French from Harvard University, has taught college-level language and literature, and has worked as a journalist and illustrator for the *Egyptian Gazette,* Cairo.

ANDREA RUGH received the Ph.D. in social anthropology from American University. She has lived in the Middle East for twelve years, including six in Egypt, and is a USAID consultant, author, and lecturer on women, education, and poverty of the region. In 1978 Rugh initiated a self-help project for poor women in Cairo that is now operating independently.

ASMA EL-BAKRY, the photographer, is a young Egyptian woman film director who has made five documentaries, worked on dozens of feature films such as *Death on the Nile* and *The Mummy,* as well as having been Egyptian production manager for "Cosmos" and the National Geographic film, *Egypt: Quest for Eternity.*

Foreword

I WOKE UP one day when I was a youngster ... and found that I was grown up." So Om Gad starts her story. "I found myself alone. I had neither brother nor sister nor a maternal aunt to turn to in an hour of need, nor a paternal aunt on whom I could call for help." The story will take us through an extended discussion of this Egyptian woman's ill-fated life, of children dying, her husband's hard work, the struggle to raise and launch the remaining children in marriage and careers. Om Gad and her husband Omar take care of cars parked in the basement of an apartment building in an affluent neighborhood of Cairo. To supplement their income, Omar makes minor repairs and runs errands for tenants while Om Gad helps with the polishing of cars and does small cleaning jobs.

Om Gad's story is one of the five oral histories found in these pages. All the women whose stories are reproduced here have in common the fact that they presently reside in an urban environment though four have origins in smaller provincial communities. In that respect they represent what is typical in Egypt in recent years, a rapid increase in the numbers of those moving from rural to urban environments. All the women in one way or another are attempting to survive in the monied economy of city life. Four of the women come from the lower social classes and one from the middle class. Class in the Egyptian context is a complicated phenomenon that does not correspond with the term in a western setting. Though it includes such factors as income, occupation, and style of life, perhaps one significant boundary between the middle and lower classes is the extent of education an individual receives. Three of the women in the stories have had little if any education; the fourth left school after the sixth grade. It was only Alice who continued on to the secondary level. The women are not self-conscious about their level of education. Om Naeema says that among the folk, "wisdom and knowledge runs very deep," but what she means is that people are well versed in what is significant to their daily lives. The lower classes harbor a suspicion that an education which at the end of university only guarantees a poorly paying job in the government bureaucracy may not always be worth the effort. Om Gad, however, is determined that her children will reach the security of positions as government employees. Dunya believes "that the potential for understanding is born into people from the beginning," and neither education nor life experiences can develop the talent if the potential is not already there. Suda leaves school when she becomes more interested in learning the practical lessons needed to prepare for marriage from her mother. Alice, expressing the middle-class view, sees the diploma of her mother as the one thing that saved the family after her father died. Alice struggles to see that all her children receive university degrees. She has no second thoughts about the necessity of education.

The women have in common their extraordinary natural perception about the world in which they live. The stories provide us with a rich mine of materials on which to reflect—these are not specially talented storytellers— rather they have absorbed the narrative skills that are particularly developed among the folk of Egypt. When we listen to the women talking about their lives, we get a sense that they have brooded a great deal over their destinies. There is a philosophical breadth and eloquence to the narratives—a richness of expression—that one might not expect in people of such substandard physical environments. These women are philosophers.

What strikes us most forcefully is the tendency the women have to reduce all the tragedies and passions of their lives to a few themes—an unrequited love, a failed marriage, the calamity of being a co-wife in a polygamous marriage, the problems with children, the difficulty of growing up without a father. The events of life are tied to the themes and to a woman's present situation, the events of the past acting as a prelude to the present. It is characteristic that they rarely speculate on the future, but their stories leave us with the sense that the future holds an endless progression of events not much different from the past or the present. Om Naeema calls life "a long chain of events"—marriage, divorce, children, jealousy, death. All the narrators seek significance in these events—each is brought in with an echo of the essential points of the story.

There is a fine difference between the way the women here tell their stories and the way a typical western novelist does. The novelist chooses carefully the moment toward which everything points. There is no single moment in these folk stories, only a series of episodes which, for example, Dunya picks out of her life—her love for Ezzo, her desperate marriage to the

Libyan, her divorce, marriage to Ezzo, her inability to conceive—episodes that go on and on, drawn from here and there—like one of the several hour-long songs of the great Egyptian singer Om Kalthum—stopping not because they have reached resolution but rather because they have reached the present moment. The burning issue remains unresolved. With Dunya, her inability to conceive means her relationship with Ezzo remains insecure. He may decide to take another wife. Even in the moment of victory, she is robbed of her security, and the reader can expect a future as fraught with perils as the past. This pattern is an Egyptian pattern, echoed again and again in art, music, and literature: the endless repetitiveness of pharaonic tomb reliefs, the repetition of musical themes with unanticipated endings, the infinite expandability of geometric designs, the string of tales in 1,001 nights. Dunya and Om Gad are artists within an age-old tradition.

The stories are carefully structured so that at the center is the narrator—the heroine—always acting in exemplary fashion, always saying the right things, always overwhelmed by a fate for which she could never have prepared or which she could not have prevented. She is engaged always in a struggle in which she views herself on the side of good. Unlike the western novelist attempting to develop characters who are shades of good and evil, our narrators matter of factly draw boundaries between the two, and characters fall to either side depending upon whether they align themselves for or against the heroine. Though the heroine stands firmly on the side of right, she is not immune to impetuous acts that may have undesirable repercussions. Dunya throws away everything in a misbegotten marriage when she feels herself spurned by Ezzo. But her moment comes when, to the accompaniment of carefully orchestrated theatrics, she publicly humiliates the Libyan and wins her release. As the heroine, she knows her moment and controls the episodes of her story to make the best use of them.

Exaggeration is not foreign to these narratives, despite Dunya's claim to have related her story "with its sad times and its tears and nothing added and nothing taken away." The stories are after all frankly presented as the women see themselves, woven through with their corrections, additions, and omissions of time past and cast in the mold of their developed themes. Where is "truth" in the stories, the reader may ask, and of course the answer is that this is but one of the many truths that reside in the drama of human events. Each woman is aware of how critical it is to present oneself to the world effectively. Not only she herself gains from this kind of glorified presentation, but so do all the others—parents, husbands, children, relatives—that make up the extended self and suffer the consequences or reap the rewards of one another's accomplishments. She must win public arguments and reduce her detractors to ineffectual antagonists. She must reiterate her point again and again—as Om Naeema does with successive stories of the evil deeds co-wives have perpetrated on each other. Both Om Naeema and Alice tell their stories as parallel to their mothers' stories and to their daughters' stories to re-emphasize in different contexts the struggle women have with their menfolk. For Om Naeema and the others this is a structural motif which forms the cornerstones of their stories. This kind of exaggeration and reiteration makes for a simplistic but convincing, moving, and effective narrative.

The stories are more than a natural art form, however. They provide a mine of information for anthropologists and others seeking an understanding of Egyptian culture. Better than analytical models, these stories give the meaning of kinship structures, decision-making vectors, cultural symbols, systems of obligations and rights, and of economic and social adaptation to particular environments. They show life-span concepts, world view, domestic cycle regularities, and values and norms without the technical terms that reduce these processes to cold and formal dimensions. In the stories customs, symbols, and values come to life as they are manipulated, within the range of deeper cultural understandings, to realize the goals of individuals. These stories do not mystify with abstractions. They may be mystical, cruel at times, sad, warm, humorous, tragic, and sometimes moving, but they are always grounded in concrete description and example.

Walking the streets of Cairo and eavesdropping on the discussions of passers-by, one gets a sense of what the compelling issues are—marriage, prices, where to find housing, children, illness, and death. It is a list not unlike Om Naeema's "chain of events." Of all these subjects, marriage consumes perhaps the most attention. It is therefore no accident that the women, when asked to tell about their lives, naturally begin with events leading up to their marriages. The serious business of life begins for women at marriage. Childhood is only a preparation and a training for that time. Even the traumatic event of clitoridectomy is presented to girls as a necessity in order to marry or "the clitoris will grow long and become like the penis of a man," the girls are told. Some women like Dunya see marriage as more than the culmination of childhood; they see it as an escape from intolerable pressures in the family home, as a solution to economic difficulty, or as a license, as women, to move more freely in the community.

If there is one crescendo in the episodic series that constitutes each narrative, it is marriage—including the initial overtures, the extended negotiations, the amassing of great piles of material goods to secure the future of a bride, and the expectation of the happiness that marriage will bring. Families are mobilized on behalf of their members to exert their most significant efforts in material and emotional terms to ensure that young people are launched in their new lives. Om Gad expresses the feeling when she asks only that God will give her husband Omar "enough time on earth to place each one of our five daughters happily in some man's house."

With all these efforts, however, the reader may be struck by how almost incidental the final choice of marriage partners seems to be in some cases. The casualness may be deceptive. What are being matched are not personalities that are compatible but characteristics that are. Every person is evaluated according to income, occupation, family background, physical attractiveness, manners, piety, and a whole host of other characteristics. Choosing one suitor over another offers advantages and disadvantages. Other family members are equally concerned and allowed an opinion because of the relations they will all have with the new spouse. Do they want to consolidate the bonds of family by marrying a son or daughter to a relative, or would they rather solidify bonds of friendship by intermarriage? Does a stranger have advantages that outweigh those of other suitors, especially because she/he has attracted the interest of the partner? In today's world parents have less say about whom their children marry, though the forms, as in the case of Suda, are often still maintained with formal marriage negotiations.

Dunya's story shows the concern with social level. Her father rejects suitors because they are "too rich" or from too high a level for her. Alice comments that a girl without a father cannot expect to look very high for a husband. Suda similarly talks about the importance of having a similar skin color as a mate, and once she rejects the advances of an educated suitor as a man not having compatible characteristics. Differences in level, they all assume, may serve as a basis for disagreement and conflict, as it in fact does in the case of Alice's son and his wife. For this reason relative-marriage often offers the advantage of pairing two individuals of relatively similar backgrounds and mutual interests.

But as Om Naeema discovers when the marriage of her daughter fails, even relatives are not safe and secure marriage partners. Her disillusionment carries over to suspicions about relatives in general.

An important concern in marriage negotiations is to secure enough personal possessions for the bride so that her husband will think twice about divorcing her and losing the use of those possessions. Even the poor make few compromises with this requirement. If the couple is divorced, the possessions provide the woman with some hope of marrying again. Poor Naeema, however, finds herself caught in a reality that is somewhat less than the ideal. Her husband does not want to divorce her and lose the furniture altogether, but he makes life so miserable for her that she has to leave him. Naeema enters the limbo women sometimes occupy, able neither to obtain a divorce nor to live in the home of the husband. Her family concentrates its desperate efforts on trying to retrieve Naeema's possessions. The possibility men have to divorce fairly easily, however remote that eventuality, hangs like a cloud over the heads of Muslim women. It is in amassing a certain amount of material wealth, in gold or possessions, that they gain a feeling of future security. Alice notes another ramification of these realities when she contends that Christian women are different with their husbands than Muslim women because divorce is so difficult for a Christian. She feels that Christian women neglect their physical appearance and do not attend to the sexual needs of their husbands as they should. Suda is the one who says, as she muses over the conversations with her married friends and relatives, "Money and sex are the most basic problems discussed among Egyptian women." Her pleasure over controlling the household budget is more than a simple desire to find a pliable mate. It means she also controls the sums that her husband might put aside for ending her own marriage and contracting a new one.

Polygamy and divorce are less common nowadays in Egypt than the stories would suggest. These practices are more common in the older generations, but economic considerations and housing shortages make both difficult for the succeeding generations. Building on these difficulties are newly created laws which require men to give prior notice to their wives of impending marriage or divorce. In the case of marriage, women can choose whether they wish to remain as co-wives or whether they wish to obtain a divorce. Women with children to raise are also given rights of occupation in the family dwelling or must be offered an equivalent dwelling. This is a strong factor in their favor in these days of severe housing shortages.

Relations between men and women are a central issue that runs through all these stories. The battle lines at times appear to be drawn firmly between the sexes as antagonists. But then we find examples of moving tenderness and mutual support between men and women. There is Dunya's male neighbor who helps her through all her trials, finding work for her when she needs it and buying his meat from her brother's shop to help the fledgling business. There is Hamed who perceptively comes to the heart of the problems between himself and Om Naeema, urging her to remain with him but offering her freedom if she wants it. There is Alice's father who patiently deals with his runaway wife. Several of the women feel oppressed by their men, but all generally resign themselves to sticking out their marriages. Om Gad says, "When I see him unwell or unhappy, I feel as if I'm in a whirlpool. If something were to happen to him, how would I bring up my children?" It is this need for a male protector and supporter that makes males indispensable to the women. They compete against each other for men to marry or, as co-wives, to hold onto the attentions of their husbands through male children. Women invest hope for future security in their sons and gain status in the community at large as mothers of many sons.

Patterns of authority and domination between men and women are more subtle and complex than a reader might expect. The reader notices immediately that control is not the fully male prerogative that we have often assumed it to be in Arab societies. Egyptian males occasionally comment that it is women who dominate them, and one remarked with some feeling, "They grind us to powder as a spice is ground with mortar and pestle." In the stories men appear to circle like moths around the light of females. This is not wholly a result of the exaggerations of the storytellers. If we take the stories at face value, women become the pivotal individuals in the everyday activities of life—partly because the family centers around them, because the accomplishments of other family members depend upon their efforts, and because it is within the family that the significant decisions are made. Women have greater opportunity to make the day-to-day decisions or at least to control the information upon which the decisions are based. What other decisions are more momentous in a lower-class context? Men, from this perspective, become the peripheral earners of income, engaged in supporting the central institution which is the family. As members of the urban lower classes or the struggling middle classes, they are emasculated by an inability to succeed more than marginally in the male prerogative of earning money. By contrast, women can succeed mightily in their roles as housekeepers, child-bearers, and nurturers—nothing in their environment per se prevents success in these matters.

It is this segregation of male and female roles that is perhaps most central in keep the whirling vortex of male and female relations in the lower classes from spinning off into a destructive disintegration. Under normal circumstances men earn money and women rear children and keep house. They need each other to perform the functions society frowns upon them doing for themselves. It is a rare man in Egypt who will admit publicly to performing women's tasks. Women, on the other hand, can perform the earning function if economic considerations necessitate it or if they have sufficient time after their other womanly duties are finished. Om Gad and Om Naeema play an important part in assisting their husbands in tasks that bring income. Dunya and Suda go out to regular jobs. Dunya's necessity comes from her estrangement from her father, her pride which does not allow her to beg from her brother, and because she has no real home after the remarriage of her mother. Suda works—the income gives her the courage to resist an undesirable suitor—but she keeps it a secret that she is engaged in the demeaning work of being a servant. Alice sews in her home and helps bring a little more breathing space to a straitened economic situation.

There is an added element that accounts for the choice between incidental and full-time work for the women of these stories. Om Gad and

Om Naeema have husbands they would shame were they to seek full-time work. Suda and Dunya (during most of the story) come from households where an authoritative male is missing; there is no man to shame. Necessity broadens the range of tasks which it is acceptable for women to perform. But neither Suda nor Dunya nor any of the others, except perhaps Alice, would necessarily consider that an advantage.

Work does not necessarily bring greater authority or independence or even a desire for them, despite what Alice feels about this subject. The picture is not so simple. Om Gad comments that it is better for a woman to stay at home. If a husband really cares for his wife properly, he never lets her go out of the house to do anything. For Om Gad this is a real sign of affection. Suda complains about a man who does not check on his wife's whereabouts. She as much as says it is no wonder he loses her when he behaves like this. For her, to be a man means to exert authority and to control the comings and goings of women. Suda believes a woman should concede the authority of the household to her man and ask his permission when she goes anywhere or when she gives even the smallest gift from his household resources to anyone.

The narrative reveals the double standard of morality expected of men and women. Men are given much more latitude in the exercise of their passions than women. The only risk to a man is a short-term one of bodily harm from angered relatives of the woman. She, on the other hand, whether guilty of provocation or not, risks her life and at the very least, her marriage chances. Her contagion carries to the rest of her family, and she can expect a life-long stigma of social opprobrium. Alice's son is encouraged to return to wife and child after his adventures in Germany, and there the matter is dropped. But a woman is expected always to be on guard. Om Naeema says, "A woman, if she speaks to a man who is not a relative, should always put it in her head to be more man than he is."

Clitoridectomy, according to folk theory, cools the passions of women. Women are highly involved in perpetuating this mutilation of female circumcision on one another, as the stories demonstrate. In fact, women are active participants in the exercise of most forms of control over themselves— it is not a system perpetrated upon women solely by men. In common with men, women fear the consequences of a lapse in behavior or the failure to properly subdue "the sensual tendencies" of women. A mythology and ignorance about the bodily functions and moralistic stories of "what happens when" contribute their share to the continuation of these practices.

As westerners, we may have come too quickly to expect that ours are the international expectations of feminism—that other women will come to want the same rights and goals we seek—or, that once a society is frankly dominated in certain spheres by men, women will be a suppressed and passive group. Nothing could be further from the truth, as the pages of this book indicate. What is important to understand is how such seeming contradictions by western standards can be reconciled into a way of life that is both consistent and fulfilling to a large portion of Egyptians, male and female.

A fatalistic nature is another one of those attributes assigned to eastern people. It is used to explain what appears to be inaction or inappropriate behavior in the face of adversity. The stories quickly reduce generalizations of this kind to the place they deserve, in the graveyard of misleading, unperceptive observations. The reality, as usual, is much more complex. Passivity is not the necessary or even the natural reaction of a fatalistic philosophy that sees all events and acts as *maktoub*, already written. On the contrary, people act because they feel themselves to be instruments of destiny. The acceptance comes after the fact when, as people say about the dead, "Nothing more could have been done than was done because it was foreordained." People feel their impotence, it is true, in predicting future outcomes, but this approach is no less sensible than that of technologically advanced societies that have come to know the narrow range of accurate prediction.

Life is not easy for the women of the impoverished urban classes, and much of their lives falls into place without the benefit of slow deliberation or the weighing of positive or negative consequences. Consequences are part of the future and as such have little bearing on the present, which is the real concern. People fall in and out of calamity as though they were unable to foresee it. When it arrives, it is the time to act.

The women here do not stand and watch their lives pass by without active interference. Nor are they reluctant to seek explanations for what they see. For Dunya and the rest, life's events are woven into a web of cause and effect that is as consistent in its rationale as scientific theories, and more satisfactory for leaving no event unexplained or left to chance. Om Naeema and Dunya both resort to modern medicine when appropriate, but if this fails, they can choose from a host of other remedies, from natural folk medicines, to visits to sheikhs and others who dispel curses or exact revenges. In their totality, the possibilities speak to the whole man or woman, physically, psychologically, emotionally, and spiritually. The point is that though the women and their families are visited by numerous and unending afflictions, they are never left without some appropriate action to take. The trick is only to diagnose the root of the problem and to select the appropriate antidote. Often it is dreams that indicate correct actions to take. After that, satisfaction comes from knowing that everything that could be done was done. We feel in these pages that women—not just men—are actively and energetically involved in manipulating their and others' lives, in responding to difficulties effectively, and in discovering solutions to problems that are realistic given the limits of what is available. We might take another look at western philosophies that discourage action because "the odds are against any improvement" or because the treatment is too restrictively focused on physical, mental, or any other narrow "cause."

Dowshah figures prominently in the narratives of this book. Dunya makes a dowshah when she attempts to win release from the Libyan; she makes another when she shakes off the attentions of a would-be suitor. The mayor of her village takes the occasion of Om Naeema's marriage to settle his scores publicly. Naeema makes a dowshah on the bus to force her recalcitrant husband to return her furniture.

The institution of the dowshah has been remarked upon by a number of writers. Desmond Stewart, in Cairo, calls the dowshah the "folk ballet of violence" and notes its function in the relief of tension. He says: "Violence of emotion cannot be abolished by law. It can be sublimated in a ritual pantomime. The vile words fly, the fierce fists are raised. But when a great number of people come flocking about them, the contestants will, with a great show of reluctance, with fists held back as though against bands of steel, allow themselves to be parted, so that till the next disturbance, the street is calm."

A dowshah is as Stewart says a "ritual pantomime"—the gestures of violence are shams and not intended to inflict severe damage. The ritual part comes in the ordered way that peace is re-established. There is, first, the provocation—usually of a two-sided nature, though to hear it from one mouth is to hear it as an affair of white against black. Second comes the "letting off steam" phase—a stream of invectives, threats of physical violence, sometimes a minor round of fisticuffs. The audience for a time encourages and abets the argument, stirring it to a red-hot heat where resolution appears impossible. In this phase people seem to recognize how critical it is to bring out into the open the feelings that have prompted the controversy. When a suitable time elapses, the mediator steps in more forcefully to listen first to one side of the argument and then the other. His goal is not to arrive at a final measure of rightness or wrongness but rather to establish that there is fault and right in both parties and to develop a formula for reconciliation. Dunya, for instance, gives up her dowry sum, and the Libyan releases her from the marriage contract. Among people who must continue to interact, there are further attempts to extract some sign that reconcilation has occurred—a handshake, a generous reduction of the demands, a gesture of friendliness. The dowshah and its resolution follow the prescribed form allowing all the participants to play their parts, to know what parts to play, and to know when the problem is finally resolved.

It would be a mistake to think that the function of *dowshah* is restricted only to tension release. The *dowshah* is also a social occasion. People gather around, social cleavages surface that under normal conditons remain hidden, and individuals have their chance to assume the respected role of mediator. And after the *dowshah* is over, there is something to mull over and discuss with friends. The satisfaction in group activity is a genuine one that extends to both amicable and hostile events. Om Gad goes farthest in expressing the joy of human companionship—even the impersonal contact of people in a city—when she remarks on the recent improvement in Cairo now that the streets have become more crowded with people.

There are a number of ways that the *dowshah* differs from conflicts in other cultural traditions, to mention the most obvious: the phasing and the timing that prolongs the tension-release period; the significant role of the mediator and the eagerness of even complete strangers to play this role; the meeting in the middle, each giving up part of what he wanted; and the readiness to make generous concessions at the end. The audience normally reacts sympathetically, regarding anger as an "outside affliction" rather than a "lack of control," and its members are willing to work out a resolution with the combatants. Community harmony is eventually restored through this process until the next *dowshah* erupts.

The *dowshah* is only one way in which hostility is expressed. The stories are rife with examples of the hexing of others or—more effective—of revenge directed at persons through harming their loved ones—a mother through her child, for example. The close connection between hostility and love is recognized in the stories. Relatives are supposed to love each other, but when they have competing loyalties, they can be the most dangerous of all—as Om Naeema points out. What stranger would care enough to harm? The most important exception is, of course, the "stranger" within the house—the wife brought in from outside the family, the sisters-in-law, the co-wives, the stepmothers. It is to these individuals one looks first when unexplained calamity occurs.

Careful attention to the details of the stories reveals important information about family life. Alice, Dunya, Suda, and Om Gad felt their aloneness because of disruptions in their circle of kin. Om Gad complained that she had no kin left; Suda and Alice felt the deaths of their fathers. Dunya had nowhere to go because of her father's hostility and her mother's remarriage. Significant consequences resulted in each case from the loss of familial support.

One has the sense all through the stories that relatives are so important and their roles so defined that it is difficult to carry on effectively when they are absent. They are the people to whom you reveal your secrets as Suda reveals the true nature of her work only to her brother, mother, sister, and maternal uncle. They are the ones who must stand with you rather than against you because they share the glories or the shame of your behavior. Flesh and blood is all the more compelling a bond the narrower the circle of kin. Parents are always ready to support their children, even when they are grown. The links between parent and child are so strong, in fact, that when a young woman marries, there is a period just after the marriage when communication is cut off from the parental home, to accustom her to life with the new family she has entered. Yet as Suda notes, families send their daughters gifts to symbolize their support. Maternal relatives—aunts, uncles, and grandparents—are the kind, loving, indulgent relatives, a step removed from the mother but paralleling her role. Om Naeema asks who is coming to the door in the night—it can only be a maternal uncle who would come in such an intimate way without warning. Paternal relatives assume a more legalistic relation. They stand together to negotiate the contracts on behalf of the family and, if necessary, to avenge the wrongs against their kin. Paternal male cousins claim their prior rights to marry female cousins. Or as in Dunya's case, one offers marriage to restore the family's good name after the Libyan incident, to demonstrate that the family stands behind its members. Relatives are, in short, the ones you hope you can rely on to act on your behalf, and in return you respond by supporting their concerns.

Relatives are so important and their contributions to well-being so specific, the stories indicate, that when some relative is missing for one reason or another, or when one wants to enlarge the circle of intimacy, others can be assigned to fill the roles. The bond is not so strong as that of specified kinship, but as long as both parties honor the arrangement, it can work. A girl without a brother, for example, may call her paternal cousin "brother" so that he will assume a protective relation toward her. "I shall be at once her husband and her brother," says Omar when he asks to marry Om Gad. Om Gad grieves over the dead son who could have been both brother and son to her. A friend of a mother is called *Khallti*, mother's sister, to co-opt her sympathy and support. A woman calling a stranger male "brother" keeps his intentions honorable, calling a friend "sister" binds her in even closer friendship. Whichever title is used, a whole host of expectations about mutual relations is implied. The extent to which the expectations are met determines the level of future relations.

Redefinitions are one way that family relations are handled. Others include what might be called equivalencies: a perception that certain relationships merge, correspond to, replace, are equal to, or represent others. The narrative of Om Naeema illustrates particularly well the poorly defined nature of separate identity. She barely distinguishes the existence of her own life from that of her mother, or her daughter. Her unexpected shifts in the narrative and her acquaintance with the most intimate feelings of the others sometimes confuse the reader into thinking that the three lives are actually one. In other examples we see people who symbolically replace or represent others, a mother of a groom who comes to observe a potential bride, an uncle or brother who stands in place of a father in performing some task. We note the need to know the name of a mother before hexing an individual. All these manipulations provide the means by which persons become merged under the protective umbrella of kinship. Individualists can stew in their own juice as Dunya finds when she resists the pressures of her family to marry and they withdraw their support from her.

What is so satisfactory about the stories is that they leave us no room for complacency about the purity of the patterns we discover. There is this exception or that, the perceptive reader will note—a maternal relative treated like a paternal one, a sister who instigates evil charms against a sister, an individual who refuses to merge her personality in the group. Om Naeema talks about her disdain for relatives who go their own way and do not do what they should. A partial explanation for some of these exceptions is found in the economic conditions of the actors. People with fewer material resources rely more heavily on other kinds of connections and exchanges, however tenuous and remote they may be. Ad hoc arrangements frequently become the order of the day. Suda's maternal uncle helps her brother find work because he happens to be in a position to do so. Dunya calls on a neighbor-stranger to help her find a means of support. Or, the exceptions may be simply the result of human unpredictability and personality difference. They are exceptions only because the culture prescribes sets of guidelines to be conformed with or resisted by each individual as she sees fit.

Reading the pages of this book is an encounter with a new culture. There are elements that surprise us in the story of Dunya, that do not meet our expectations, perhaps, of the life of "traditional" women in an Arab society. Reading Dunya prepares us to look for parallels in Om Naeema, Om Gad, and Suda. The story of Alice gives us broader insights into how similar themes are carried out in a different social stratum of urban life. Which are the consistent patterns of behavior among these women, and which are the idiosyncratic ones that come from their own individual personalities? Dunya, with her flamboyant personality, is perhaps the most active in rearranging events to satisfy her own view of how they should be. But she does it in an impetuous way. Alice moves toward her goals with sustained effort and a great deal of perseverance. Om Naeema and Om Gad, by contrast, only mildly raise objection to their lot; their typical response is accommodation. Om Naeema's one resistance, brought on by her desire to have children, precipitates serious illnes and she quickly resigns herself to her marriage. The women may react differently to their afflictions, but at the heart of their responses are some of the same guiding principles: that it is a tragedy to be childless or have few children; that a woman who does not have a husband is somehow a reduced human being, subject to continuous social pressures and a restricted existence; that conflicts have certain patterns of resolution; and that relatives are expected to perform certain kinds of tasks. The women also have in common their other-directedness: they view themselves as always "bounced off" other people—their mothers, husbands, children, friends, and enemies. We weave our conclusions much as the student of culture does, by seeking the parallels, by learning what disappoints the expectations of the women, by considering what causes conflicts, by what is abnormal, and by what is usual.

The stories are the next best thing to being participant observers in a culture not our own. Like participant observers, readers should expect to find themselves caught up from time to time in an emotional and empathetic experience. It would be unfortunate to analyze the stories from too critical a perspective and thereby lose the freshness of the image they present.

Some readers will want to know more about the mechanics of how the histories were gathered and about the relationship between the collector of the stories, Nayra Atiya, and the women themselves.

Nayra and I arrived at about the same time in 1976 for an indefinite stay in Egypt—Nayra returning to her native country after a teenage and adulthood spent mostly in the United States, and I as an American an-thropologist beginning research in a lower-class neighborhood of Cairo. For the five years I remained there we were close friends, experiencing Egypt in sometimes very different and sometimes very similar ways.

As an Egyptian returning to her native country, Nayra came with a fluency in colloquial Egyptian Arabic that enabled her to translate the his-tories so skillfully as well as enabling her to communicate directly with the women. But because she had left the country as a child, there were some gaps in her understanding of Egyptian culture and society that are necessary to a flawless interaction in the society. For us, who are her friends and readers, this turned out to be to our advantage for it left her with an outsider's perspective open to discovering the subtleties of human relationships in the Egyptian context. Because she was a relative newcomer to adult Egyptian life, she saw some aspects of it more clearly.

The lower social classes that Nayra met first as shoemakers, car watchers, plumbers, shirtmakers, or doorkeepers were generally perplexed by her. "Where are you from?" they would demand to know and then would refuse to accept the fact that she wasn't an Egyptian. The more candid of them would explain that her manners and courtesies toward them were simply not those commonly found in members of her class. What they meant was that a manner of speech exists that divides the classes in Egypt and that she did not conform with this pattern. I think Nayra felt it a challenge to overcome these barriers of class and form intimate relations with the world of the urban lower classes, a world little known to Egyptian educated elites. The oral histories leave us with no doubt that she was able to create an atmosphere of openness and trust with the women she interviewed.

With the presentation of only five stories (four, in fact, if only the lower-class histories are counted), it is clear there is no certainty that the average or even a representative view of the lower-class woman has been conveyed. However, my experience working among the lower classes convinces me these histories ring true as representing these classes in their manner of speech, in the way they articulate their experiences, and in their preoccupations. If there is a bias, it is in favor of subjects that have taken the initiative to work on their own. It is more common for women of that class to confine themselves to aiding their husbands whenever possible in their economic activities much in the way that Om Gad helps her husband with the polishing of cars or Om Naeema helps with the fishing. Each person, it is true, is unique in some way but unique in the sense that every person is unique. They are certainly not exceptional as Egyptians.

Given the circumstances Nayra faced, it was impossible to impose strict control on the conditions under which the oral histories were taken, nor was it ever her intention to do so. They were collected instead in a manner that was determined by what was most comfortable and natural for Nayra and the women. She recorded the histories on tapes first, some over a period of months, others in much shorter sittings. Some women were voluble with little urging; others needed nudging and encouragement to loosen their tongues. After transcribing the tapes in English, some editing and cutting was required to avoid an overly repetitive narrative. A certain amount of repetition was preserved as in instances where a woman gave several examples to illustrate a point or she mirrored her own story in that of her mother or daughter or both. This is characteristic of the way narrators convey their thoughts.

Nayra is not a trained anthropologist. She is a painter, a poet, and a writer. If she were an anthropologist, one might suspect her of fastening on certain events such as marriage, death, birth, and circumcision as significant because of her professional biases. Instead, the vivid details of these events have naturally flowed out of the narrative, not selected by her, but chosen by the women themselves as the subjects around which to organize their discourses. These subjects are not exhaustive of what interests the women but rather are what they consider the essential points that must be covered for a complete story of their lives. In their own way the women have validated the concerns anthropologists have felt to be significant for a long time.

Cairo, Egypt   Andrea B. Rugh
Fall 1981

Preface

𝒥N THIS BOOK five contemporary Egyptian women, in age from their early twenties to mid-sixties and all of the mid- to lower socioeconomic classes, tell their life stories. From birth and childhood to puberty, clitoridectomy, marriage, adult life, and children, we are allowed a generous glimpse, through these very personal accounts, into the details of five women's daily lives. We become acquainted with their families, share their thoughts, dreams, fears, tragedies, and disappointments, as well as getting a good dollop of folklore, superstition, manners and customs, and general information.

Dunya came to clean for me six days a week one year when I lived on a houseboat on the Nile in Cairo. I began to tape record her stories some months after she came to work. Before that time we had talked off and on informally. As she traveled, feather duster in hand, from cabin to cabin, she would stop to chat or to tell me about her neighbors and herself. Dunya was a talented raconteuse, and when she spoke I dropped everything to listen.

I felt I was being allowed a privileged peek into a society I knew almost nothing about and which I longed to understand, as much as I longed to become intimately acquainted with an Egypt I had left to go to the United States as a child some twenty-five years earlier.

As I speak fluent Cairene Arabic, Dunya and I communicated with ease. She shared her world with me and, in my own way, I reciprocated.

It was to round out some of the themes, such as growing up, love, marriage, family, and expectations, which ran through Dunya's tale, and which I suspected could not be unique to her, that I began to speak in the same way with other men and women around me. They were by and large picked at random from among Egyptians I saw over a period of three years, 1976–79, mostly in the course of ordinary daily activities.

From these I chose the life stories of five women: Dunya, Om Naeema, Om Gad, Suda, and Alice. Only Alice, a middle-class woman from upper Egypt who often came to visit one of my aunts, and Suda, a housekeeper in an upper middle-class home in Garden City, could read and write. All the women are Muslim with the exception of Alice, a Coptic Christian.

Dunya was in her twenties and well proportioned. She had generous features, brown eyes with a slightly oriental tilt, and a full mouth. Her teeth were small and perfect and her skin very white. Her proud carriage and spirited demeanor gave her a regal appearance even when she was engaged in the most menial task.

She dressed in layers like many traditional women or women of the lower and lower middle classes in Egypt. She wore long, sleeveless cotton frocks under her long, black street dress and a flowered kerchief snugly tied over her head and forehead under the black street veil. These light-colored garments, always neat and freshly laundered, she wore at home or while working. The sleeveless dresses, she told me, were considered immodest by her neighbors. She did not care, however, and said, "They'll always find something to criticize in you. Let them say what they please. I know myself and I don't have anything to be ashamed of."

Alice, pronounced "Alease," was dark and small but strikingly sturdy and rather unusual. A woman with grown children, she moved to Cairo with her husband, initially to be nearer their children, and set herself the task of bettering the lot of poor women, both Muslim and Christian, by teaching them to sew, knit, or go into business for themselves. All the while she preached financial independence as the only way to self-respect for any woman. Alice's messages, based on a hard apprenticeship at life's hands, were: a woman with money in her pocket can demand respect and get it; a woman with none is forever a slave. Alice herself knitted and sewed for charity bazaars.

She had a marked dislike for members of the middle classes, whom she considered by and large selfish, petty, and unloving. This dislike was matched in intensity only by her hatred of what she considered another oppressor: man. She found men equally selfish and generally as disloyal to those who loved them as were most members of the middle classes to their friends and relatives. Bitter personal experience had led her to feel nothing but contempt for both, although, on meeting her casually, this did not show. She was outwardly friendly to all.

She had no car and would walk miles each day to visit the women who needed her. She took them and their children to hospitals and gently bullied or bribed her way in through the throngs to have them see a doctor. She made a point of catering to their needs while trying to teach them to help themselves. When I joined her on her rounds from time to time, I noticed that she was not only cast in the role of teacher but also of matchmaker, healer, mediator during quarrels or family disagreements, friend, and general problem solver.

"The poor," she told me, "really appreciate what you do for them and are usually more generous with the little they have than those who are well off and who will conveniently forget a good deed when it is time to reciprocate."

Om Naeema, in her fifties and the wife of a fisherman, watched my comings and goings with interest from her mooring place near the houseboat on which I lived. For a time we exchanged polite greetings. This was easy to do as greetings follow a prescribed pattern in Egypt which, once learned, becomes a formula. We talked guardedly at first. She and her husband then invited me to have tea with them on their boat, and I reciprocated. Then I offered boxes of sugar, a package of tea, and they would leave an enameled plate full of fried Nile fish for me in the kitchen. Gradually, a friendship developed based on mutual respect and concern.

Their rowboat, about five meters long and less than two meters wide, was their home away from home and their breadwinner. Besides their fishing gear, they carried with them at all times a primus stove, a small candle lantern, a tiny blue enameled teapot, one minuscule glass with a fluted surface from which we drank tea made from river water, in turn, and a porous buff-colored water jug, *olla*, slung over the side of the boat.

They also had a tarpaulin which went over the top of the boat to cover them at night, a couple of blankets, some cooking pots, enameled plates and bowls, and one change of clothing and their street clothes. For the fisherman the costume was a heavy brown *gallabeyya* cut very wide at the sleeves, peasant fashion. For Om Naeema it was a black velvet street dress which went over the long-sleeved, flowered dress with a yoke she wore on the boat, a set of cut glass beads around her neck, and gold, crescent moon-shaped earrings. She had a new flowered cotton dress made at feast time, as prescribed by tradition, whenever she could afford it. Her husband worked in his underclothing, consisting of vast pants caught at the waist with a string or elastic, a knee-length shirt, cut wide and round at the neck, topped with a *sedayree*, or a vest made of plain cotton at the back and shiny, striped cotton at the front with a string of tiny buttons, like marbles, running up and down the edge, one very near the other. On his head he wore at all times a rough, reddish brown skull cap, very much the color and texture of the loosely woven fibers at the base of the fronds of a date palm, used in Egypt to make cheap, thick brooms and sturdy ropes.

Om Naeema and her husband divided their lives between their boat and a home in their native village in the Delta, where they went at feast times and where their only daughter spent much of her time.

Their chief worry and problem, their divorced daughter, has recently been solved. She remarried and lives with her husband in Cairo, where they can often visit her and more easily watch over her welfare.

Om means "mother of" and is used as a term of respect. Om shows that a woman has fulfilled her calling, that of becoming a mother. Sometimes a childless woman will be referred to as Om el-Ghayib or "mother of the absent one," in order never to use her first name which would show disrespect or be a way of belittling her. Abu means "father" and is used in the same way. These terms are used when one is talking to an older person. One may also use the terms Khallti or Ammitty meaning "auntie," or Khali or Ammi meaning "uncle" for the same reasons.

Om Gad and her family lived in three rooms at the back of the garage where I used to park my car. I met her in 1976, and saw her daily as I came and went, taking time to chat with her and her husband when parking my car or taking it out.

Their existence, unlike that of the fisherfolk, was molelike. I think for that reason they often fled to the street for air except at the time of the soap operas on television in the evening, when they all huddled in one room to watch. Their rooms, dark and dank, were painted a jarring turquoise color. The smell of cooking, mixing at close quarters with too many lives, produced an unhealthy atmosphere which reflected itself in the pale, haggard faces of the members of that family.

Om Gad was short and fat. Despite the unhappiness of losing children and the difficulties of life behind the garage, she felt she had managed her family's affairs quite successfully. Her large brown eyes held none of the sadness she speaks of in her story, although when telling me of the death of her young son, she wept bitterly.

Om Gad wore the traditional long-sleeved, ankle-length cotton dresses of her people. She shuffled around in bright purple plastic slippers and wore at all times a black or white head scarf tied low over her forehead with a knot at the top, her thin braids hanging at the back. Her black overdress was reserved for trips to the family house in Giza, in an old pistachio-colored car, a new acquisition she speaks of proudly in her story.

Her husband was as thin and dry as she was pudgy. Behind his apparently cheerful greeting, morning and evening, lay a tremendous sadness.

Suda, who worked as a housekeeper, was always pleasant, efficient, and above all a woman with a mind of her own. She was in some ways like Om Gad. She wanted to marry, stop working, and set up a home with all of the modern conveniences now available in Egypt to anyone who can pay for them.

She planned to work only until she had saved enough money to get what she wanted. This included among other things, a refrigerator, washing machine, television, and radio-cassette player. Suda, like many young women of her class today, liked to dress well. The growing ready-made clothing industry in Egypt makes this easily possible. Suda was neatly put together in short skirts, high-heeled slippers, attractive polyester knit blouses, and scarves to match. She never wore the same outfit two days in a row during the time I knew her and was pleased to be complimented on her snappy wardrobe.

As Suda's ancestors were from the Sudan, she was very black, tall, and graceful. Her good looks were enhanced by intelligent eyes, which could turn stubborn when she had her mind set on doing things her way.

She, like the others, found it amusing that I should be interested in including her life story in a collection of stories about Egyptians. She did not consider herself in any way extraordinary and therefore worthy of special attention. She was willing though, like the others, to sit down and tell me about herself, always laughingly, as if it was a big joke.

My relationships with Alice, Om Gad, and Suda were less intimate than those I had with Om Naeema and Dunya, whom I saw daily. Later, however, I moved from the houseboat and Dunya also moved, and I have regretfully lost track of her. I was able to find Suda last summer, however. She had stopped working. I left a message with one of her girlfriends who still worked for someone I knew, asking if I might see her. She came to meet me and took me to her home where I met her mother for the first time and her youngest sister. She had married and was expecting her first child. She spends the entire day with her mother until her husband comes to fetch her at sunset when they go home to their own flat, just down the street. She had planned her life carefully and has done just what she had set out to do. I see Alice from time to time and pay Om Naeema and her husband, Hamed, visits on their boat on the Nile.

As I was writing these stories, my closest tie was with Om Naeema. We saw each other casually, going and coming, and this gave our encounters a pleasant informality from 1976 to 1979, when I moved from the boat.

The women who told me their stories did so, I believe, because a sense of trust was established between us and because it helped us all to talk out many problems. I shared many of my thoughts and experiences with them and tried to draw on their wisdom for solutions to some problems and for a better understanding of many aspects of Egyptian life. They reciprocated. In some cases I was comfortable enough to ask to tape record their stories within a few months of our getting acquainted. In other cases it took one or two years, especially with the women I saw only from time to time, like Alice and Suda. In all cases I explained at the onset that I was collecting stories about

Egyptians and would like to include theirs in what might become a book. They all agreed.

I have changed the names of all of the women to protect their identities and have mostly included only general photographs to illustrate the text for the same reason. The photographs, while nonspecific and do not identify the subjects, are representative.

All five women told me their stories in Arabic. I translated them and then arranged them, trying to keep to the sequence of events in the original story and cutting as little as possible. Throughout, I made an effort to convey in English the style of the storyteller, the spirit in which each story was told, and the drama which makes up the fabric of each of these lives.

My goal in recording these stories was to get better acquainted with my native Egypt through some of its people; sharing them with readers was an afterthought. The five chosen here are not representative of all of Egyptian society by any means. They were not picked to represent any particular social class or type of person. Rather, they are people whom I met at random. Their stories touched me. The richness of detail in their lives and their way of recounting these gave added perspective to my efforts to understand Egypt and my people. From these stories I was able to draw a number of conclusions about Egypt and Egyptians for myself. Being neither an anthropologist nor a sociologist, however, I defer analysis of these offerings to those who are trained to or wish to make them.

I included no men in this book in order to keep to a theme and also because those most accessible to me as a woman and those I was most easily in touch with were women. The fact that four of these are from the lower or lower middle-class and only one from the middle class is pure coincidence.

The *khul-khaal* of the book's title are heavy silver or gold anklets, not unlike shackles, worn by married women. These are often removed when they are widows. They are an image appropriate to the content of this book because of their symbolic as well as material meanings.

The *khul-khaal* bind but can also be used to advantage. As an ornament, their presence on a shapely ankle and the ringing sound they make when a woman walks can be seductive. In a popular Egyptian song the phrase "the ringing of thine anklets has deprived me of my reason," shows how they can be a way to a man's heart. The Koran acknowledges this by warning women against striking their feet together "in order to draw attention to their hidden ornaments."

Materially speaking, an average pair of anklets in silver are worth about E£20. They serve, as do other items of jewelry, as a hedge against misfortune. We see in Alice's story, for example, how she sells bits of her gold chains to make ends meet.

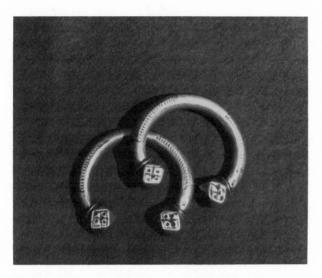

Khul-khaal. Photograph by Margot Badran.

I should like to express my gratitude to the women who enriched me by sharing their life stories, their wisdom, and their experiences with me. They gave a very definite flavor and richness to an Egypt I left as a child, returned to as an adult, and shall, I expect, always be in the process of discovering.

I should like to take this opportunity to express my appreciation and thanks to the friends and relatives who, through their encouragement or direct help made the creation of these stories into a book possible.

To Andrea Rugh for first reading the manuscript, expressing her enthusiasm for it, as a professional anthropologist, suggesting that I try to publish it, and kindly writing the foreword for the book in the midst of a very busy professional schedule. To Asma el-Bakry for unfailing encouragement and for criss-crossing Cairo and outlying areas to take photographs for the book. To Jeanne Tifft for allowing me to use one of her fine photographs. To Margot Badran for her enthusiasm and perceptive comments. To Elizabeth Taylor and Essam Awny for providing me with a cheerful place to work one difficult summer. To Mary Megally for volunteering long hours of typing. To May Trad and Ruth and Norman Daniel for providing me with a change of pace when it was most needed. To Pauline Sadek for completing the typing of the manuscript in record time. To Nathene Loveland for invaluable advice.

To Martin Rose, Nelly Hanna, William Eshaq, and the late Ali Omar for friendly comment. To my children, Adam and Katrina, for pushing me to the finish line. To my aunts Nina, Suzy, and Lucienne for looking after me during the vital final laps. Last but not least to my parents who, from a distance, lent their unfailing and much needed support. To my beloved Egypt for timeless riches.

Cairo, Egypt   Nayra Atiya
Fall 1981

Khul-Khaal

1

Om Gad

WIFE OF THE GARAGEKEEPER

"Blood has to come out. It stands for honor."

I woke up one day when I was a youngster and opened my eyes suddenly and found that I was grown up.

I found myself alone. I had neither brother, nor sister, nor a maternal aunt to turn to in an hour of need, nor a paternal aunt on whom I could call for help. My paternal aunt died before I was aware of myself as a person. My paternal uncles died too before I realized that I was a member of the human race.

I was born in a village in Giza. Our roots run deep in that village, and we have no other village that we call our own. The lives of my father, my father's father, and his father before him ran their course within the confines of that village. So when we emerged, we found ourselves part of that village and none other.

When I awoke then I found myself to be an only child. My father had been married once to his paternal aunt's daughter, the daughter of his father's sister. She had borne him three daughters. All died. None remained. This was before I was born. His first wife died, and he married my mother.

My mother bore him eight children. They were three boys and five girls. None of these died young. Some were six years old and others seven when they died. The would suddenly disappear without illness or warning of any kind.

When my mother became pregnant with me, fearing the same fate for me as for these other children, she went to a wise man to ask advice. Sheikh Ali, the one who knows, lived in a village nearby.

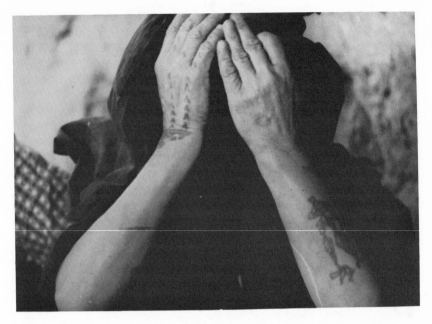

Tattooed arms of a Bedouin woman living in Cairo. Photograph by Asma el-Bakry.

She went shortly before giving birth to me. The *Sheikh* said to her, "Remove any differences you might have with your heavenly sister." We believe that each one of us has a *Kareena*, or a heavenly sister or brother. They are spirits who move us to do things we ourselves might not otherwise do. I may refuse a glass of tea, for example. If she wants to drink it, she will hold a grudge against me for refusing it. She will eventually take her revenge. If I become pregnant, for example, she will cause me to have a miscarriage.

My mother was afraid of her spiritual sister, and that is why she went to see the one who knows.

He said to her, "When you give birth make sure you have on hand a black-colored duck with no markings on its body. When the child is born, have a basin ready into which you'll catch everything which comes out of you. Don't let any part come outside it or let the afterbirth touch the ground." Then he told her that the duck should be slaughtered, plucked, and cooked whole, with not a bone in its body broken. He said to her, "After giving birth you must set yourself to eating this bird without breaking the bones. Pick it clean, and when the carcass is bare and looking like an altar of bones, get a meter of white cloth, *farta beyda,* and place the blood and afterbirth and the duck's carcass in it. Add a piece of bread and some salt, tie up the sheet with a firm knot, then dig a deep hole beside your house, at the roots of the house, and bury the lot there. The child will then survive."

Although life and death are in the hands of God, and it is he who moves mountains, my mother did as she was told and I survived. I lived.

When I was a baby, she breast fed me a long time. She felt she must do so because it was such good fortune that I survived. But because she fed me so well, by the time I was five years old I became fretful. I would kick and cry and fuss a great deal, and so she had me tattooed to calm me down. She took me to someone who does this. She had me tattooed on the forehead and on my heels. The tattoo on the heel is now almost gone, perhaps as a result of frequent washing.

At the time of my tattooing, my mother gave birth to another child. It was a boy. She called him Hassan. He died when he was six years old. She then had another daughter who was healthy and beautiful and already crawling when God remembered her and took her from us.

My brother Hassan was handsome. If you were to see him, you would say he was the son of kings. His face was full and ruddy like an Englishman's. Someone gave him the evil eye.

People in those days were few and far between, and they were full of mystery and often full of envy and ill will. You felt alone in those times. Not like today when the streets are crowded and full of warmth and security.

If you walked down a street in our village in those days, it would be a long moment before you met a man or another woman or child coming toward you. Ours was a native quarter. It was built around narrow alleys and dead-end streets and dotted with tight clusters of mud brick houses. We all knew each other, but an underlying sense of fear wove itself into our lives.

People when they saw my brother Hassan would say, "Oh, what a beautiful child! How can someone like you have given birth to such a jewel." They would carry on in this way and cast an evil spell on the boy.

At that time the country was full of English and African peoples. They would come to the fields around our village, and when they saw my brother they too would go on about his looks. He would ask them for cigarettes to bring to his father, and in return he would shuck and roast corn from our fields for them. He was very clever. He would bring his booty to his father and ask him if he'd brought him sweets called *basboosa* and *boghaaza*.

The foreigners didn't mean any harm by their compliments. They didn't have our concept of *hassad*, or the evil eye. It was one of us who did my brother in.

I was about ten years old when Hassan died. I rolled on the ground and cried at the loss of the handsome brother who stood beside me.

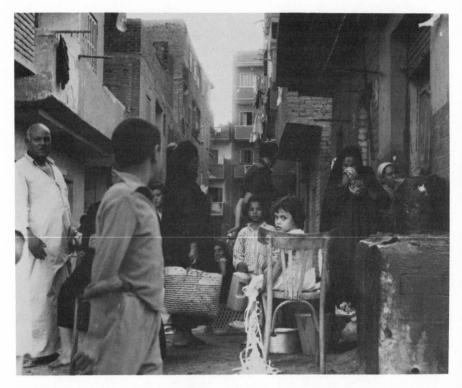

"Ours was a native quarter. We all knew each other, but an underlying sense of fear wove itself into our lives."—Om Gad. Photograph by Asma el-Bakry.

Hassan had the habit of getting up in the middle of the night and asking for a drink. We would get up and prepare a glass of tea and milk for him. This became a nightly ritual.

One night my mother woke up suddenly, missing the child's call for tea. She noticed that his lamp was off, and no sound came from his direction. She got up with a start and called to my father, "Ya, Omar. Ya, Omar." So my father cried back, "What's the matter, woman, what's the matter?" So she answered, "The lamp is not lit, and the boy did not wake up as usual to ask for his tea." My father and mother got up and turned on the light. When they did, they rolled the child over and found him dead.

There had been no illness, no warning. It was a shock. They woke me up, and I began to scream. My mother flew out of the house, wailing. She ran to her mother's house and the houses of her relatives. We all lived in the same area.

It was about two in the morning, and my brother used to wake up at midnight for his tea. The streets were dark and deserted.

My mother filled the streets with her crying. Her brother woke and said to his wife, "Zeinab, can you imagine that the crying you hear is that of my sister? Is it possible?" His wife got up and threw open the window and looked out. It was indeed my mother. Her sister-in-law rushed out of the house and said, "What's the matter, what's happened?" My mother answered, "O cursed one, *el be'eeda,* the son of the cursed one has died."

People woke up and came out of their houses. But what can you do? There is a saying among us that if you are patient you shall be rewarded for your patience, and God's will shall be done; if you are not patient, you will be the loser, but his will shall nevertheless be done.

Not long after that I was engaged to my paternal uncle's son. As I was an only child and my husband had only one sister, we felt quite alone in the world. My cousin was determined to fortify the link between our families by marrying me. He said, "I shall marry her, and be at once her husband and her brother."

He spoke to my father, and my father said to him, "My son, she is your first cousin, and come what may you have priority above anyone else. You are a brother to her."

As my father's house had only my parents living in it, it seemed empty with all the children dead and gone. My parents were companionless, and so my father said to Omar, "My boy, this is your home. You have a place in it, and you shall have your own room." So it came to pass. I was thirteen and had neither breasts nor had my period come yet.

My period came eight months after I was married. Right after, my first child, a daughter, was born. This is the one we call Fatma, Om Reda.

I had another girl after this one. She refused to nurse. She turned away from the breast, and when I tried to bottle feed her, she died. She was six months old.

Another daughter was born later. She is now a clerk in one of the ministries. After her we had a son, Mohammad, who died when he was eight months old. He was also given the evil eye. We seem fated that way in our family. My father had not died then. No sooner had we gone to the cemetery for my father than the boy got fever. The sun didn't rise on him before he was dead. Our mourning was doubled.

We had to go on living. My mother was alone, and I was an only child and the only support left her. Could I leave my mother then in the care of her brother's son or daughter? It wouldn't do. She was our responsibility. I said to her, "Consider that we are in my father's house and that we rent rooms here. We carry you in our eyes." So she stayed.

Omar, my husband, had been working as a caretaker, car washer and part-time driver in garages by then. He has been in his present job twenty years, although we have lived behind that garage only five years.

One night my dead father appeared to my paternal uncle's wife in a dream. He said to her, "So and so hearken. My daughter has given birth. Go to her and tell her to dress the one to whom she has given birth in black. Tell her to cover his face with a black cap. Tell her not to show him to anyone and not to let anyone else hold or carry him. If she does this, the child will live."

She came running and told me these things. She said to my mother, "O so and so, who is it who said that the dead are not aware of the living! Hearken, your husband came to me in a dream last night."

I did as I was told. I kept the baby covered and dressed in black until he was nice and big, and he survived.

I then had a daughter, Sana. When she was eight months old she had fever, and I took her to someone who gave her penicillin injections, and lo and behold, instead of recovering she became paralyzed. She got polio. I stood her up on my knee one day, and suddenly her leg gave way. I was shocked. My nerves gave way. That this should happen to her, and she being a girl and a woman, I knew would have grave consequences. No man would want to marry a cripple.

I took her to Abu Reesh Children's Hospital, and there the doctor asked me if she'd had fever and if I'd given her a penicillin injection. When I said I had, he said, "Well, my good woman, you can only put your trust in God now to heal her."

I continued to take her to hospital for physiotherapy. I took her every other day for three years. She then put her foot to the floor one day, and God had mercy on her. She walked. But she has a slight limp. We sent her to school, and she is now studying accounting.

I then gave birth to another son. I named him Ali after my father. We had by then moved to the rooms behind the garage. One day when he was about thirteen years old, during a *moosim* or a feast time, I decided to do some special cooking to take back to our relatives in the village.

I found Ali sitting more quietly than usual. I said to him, "What's the matter, little brother?" He answered, "Nothing. I just have a little cough."

He sat and shelled peas with me. His sister cooked them, and he ate as usual and went out to play with his friends. I took the food and went to the village. It was about five o'clock.

At nine o'clock I suddenly saw the boy's sister, Sana, the one who limps, coming toward me. I was alarmed and cried out to her, "What brings you at this hour?" She said, "Ali took a nap this afternoon. When he woke up he said to his grandmother, 'I want to urinate.'" So she answered, "Get up and urinate then, my child." He started to get up, but his legs wouldn't hold him. He cried out, "Help me, Grandmother, I can't stand!" He fell in a heap on the ground, and his grandmother cried out and ran to him. The neighbors gathered. My mother cried, "Help me, help me. Look at the boy!" So they carried him and ran with him to a doctor. By the time Sana reached us in the village and his father and I got a taxi and rushed back, we found them bringing him back dead in the doctor's car.

I can't forget him. He is on my mind at all times. He was a boy like my beautiful brother who died. He was a man already. I didn't see him. His father didn't see him. He was just taken from us with no warning. That was five years ago. I was desperate. I covered myself in mud, and my sorrow burned me like fire.

His father has never recovered. He is a broken man. He continues to struggle because of the children he must raise still, but his back is broken. He's not one to show his sorrow. He holds it in, and it devours him.

I stayed two years in a state of collapse. I couldn't eat, move, or do anything. They had to force me to eat, and it was all I could do to take a little milk now and then.

I loved Ali more than the others because he was named after my father. He would have been a brother and a son to me today. All I have to my name now are those few bits of children and my man.

I used to say to myself before my son died, "My father is dead, but I have planted another Ali in the house." But God did not grant him life. I suffer because my father's name has been mowed down twice.

When Ali was alive and I called out his name, my heart was at peace. I would feel a great happiness come over me, and his name would spring from my lips like the ringing of bells. My heart was full, and I was expansive.

Ali was a wise child. He was as stable as a rock. Whatever happened in front of him he would keep it to himself like a man. I would sometimes say to him, "My boy, you saw such and such happen. How could you keep it from me?" He would wave his hand grandly and turn away in a gesture of contempt and say to me, "How do I know?" When I saw him sweep the air like that with his hand, I was overcome with pleasure. He was a real man. Nothing moved him. So when I spoke to him questioningly, he would say, "Don't ask me anything. How do I know?" Saying this he would run away from me. He wouldn't stay around to be asked questions like a ninny.

When I saw him go out on the street to play, a sense of greed would consume my heart. I would go after him like someone who is hungry goes after food. I would look for him in the street, and when I found him and he

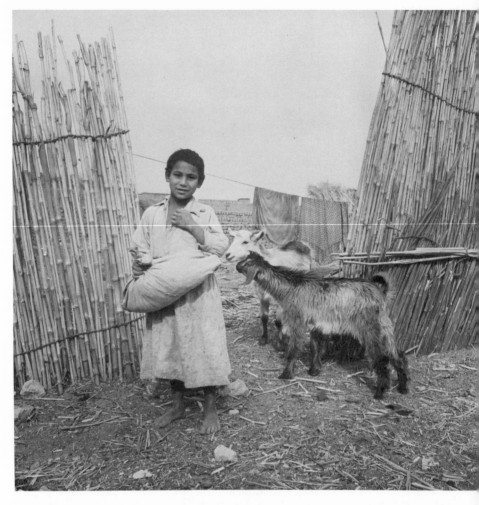

"I loved Ali more than the others because he was named after my father."—Om Gad.
Photograph by Asma el-Bakry.

was before me once again, my heart would be at peace. The fire which
consumed me when he was out of sight would subside when I saw him, as
suddenly as it had been ignited.

One time when his father drove some people to Suez he had an
accident. He had the boy with him and told him to say nothing in order to

spare me. But a few months later when the chance of giving me a shock had passed, his father mentioned it. He said, "Can you imagine, Om Gad, that when I was in Suez I had an accident!" I answered, "O merciful Lord. O calamity! What happened?" He said, "I ran into a child. But I was lucky. God was watching over me, and nothing happened." I said, "Was the child hurt?" and he said, "No."

I ran to Ali and called out to him, "Come here. Why didn't you say anything about the accident?" So he waved his hand without hesitation, and with a manliness which went straight to my heart he said, "So what of it? What did you want me to tell you?" and left the room. He was as solid as a man of thirty or forty. He was also handsome—a real body—handsome and godlike.

After he died I would go to the cemetery and in my sorrow wail and cover myself with dust. I was on fire. I was like an oven. His father still weeps but quietly. Men don't wail and cover themselves in dust like women. He holds in his pain and shows nothing. But the shock has dismantled him.

In these circumstances a woman has to be patient. We've been together thirty years—thirty years since I took him. And because he's my first cousin, his sorrow pains me doubly, and his happiness concerns me all the more.

When I see him unwell or unhappy, I feel as if I'm in a whirlpool. If something were to happen to him, how would I bring up my children? I look to God and say, "You see and know all. It's enough that he should have the strength to raise up these last few children. I require nothing for myself."

Fatigue and discouragement have affected him. There's no rest, not even a day off to collect himself. Cars have to be tended and washed daily. But on days when his back gives out and still he tries to get up, I stand before him and swear saying, "By God, you'll stay in bed, I'll go out and do what I can, and leave the rest to God."

If someone complains that his car is not clean, I try to smooth things over by saying, "By God, Sir, Omar is ill, please let it pass." When he stays in bed and stews, he can't stand it. He hates me being forced to do his work.

This is our life, everything that happens is God's will after all. We accept it. I just hope God gives Omar time enough on this earth to place each one of our five daughters happily in some man's house.

Daughters are a serious responsibility. We have only two sons left; the eldest is Gad. Our eldest daughter married, but it turned out badly. The one she took was a poor man. I took him under my wing and built him up and set up a home for him. I did this thinking, "I'm preparing a nest for my daughter. It's enough that she be in a man's house even if he is a poor man of humble origin."

I thought that even if we had to feed them, it was enough to be able to say when the neighbors asked, "Where is your daughter going to or coming from?" "She's going to her husband's house or coming from her husband's house." But the marriage was a failure.

His parents began to plot to dispose of the furniture we had provided the couple, and the whole thing soured. She had a son, Reda, by this man. That is why we call her Om Reda.

After the boy was born, his folks worked on him saying, "Divorce her, divorce her," until he did.

She and her son, Reda, now live with us. She had this boy one year before I gave birth to another son, Saad, who is now six years old. He will be going to school next year.

When Saad was born, I had four men in the house. I was happy. They filled the house with their presence. Their comings and goings were my joy. They made me feel needed and gave me hope in the future. But soon people began their round of envious chatter. Before Saad was born, I'd had a son who died when he was one year old. "Oh, she's had another son," they would say with envy in their hearts. "Oh, she now has four men in her house." This way people began to cast the evil eye on us, and the thirteen-year-old and the baby both died.

I was heartbroken. They had given meaning to my life and provided the house with a soul. But God didn't mean for my happiness to last. The light in my heart is dim with the losses I've suffered. Even our daughter was returned to us after seven years of marriage. Unlike the other children, she didn't go to school. She's a poor creature who has nothing.

Gad didn't do well in school, so we got him a job as a messenger in a company. The army then took him, and when his three years in service are over, he'll go back to his job.

We got our other daughter a job in one of the ministries as a clerk. The youngest girl who had polio didn't get high enough marks on her exams to go on to high school, so we said to her, "Never mind, child. You see that your sister is a clerk and is content and has a job. We will find something for you to do."

Each one of the children must have an education with which to make his way in the world. We are not certain to be able to support them forever. We still have my father's house in Giza, and we have built another house there which we rent. We work hard in order to be able to leave behind us something for the children.

We have to work hard. In the last five years we came to live with Omar in the three rooms behind the garage. I've helped him with his work, although I was not accustomed to working, and he never subjected me to the hardship or vexation of a job. In fact, he kept me so well that I never even slipped out of the house to go on an errand. He really cared for me. That's the way he showed it—by keeping me home.

I used to be pretty, and I never went out. But since my son Ali died I have lost my looks, and I have to help my husband although he doesn't want me to. But what with Gad, our eldest son in the army, and Omar broken by hardship and sadness, I decided I had to help.

With us if a man cares for his wife properly, he never lets her go out or do anything. This is the real sign of his affection. It is shameful to let her out. It's different with our educated daughters of course. But I feel contented with life this way.

The owner of the building takes half of the rent paid to the garage, and we take the other half. The owner also gives us a salary of E£15 [about U.S. $25] a month.

There are some occasions in life which are unforgettable. One of these was my circumcision.

I was sitting with my maternal first cousins. There was a barber in the village who specialized in this operation. Circumcision is absolutely necessary. I don't know why, but it is a tradition. These parts in a woman grow bigger the older she gets. They are ugly and deface her. It's true that God created us this way, but when we woke up to ourselves we found this custom handed down to us from our grandfathers and theirs and from those of whom we are not even aware and those we no longer know. We emerged into this world and found this habit already existed. It's just so. My people do this, and so I must do like they do.

I was nine years old when I was circumcised. One day cousin Zahra came running up to me and said, "Come on, come one, we are going to be circumcised." She was happy. We are told it's a big event. Our parents prepare us by saying, "We'll slaughter a chicken for the occasion. We'll feed you some sweets," and so we children rejoiced at all these possibilities. When my cousin came to call me I was overjoyed. I got up and ran with her. It was a feast!

Although I'd heard a child scream when being circumcised I wasn't afraid. Some of our cousins had already been circumcised when we arrived at the house. They were sitting there laughing. It only hurts the moment the razor hits, then the stinging goes away.

My cousin Zahra sat first. I heard her cry out. I was a little frightened then. I said, "I don't want to be circumcised." So they got hold of me, and my maternal uncle's wife sat behind me and held my legs apart. I was sitting on the floor on a piece of rug. The barber stood in front of me and did the operation. I cried out once, then they made a bandage of cotton and gauze and placed it between the "sisters" [labia] and said, "Don't bring your legs together or the wound will heal over. If this happens, when a woman gives birth she is torn."

We did as we were told. Every day we washed the wound with water and disinfectant and then sprinkled a powder made from the little insects, soos, which nest in the dried twigs of the cotton plant when it is stored on the roof of the houses in the village. We use it as fuel in the ovens. It is called soos afchet el kotn. We didn't use mercurochrome or sulfa powder as they do now.

After seven days the wound healed. We washed in the nearby canal, because we believe that Nile water is healing. We also dabbed a little oil on the wound. This was sometimes not so good. It prevented the wound from drying.

Circumcision can be performed at any time, but usually we avoid doing it in winter because cold makes healing more difficult. The skin is hard and stiff. Summer is better because you can wash more easily and not be cold. Summer is also gentler.

When they came to get me for the operation I went. My mother stayed home. She trusted her sisters and let them take care of the operation. We are all the same. But some siblings are good to each other, and with others there are misunderstandings and no trust.

My youngest daughter is eleven. She has not been circumcised. She is in fourth form at school. She doesn't know it's coming because she's a little absent minded. But mostly the children all know about it. They talk to each other. It's a necessity, a tradition for boys and girls alike. Her eldest sister will take her to the Imam el Shaf'ee, to a man there for the operation. She took her other brothers and sister to be circumcised there. She took them and set out in a taxi at six o'clock one morning. She had them circumcised then brought them back. It's not strange that the operation should be done by a man. These are only children, and he doesn't know us from Adam anyway.

My eldest daughter was circumcised by a midwife. But her knife was blunt, and it took three tries by the end of which the girl was a wreck, and I was a jumble of nerves. Usually men are better and lighter handed.

I remember saying to myself when the midwife was operating, "Why didn't you sharpen your instruments, why didn't you get new razors?" But I couldn't say anything, and the girl suffered. It took her a long time to recover.

The children who were circumcised at the Imam el Shaf'ee were healed within seven days. I washed them and applied mercurochrome to the wounds regularly. I changed the bandages every day, and they got up safe and sound in no time.

It's best to do this when the children are fairly young. I knew a woman who had it done just one week before her marriage was consummated. It was rough. They dragged her off because she looked unseemly. If you opened her up, you would see her parts hanging out. It disfigures a girl.

Circumcision doesn't affect sexual desire. Some women just want a man all the time. Others don't. There are some women who want a man with them morning, noon, and night. If a night passes when he hasn't "bathed" with her, as we call it, she becomes angry, nervous, and ill humored. Other women are more reasonable, not wanting to make an issue of sex. Whether the man "presents himself" to her or not, she'll not mention it. She won't embarrass or shame herself by saying anything or asking for anything.

When a woman gets married, is it because she's hungry, thirsty, or naked in her father's house? Not usually. She gets married because in her father's house one thing is lacking. Marriage is meant only for that one thing, sex. That is the purpose of marriage and that alone.

When I was married, I didn't know what sex was about. I was young. Not like today's children, who know everything about everything. I was thirteen. I had neither breasts nor had my period come yet. I was a kid, but I was plump.

The neighbors looking at me would laugh and say, "Good Lord, what in the world can he do with a girl like that? What does she understand of what a man wants?" They would then turn and looking at my childish figure would say, "Good heavens, child, what will your bridegroom be able to hold on to? Do you even have a hint of a bosom?" They would go on in this way. Despite the comments of the women, youthful marriages were not so unusual in my day.

The females of my family came the day of my wedding and held me for the defloration. People don't do that much any more. This first night is between the man and woman now. But then they did. It was the custom.

They dressed me in white on the day my marriage was to be con-summated. They wrapped me inside a *melaya laff,* a very large piece of black cloth, like a sheet, which women used to wear on top of their house dresses in native quarters to go out on the street. They didn't want to have me looked at by everyone. I was covered and walked like a little black bundle the short distance from my father's house to my husband's house. When I got there, the family sat me down in front of the house on a chair and took off the black sheet. People began to come and recite verses from the Koran and give money presents, *no'ta,* and the music and drumming struck up. This went on all night.

At the end of the night, my paternal uncle's son went up to my bridegroom and said to him, "Come along now and carry your bride across the threshold." So he took me into the house and laid me down on the bed. He carried me easily. He was twenty-five and a man already. I was half his age, thirteen.

I then saw the womenfolk all sitting around on the benches which lined the room, my maternal uncle's wife, the wife of my mother's paternal uncle's son, and others. I was astonished to see them lined up. I said to myself, "How amazing. What are they sitting around for?" Then one of them said to me, "Take off your underpants." I said, "What do you mean? Where do you think I've left my manners? What sort of shame do you want to put me to?" So they laughed.

They looked at me and twittered and whispered and laughed. Each had her say, and they bantered back and forth. "She's a child, Sister," one would say to the other. "She's so young, Sister. Does she know the first thing about marriage?" "Whatever came over her mother and father? How could they give her away at that age?" "Well, you know how it is. The groom is her paternal uncle's son and her first cousin. Her parents couldn't say no to him when he asked for her. They couldn't keep her from her cousin." I stood looking, Omar smiled and seemed pleased. The women gossipped. Suddenly they got up and seized me. One of them took off my underpants by force. These were not like today's with elastic at the top. They were constructed with a cummerbund which was knotted snugly at the front and back. They ripped off the cummerbund and held me down for him on a rug on the floor. I was shaking and crying. They held my legs apart. One of them held me firmly from behind. One woman gave my groom a clean white gauze to wrap around his finger. He knew what to do and seem pleased by my ignorance.

Men are never afraid. They know everything, not like women. He inserted his finger into me, and I screamed. He did this a couple of times until he drew blood. Then he took me and threw me on the bed. I was limp. They gave me a glass of sugared water to revive me.

First he has to puncture a little membrane, like a grape, which is delicate and gives out its blood as soon as it is poked. Second there is something like a kidney which is tougher and requires a few jabs of the finger to give out its blood. Blood has to come out. It stands for honor. It stands for enormous honor. A girl's honor is worth the world. Her happiness is built on it. It's destroyed without it and can never be repaired.

When the women saw the blood come out they said, "Enough, Omar. Stay your hand now." So he did. When this was done, each one went her way, and I was alone with him. He closed the door behind them. Suddenly I saw that he was undressed. He had taken off his underpants. I had drawn myself up into a ball on the bed. I was cowering, stuck like a fly against the wall. He said, "Let's go."

It is our custom to have dinner brought in to the bride and groom after the defloration. It usually consists of a pair of male ducks and a tray of baked macaroni with minced meat. The women had prepared the food ahead of time and left it in the room. He brought it out and cut the duck and dished out the macaroni and offered me a plate, saying, "Eat this." I refused, saying, "I don't want to eat. I'm not hungry." He tried to cajole me, saying, "Have this little morsel." "This is a nice piece." "Here, eat the liver." The liver is a delicacy. But where is appetite at a time like this?

When he saw that I wouldn't eat, he ate and removed the food. I had shrunk within myself. I didn't know what to expect. He was naked. I was dressed. He tried to persuade me to take off my clothes. I refused. Finally he said, "Well, at least take off your dress." I said, "I'll sleep in my dress." He insisted. I was afraid. Finally I got up the courage to say, "Shame on you. What are you sitting there naked for? Get up and get dressed." He answered, "My girl, this is what marriage is all about. What do you think we get married for?" So I said, "I don't know this sort of marriage." I was embarrassed. I kept my eyes on the floor. I didn't want to look in his direction. I didn't want to see him.

When he saw that it was useless, he got up and put on a white cotton night shirt and lay down. He put his head on the pillow and pretended to sleep. When he began to snore, I was reassured.

I got up slowly and moved away from him. I crept to the wardrobe and got out a fresh pair of drawers and put them on. I tied them with a double knot back and front. Slowly I went to one of the couches in the far end of the room and lay down and fell fast asleep the way a tired child does, a sleeper, dead to the world.

Suddenly I felt myself being moved. He had carried me back to the bed and was on top of me. I felt a pain and woke up as he penetrated me. He was strong and vigorous. I was a girl. My underpants were gone again. He had slit the knot in the belt with a razor blade while I slept. He was on top of me.

I screamed. He put his hand on my mouth and said, "For shame. Don't cry out like that in the middle of the night. What will people say?" So I lay still. He finished his business and got up.

Later in the night he wanted me again. I said no. I was afraid. I got up and sat upright on the couch. Every time I dozed off, I'd jerk myself awake, fearing him. He was young and full of passion. I was terrified. So it went all night.

Once, twice, three times, and I got used to him.

Seven or eight months after I was married my period came. It dropped in on me one day like an unexpected visitor, between the time for afternoon and evening prayers. My husband was asleep. He had then started to work as a caretaker and car washer in various garages. It was night work. He slept in the day time. He was just about to get up then. I was up and going to wash myself when it came. I was dousing myself with water. I saw blood.

I ran to my husband in surprise and cried out, "Omar, help me. I was washing myself, and I saw blood on my finger." He said, "What blood?" I answered, "I don't know. I don't know what it is." So he said, "Maybe it's what they call *el-dahr* [the back]." I began to feel my back. I thought he meant that I was wounded. I didn't know. I was ignorant. But there was no blood on my back. I said to him, "You must stop at my mother's on your way to work and send her to me right away or else take me with you." So he said, "You stay. On my way to work I'll stop by my paternal uncle's wife—that is my mother—and send her to you. She'll tell you what's happened."

My mother came. I said to her, "This and this and this is what happened." So she said to me, "That's your 'back.' It's come." I answered, "But my back isn't wounded." My mother laughed. She was a mature woman and knew. I said again, "But woman, there's nothing wrong with my back. What are you saying?" So she said it was my period, that I could now start having children, and told me not to wash until it was over.

When it was over, I bathed and became pregnant right after with Fatma, my eldest daughter.

My period never gave me any trouble. I neither use cotton pads nor anything else. If I do, it stops. So I just wear my underpants, and when they are soiled, I wash them in boiling water and change into clean ones.

My daughters, on the other hand, have a hard time with it. One of them complains of cramps and rolls around in pain. She can neither go to work nor get out of bed for three days. She takes some brown tablets that her fellow-workers get for her from Saudi Arabia to ease the pain. With me it stays three days and is gone. In the past the flow descended on me like a sea in turmoil. I could feel it flow at the source and catch myself just in time to change my drawers. Now it's just a trickle. It barely soils my pants.

One of my daughters can't take anything for relief, not even a hot glass of herb tea, *yansoon* or *helba*, or any of the soothing hot drinks we have. We went to see a doctor about the pain, and he said it would pass when she married.

Before my first child was born I prepared myself for the occasion. It is the custom with us not to wait until the woman gives birth to stock the house with food for her. Once I've passed the sixth or seventh month of pregnancy, I make sure I have poultry in the house. This is our custom. We keep chickens. Every house has a place to keep poultry. I'd get a pair of ducks for example. The ducks would eat the leftovers of the house. I'd get a pair of rabbits and put them in with the ducks or a few chickens. Enough for the whole family to feast on when a child is born. Surely I'd not eat alone and let the rest of the household look on. All must eat.

Whatever scraps are left over from meals—a bit of bread, a branch or two of some greens—it all goes to the animals. It's like an investment. When a woman gives birth, she's then all ready to provide for her needs from her own house and doesn't need to run off to the chicken merchant or the butcher's for what food the household requires at that time. After giving birth she must eat well.

My labor pains began one day, and the child was born easily. My pregnancy was difficult, and I couldn't hold down any food for nine months, not even a glass of tea. I slept, woke up, vomited, and did not feel comfortable until the fetus came down to earth. Then it was as if nothing had happened. The births of all my children were easy—a matter of half an hour, and the child would be on the ground. I'd then get up. The women attending me would heat water and bathe me and the child. They'd dress the child with garments I had prepared ahead of time. A couple of suits usually. They'd spread something on the bed, a piece of plastic to protect the mattress from the bleeding, and I'd lie down again. So it went. They'd bring me a glass of *helba* to drink first thing and then kill a chicken or a rabbit, stew it, and feed me. They fed me well until I regained my strength. My mother was always with me these times.

I had three children die on me and miscarried once. I have seven children now. Seven and four, that's eleven. I'd have had eleven children if all had lived.

My grown son died. The boy who was eight months old and the girl who was six months old died. When I miscarried, it was a boy, and I had been six months pregnant. It was very hard, and I was unwell. When I saw that he was born dead, I said to him, "Go. God give you sustenance."

The son who died when he was eleven years old was born on a Friday. He came into this world at dawn, when the day is as if covered in gauze. I had a cousin, *Bint Khaali*, who rejoiced at the birth of boys. We had relatively few boys in the family. She had an only daughter with no brothers. She herself had no brothers. I had none, and my mother had none. She was with me when I gave birth to the boy. She called my husband and said to him, "Come here, my boy. God has been generous to us. Come here, Omar. Come, my fellow, come. Come and cut the cord of your son. Come and cut it so he can grow up and be like you." So he took hold of *ibrit baboor,* a sharp, flat bit of metal with a short needle point at the end used to clean the eye of the primus stoves—we have a custom of cutting the cord with this instrument—and cut his son's cord. He did it for Gad, too. Men rejoice at the birth of a boy.

Our people prefer boys, because a girl's life is difficult. It's difficult in every sort of family and among all nationalities. A girl's life is not like a man's life. She has no assurance of being happy in her marriage. And her main

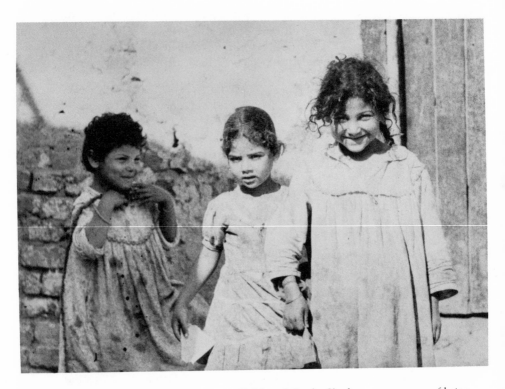

"Our people prefer boys because a girl's life is difficult. She has no assurance of being happy in her marriage. A girl's and a woman's lives are a trial whatever happens."
—Om Gad. Photograph by Asma el-Bakry.

purpose in life is to marry and to have children. A girl's and a woman's lives are a trial whatever happens. I don't know why.

Every woman wants to be happy. She wants to be happy with her man. She wants him to love and care for her. She wants him to treasure her and look after her. He shows his love in this way. If she speaks to him, he listens and takes her opinion into consideration. He trusts her. There are some men who when their wives speak will say, "Oh, don't listen to her." This hurts a woman and shows her that for him she's no more than a statue. She's not human.

If a woman makes a mistake, for example, her husband should not be hard on her. He shouldn't punish her. Everyone makes mistakes. There are some men who will complain about their wives to others, saying, "My wife

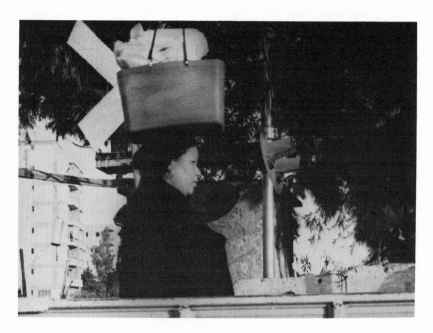

Going home from market carrying a now-popular type of shopping basket made of plastic. Photograph by Asma el-Bakry.

does this or is that." That's not love. If he makes a mistake, she should also be tolerant and not speak to others about his shortcomings. If they let out secrets about each other, this is not love. It is said that a married man and woman must be like a tomb. What happens between them stays between them. Without this they cannot be happy.

If God gives a man a piaster [about U.S. 15¢], a good husband will say to his wife, *"It faddalli,* have this," and offer it to her. If she is *bint nass wa assela,* that is, well bred and of good stock, she'll take good care of the piaster he gives her. She'll make it pay off. A good wife will not adopt the attitude of "God gives, and God taketh away. God will provide." She must make of that one piaster, ten piasters. She must put it to work so that it will be useful to her and her children. One can never be sure of what life holds, and it is a wife's job to make the money her husband earns go a long way.

My man never says to me, "What have you spent, or what did you buy, or what did you do?" When he gets paid, he brings me the money. He says, "Here you are, Om Gad." If I get some money from one of the tenants in our building for doing some little job, I go to him and say, "So and so gave me this sum." There are no secrets between us.

I wish we could stay in our house in Giza. I wish that my husband would go to work like before and that we lived at home. I wish I could be happily settled in my own house. Instead we live in back of the garage where he works. We have three rooms, and our own house is closed up. Our furniture and things are in it. When I open the house now and then and look in, I feel sad. I am sad and I leave. But then I console myself by saying, "Is the house alone going to feed me? Can I cut away parts of its walls to live on and make a living for the group who depends on me? No, I have to work. I have to stay here and make a living."

Our problem is that we are modest people with no capital. We have to work hard to make ends meet. Behind the garage we lived in two rooms first. Then we got fed up. We were cramped, and what compensation did we have for living this way? The tenants in the apartment building pay the same pound every month now [about U.S. $1.50] that they paid five years ago. For this they get their cars washed daily and guarded at night. So I went to the owner of the building and struck a bargain with her. We would stay on getting E£15 a month salary, plus what we got from each tenant if she agreed to build us an extra two rooms at her expense. She agreed.

My husband, whether he's well or not, has to get up at four in the morning daily to wash cars. He drinks his glass of tea, prays, and goes to work. I get up to help him. The children can only help us a little. They have to build their own lives. Besides, they are ashamed of this work. Our daughter especially has trouble with what her father does. She works at one of the ministries and has had a number of men come to her with offers of marriage. But the first question a young man asks now of a prospective bride is, "What does your father do?" What can she answer? "My father works as a garage attendant?" She can't. It would embarrass her. This is a generation of government employees. They have been educated. They have diplomas. They look down their noses at anyone who works with his hands.

My daughter is in an awkward position. She is in conflict because she doesn't want to have this question put to her. Her schooling is an advantage and a drawback.

A prospective bridegroom presented himself to our daughter recently. He is from humble origins like we are. His people are modest like us. He's employed by a bank and is doing a correspondence course to improve his lot and get ahead. Every diploma you get earns you more respect. God help him succeed in his endeavors! He earns E£32 [about U.S. $60] a month. There are extras with his job, and he sits at a desk. This is probably the only kind of man she can marry. Someone from the same background as us but who has improved himself like her and has diplomas to match hers.

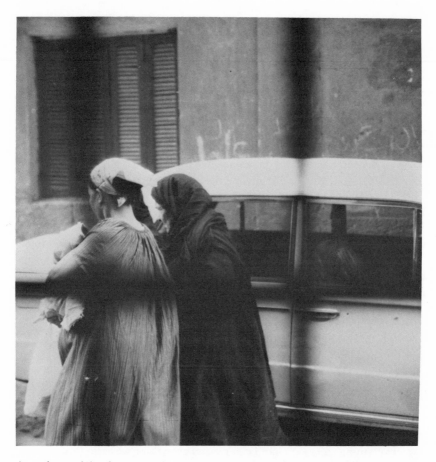

A mother and daughter going for a visit in a popular quarter in Cairo. Photograph by Asma el-Bakry.

Our daughter earns E£20 [about U.S. $30] a month. It's not enough to keep her. It's hardly enough to buy the clothes she needs for a working girl and the tea she buys for herself and offers her colleagues at work. We support her a little on the side. What can we do? My man struggles, and I work alongside. He can never rest. Children are a trust and a responsibility.

He gets up in the morning to wash the cars. I'll do a few of them with him or help him wipe them dry. If one of the tenants needs something, whether in our building or one of the neighboring buildings, he calls on my husband. There are some ladies who can't drive but have cars. They will sometimes say, "Come drive us to town, Omar." So he obliges. He spends an hour or two or three with them, and God rewards him with a pound or so. Someone wants a window or shutter fixed. He will do it. He'll get fifty or sixty piasters [about U.S. $1] for that. He'll put a washer in a leaky faucet and get another twenty-five piasters, and so on. It adds up. It keeps us going, and we have many mouths to feed.

Everything has become so expensive, the thing which cost ten pias-ters last year now costs fifty, and what was fifty piasters is now a pound. So our burden is heavy.

We can't let a child go hungry. We can't say to a child, "We haven't the money to feed you." So if anyone needs his services, the man has to run whether he is able to or not. He must say "yes." He says, "The piaster which I earn is better than the one I leave unearned."

We finish the cars at about eight or nine on the mornings when I'm with him. The rest of the day I cook, wash, and take care of the children. Those of us who are home prepare for the ones at work. If there is washing to be done, we do it. Everyone pulls his weight. The one who drinks from a glass rinses it out. My eldest daughter washes up and tidies the place.

We have five small rooms now and a bathroom. We have a place where we put the *butagaz* stove. We cook there. We have to make do. People can wish for things, but everything is in God's hand in the end. Our daugh-ter's husband left her seven years ago. We are bringing up her son, along with our children. His father is a son of a bitch. He married and had a child and doesn't even ask after him or give anything for his support. What can we do?

Our daughter who is working at the ministry has now had an offer of marriage from the man whose family are people like us. We've accepted him but are at a loss as to how to prepare the girl's trousseau and required furnish-ings. Everything costs so much. I can't spend everything we earn. If there is an emergency, who could I borrow money from? I keep suggesting she marry one of her colleagues, someone better off than this man, but she refuses on the grounds that her father's job makes it impossible. So I say to her, "Tell him you father is a driver." That would be acceptable. She answers that if the man asks to see her father's papers to prove the validity of her word, he would notice that his driver's license is only for a private vehicle. He would ask the neighbors and investigate to find out how Omar made a living. He would then think this marriage below him. We would suffer rejection and humilia-tion, so why put ourselves in this position? We stick to our own.

We bought an old car this year for E£ 500 [about U.S. $700–800]. It belonged to one of the tenants. I paid E£400 which I got by forming a cooperative. I contributed E£20 to this cooperative. My maternal first cousin and a few trusted friends each paid E£20 to make up the rest of 400 pounds. Each month I put in E£20, as do the others. The lot goes to each one in turn. We can only make big purchases like that by forming co-operatives. These are very common among people like us because no one has ready big sums at one time. I bought the car from someone who has two cars in the garage. They pay E£5 a month for upkeep of each car. Now they keep those ten pounds to make up the remaining hundred I still owe them. I'll have my debt paid in five months.

It's useful to have a car. When I go to our house in Giza by taxi, I pay at least fifty piasters, round trip. I have a long wait on the street sometimes. If I want to take something to the house or if I leave the children there on their holidays and want to take them some food, it's hard to get back and forth. Taxis don't stop readily for passengers.

One day these tenants told Omar they wanted to sell the car. They asked him to look out for a buyer. It is a Ramses car, a very small Egyptian-made Fiat. So when he mentioned it to me, I jumped at the opportunity. I said to him, "Look here, Abu Gad, it's our turn to get the 200 pounds from the cooperative. Why don't we buy it?" We were getting the money to get our daughter ready for marriage. But as the bridegroom had not really "formed" himself yet and was still paying out money for his newly married sister's support, we thought the preparations could wait. He was still paying installments on his sister's furniture, to help his father out. We could wait.

Omar then went to see the car owner. He asked how much she wanted for the car. She said E£600. He came back to tell me. I told him, "We'll buy the car." He said, "What are you going to buy this car with? You just want to buy everything which comes your way. Buy, buy, buy." I answered, "Just wait a minute. Instead of having to take public transportation and taxis, we'll use the money we have from the co-op for this. God will provide when your daughter is ready to settle down." He said, "People like us don't have cars. We'll be the laughingstock of the street. People will snigger and talk and refer to it as a donkey cart. We have to know our place so that we will not be ridiculed!" But I insisted. Let people say what they will. Why shouldn't we improve ourselves? So I went to see the owner.

When I confronted her with the idea, she laughed. Omar was right. But I said to her, "Don't laugh, Lady, just because we're humble people wanting to better ourselves. Even if we took this car for nothing, it would not make a difference to someone like you." So she agreed to sell it to us saying, "You're good people, and everyone likes you." I said, "God bless you. I'll take the car for 400." She said, "No, I'm asking 600." So I told her we didn't have that, we'd been so long in her service that she should have some consideration for our circumstances, and words of that nature. She wanted to know where I'd get the money. I explained about the cooperative and said, "I'd be sorry to see the car sold outside." So she agreed to let me have it for 500. I couldn't argue with that. I said, "I'll give you 400 now and you deduct 10 pounds a month from the garage rent until the remaining 100 are paid up." She said, "Well, don't let me down." I said I wouldn't, these agreements being sacred.

She thought then and said, "Why don't you add another five a month to the deal?" I said I couldn't. I'd be paying 20 each month to the cooperative and would have nothing left over. I said to her, "If some month, God forbid, I'm unable to pay you, you would let it pass, I'm sure. But I can't fall back on payments to the co-op, because just as I relied on others, so others are relying on me. One can't fail to pay a co-op." I told her to keep the car in her name until we'd paid up, but she refused, saying she trusted me. I said these things were all in the hands of God anyway and went away satisfied to tell Omar, Abu Gad, the news.

She took her money, and we went to register the car. Omar wanted to put it in my name, but I refused. He said we could put it in both our names. I said to him, "You're the man, and you're responsible. Put it in your name." So he did.

We rent my father's house in Giza for E£9 a month. It's a mud brick house, but I haven't the means to rebuild it in fired brick. It has two rooms. We rent it to a construction worker and his wife. She works too, and on the first of each month without fail they pay the rent.

Our own house is made of brick. It has four rooms. It has tiled floors, painted walls, electricity, and water. We have stored our divorced daughter's furniture in one room. Every few days we go there to clean the furniture and stay a while. The children go there on their holidays.

We don't think of renting it because I don't know what the future holds. Supposing we leave this job? Where would we go if the house was rented? Once you have a renter, he will never leave.

This is our life. There are twelve of us. We struggle to get by. We eat bread alone for 30 piasters a day. God willing, when we can, we buy two or three kilos of meat twice a week from the government cooperative. We can't afford to pay the prices at the regular butcher's. Meat there costs twice as much as at the government stores. Along with this I buy some vegetables, some rice or macaroni which all comes to about two or three pounds a week [about U.S. $5]. We spend about ten pounds a week on food. We also take a kilo of milk a day for thirty piasters, tea for seventy-five piasters, a week, and sugar every two or three days for thirty piasters.

From time to time we buy fruit for the children. We often do without ourselves because after all we are grown, and we have to watch every penny. But a child is not like an adult. When a child sees something, he wants it.

You can't deprive a child. But from time to time we all share. If God rewards us with a watermelon, or a kilo of fruit, for example, we sit around and eat it. We don't have a fridge.* Everyone takes his share.

We have a television. I bought it by forming another cooperative. I'd put away 120 pounds one time. God was kind to me. I didn't have it in mind to buy a T.V., but it came my way. I hadn't thought of it, because it was at the time of the death of my son and I was mourning.

A German who lived in the building across the way from us was going home. He was selling his things. He told his Nubian cook about it. The cook came and said to me, "Om Gad, this man has two radios and a T.V. and an air conditioner to sell." We hear of these things by word of mouth, like that. News travels fast in the street. I said, "I don't want a T.V." I was too unhappy to think of such a thing. I wanted the radio to listen to the chanted Koran. Listening to the chanted Koran would be a consolation and a comfort. The cook said the radio was going for E£35 [about U.S. $50]. I said, "If you can get it for E£25, I'll take it and give you five pounds for your trouble." He agreed.

In the meantime, another cook heard about the merchandise and decided he wanted the lot. He paid E£180 [about U.S. $200] for it. He said to the other cook, "If Om Gad wants the radio, she can pay E£35." I was angry and didn't agree.

There was a young lady who stayed with the German and she spoke Arabic. So I went up to see her and told her the story and asked her to mediate. She told the other cook to give me the radio as agreed. He raised his voice and abused her. She called the German and said to him in their language, "Give this man his money back. He's insulted and threatened me. He'll get nothing." Hearing this, I ran down to get the money for the radio. God was watching over me, because for some reason I decided to take some extra cash along and maybe get the T.V. as well.

The cook who lost the deal came down after me. He began to shout and scream in the street. I said to him, "Don't shout. The radio was promised to me, and you undercut me." I left him fussing and appealing to anyone who would listen and went back up and asked the lady how much they wanted for the T.V. and radio together. She said the cook had paid 180 pounds for all the appliances. I offered her 145 pounds for the radio and T.V. She said, "Well, where's your money?" I said, "Here it is." So she said, "Keep your

*Since this story was told, they acquired a good, locally made electric refrigerator, which sits prominently in Om Gad's bedroom.

money now and come get the things in three weeks when we leave." I said,
"No, you take the money now." I wanted to make sure they would not change
their minds.

When I went back down, the cook was still making a scene on the
street. People gathered to watch and listen. I said to him, "Look here. You
were rude to that lady and tried to cheat me. Nothing is gained by force. You
have to be courteous. You harmed yourself." But of course I said nothing to
him about the T.V. I figured that he and the other servant had cooked up this
scheme to their mutual benefit. I was happy they failed.

After three weeks I went up to the German's flat. It was a Tuesday.
The cook opened the door, and the man was there. The T.V. and radio were
ready. The man gave me their catalogs and a bill of sale written in English. He
said, "Go get someone to carry them for you. Where is your husband?" So I
said, "Downstairs," and ran down to get him, shouting, "We're getting the
T.V. and radio today!" He laughed and came up with me.

A day later the other cook came and jumped up and down with
annoyance and made another scene. He couldn't swallow his defeat. I said,
"Stew in your own juices. These things were obviously meant for me, or God
would not have turned the tables on you as he did." Today this T.V., a Sanyo,
is worth 200 pounds. This is how one makes a piaster worth ten.

I thought, "God had me in mind when this happened." When I form
a co-op, I always say, "Let it collect. When the time is right, God will open
the door through which it is meant to go."

The day I built the new house in Giza, I had only 300 pounds [about
U.S. $500] in my pocket. It cost me 2,500 pounds [about U.S. $4,000] to
build. It's there for the future and for the children.

The idea came to me one day like an inspiration. I said to Omar,
"We're going to build." He cursed, saying, "What are you going to build with,
woman? Is 300 pounds going to build a house?" So I said to him, "Look here,
we're going to make an effort, and God will strengthen us. We'll throw a
stone and run after it. God is great." So I ran, and God rewarded us.

I formed another co-op for E£20 a month later. My maternal first
cousin, *Bint Khalti*, lent me some money, and the house is all but paid for
now, and the car has just two months to go.

We have to struggle and argue with life until we reach the limits of
what is in store for us.

I thank God for everything and trust in him. But nothing I have
suffered in this life affected my body and my spirit as did the death of my son.
It still affects me. When he died and I saw myself completely undone, I
thought I would be lost and the children lost in my wake. I made an effort and
said to myself, "My girl, God give you patience." When I feel a tear crop up in

my eye, I repeat to myself, "God give me patience, God give me patience" and read the opening passage in the Koran, the *Fatha*. This sustains me.

I try to cool myself down when grief consumes me. I get up at once and don't let myself stew. I go out on the street. I stay there for a while so that the devil will not get hold of my thoughts and flatten me out again. Going out on the street is like dousing a fire with water. When I am on the street I feel better. I am in the open air, and there are people about to distract me. The street is a refuge.

We have to work and to live. We have to bring up our children. My dead son was everything to me. I wanted him to live. But everything in this world is in the hands of God. We live and accept his will. Our faith in him sustains and strengthens us.

2

Alice

THE CHARITY WORKER

"Money gives people room for love and hope. The lack of it occupies their minds completely and leaves room for nothing else."

I AM FROM the town of Minya, a town known for its hard-working people.

I was born there, and my mother was educated at the English school, as was her mother. The English planted the spirit of learning in these mothers, who then took an interest in educating their daughters.

My mother was the first to receive a diploma in our family. These eight or nine years at school marked her for life. She was taught English and handwork quite well and philosophy and sociology very well.

From mother to daughter the desire to learn was instilled. It served mothers and daughters well, especially in times of trouble.

My mother married my father, who was then a government employee. He had been French-educated by the Jesuit fathers.

My father's mother and my mother's mother were maternal first cousins. Relatives, in our part of the world, always seek each other out as marriage partners. Theirs was an expected union.

My mother was married five years and had had three children when my father died. He was killed in a car accident while we were on holiday in Cairo. We returned to Minya as soon after as we could to escape the humiliation of being cared for by my mother's family.

My mother's education proved to be a lifesaver. We had no income and no independent means of support save the rent from part of our small house in Minya. That was hardly enough to keep us. I was two years old when my father died, and I remember very little of that time save what my mother told us later.

We buried my father in Cairo and went back to Minya.

When we got home, my mother was offered a teaching position at the school where she had been a student and was welcomed by the staff with open arms. When we were old enough, she enrolled us there too—the girls in the girls' section of the school and her sons in the boys' section. We continued to live on the first floor of our house and rent out the top.

During my second year of high school, Saad, who is now my husband, came to my mother and offered himself in marriage to me.

He worked in a stationery shop. He had not finished high school but was very bright. As our father was dead and my mother's life was a struggle, she was inclined to accept him. A woman alone with daughters to marry cannot look as high in choosing a husband for her girls as one with a family of men at her back and a husband.

I was the eldest of her daughters and therefore the first to be married. She consulted me on the matter one day. I liked him, and she gave me to him.

When final agreements were reached, Saad bought the *shabka*, which is the gold jewelry given by the groom to the prospective bride to seal their engagement. He gave me a gold filigree bracelet and said to my mother, "I don't want anything from you." To me he said, "I know your father is dead. Your means are limited, and I propose to shoulder the costs of setting up a house." This meant that we didn't have to provide the furniture, like the bedroom suite which is usually the bride's family's contribution to the couple. The household must be fully furnished before a couple can be married. The furniture bought before the wedding is meant to last a lifetime.

I was married.

My mother gave notice to the tenants and offered us the second floor of her house to live in. We paid her a very small rent in exchange. Saad continued to work at the stationery shop, and I stayed home. His father and mother were dead. He was responsible for his younger brothers and sisters, and as soon as we married, they came to live with us.

Saad's salary was modest. From the beginning life was a struggle. He left the house at eight in the morning and came home for an hour at lunch time then went back to the stationery. He worked until nine or ten o'clock in the evening. Sunday was his day off.

When our children were born, they hardly saw anything of their father because he was gone so much. I pondered the situation. I was not satisfied and thought that Saad must go back to school to further himself and improve our lot.

He had a natural yen for learning, and when I proposed the idea to him, he welcomed it.

He set out to finish high school first. Then while continuing to work at the shop, he took a correspondence course in the humanities through a university in Cairo. He studied hard and went to Cairo only to sit for exams.

When he graduated four years later, the direction of our lives changed. He presented himself to the Ministry of Education and was assigned as a teacher of English in one of the public schools in Minya. Our situation improved.

I had had five children by then. Two boys and three girls. One of the girls died when she was a baby.

Saad taught and I stayed home. I felt restless and wanted to improve our lot even further. I had some gold jewelry then and had saved a little money. I gave this to Saad to sell, and with the money we bought our own little house. But that was not enough. I felt I had to do something as well. I had not graduated from high school. So I learned to sew. I saved some money and bought a machine and set myself up in business. Many customers wanted my services. I did well making a dress for a pound or seventy-five piasters.

When my eldest daughter came of age, she earned a degree in art and married very quickly. Her husband was a teacher. It was a love marriage, and they moved to Cairo.

My eldest son finished high school successfully and entered the college of engineering.

Each of these children had expenses for clothes, books, and spending money. So I sewed and helped my husband and children in this way.

I wanted the children to dress well, eat well, and live well. I educated them all. My youngest daughter went to the school of commerce at the university and was clever. She now works in a bank in Cairo. She married a pharmacist, and that too was a love marriage.

My youngest son is a government employee. But he was not satisfied with his lot. He wanted more. He didn't want to live a middle-class life like so many others. He sought his fortune outside Egypt. He went to one of the Arab countries to work for a firm. There he earns a very good salary.

I've lived a good life. But it hasn't been easy. There was the responsibility of raising the children and the heartache of losing a child, plus all of the difficulties of married life. After the children had grown up, we moved to Cairo. I had grown weary of sewing but had a keen interest in people and their problems. So I joined a church organization designed to help the needy. Although I teach sewing to poor women, my real fulfillment comes from looking after the social, health, and financial needs of these women. Having struggled myself, I am keen to talk to them about their problems. They have my full sympathy and understanding. I try to advise them on how to further themselves. I am also a good matchmaker, and I help families in this way as well.

I am trying to instill in these women the spirit of independence—in

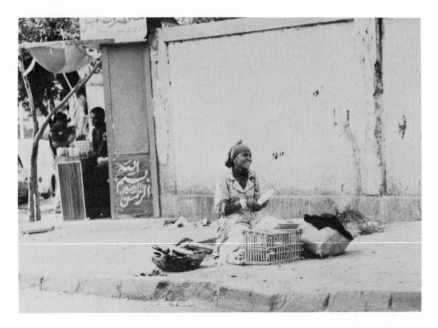

"I am trying to instill in these women a sense of independence. I want them to do some work which is of use to them, provide them with an income."—Alice. Selling corn to passersby on one of Cairo's streets. Often shucking and roasting corn on a fire made in a small metal basin is one of the first signs that summer has come. Photograph by Asma el-Bakry.

other words, how not to extend their hands and beg for money. I want them to learn to do some work which will be of use to them, provide them with an income, and give them a sense of accomplishment. Some make things they can sell, like homemade noodles. Others raise chicks to sell, and the rest learn to sew, knit, embroider, and crochet. These skills are always in demand. These skills also free them from total dependence on their husbands or families.

Some of the women even work in homes, earning E£1 or 1.50 per day. The spirit I have tried to instill is taking hold. Women are jealous of one another. The competition keeps them interested. Their work keeps money in their pockets.

To grow up fatherless as I did in our society is very difficult. This was my lot.

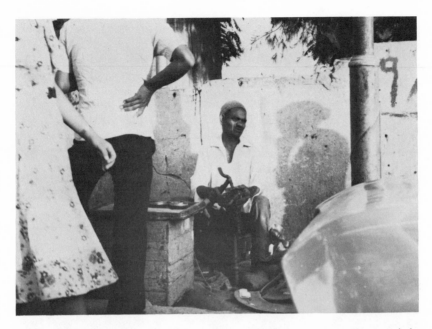

The neighborhood shoe repairman sets up by the railroad crossing. Photograph by Asma el-Bakry.

When I came into contact with other children and saw how they were cuddled and spoiled by their fathers or taken to another city for holidays, it cut into me pretty sharply. I felt that to be deprived of a father was a calamity.

When I saw my mother struggling to bring us up, it made me suffer. But this perhaps had a positive effect on us in the end. It taught us all very early on to shoulder responsibility.

When we were young, we went to school and returned home at four or half past four in the afternoon. We studied and had Sundays off. I helped my mother with cleaning the house, and on Sundays we went to church morning and afternoon.

In summer my eldest brother formed a sort of little club for us at home. We were not allowed to go out. We had neither garden nor balcony to play in. To compensate, my brother made us a chess set out of plywood. He taught us to play chess and dominoes. I'm convinced this helped improve our skills in mathematics. It forced us to think and plan and use our minds. I was about twelve years old then.

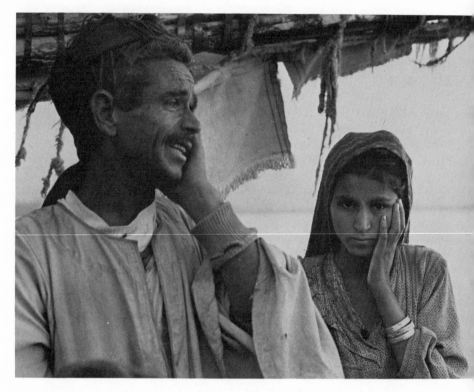

"I felt that to be deprived of a father was a calamity. It taught us all very early on to shoulder responsibility."—Alice. Photograph by Asma el-Bakry.

When my mother was short of money, she would weep and talk to us of our father. She would say, "Your father was unusual. He liked music and played the violin."

She said this. But I'm not sure she really liked it. She was very stern, and my father was gregarious. He and his friends had parties, played music, and drank wine. My mother's conservative spirit made it hard for her to accept the gaiety. These parties led to the sort of talk which offended her.

Her education and her nature made of her a moderate person. She was reserved and straight laced. I remember her wearing a small white metal bow pinned to her dress. It was a sign that the wearer neither drank alcohol nor smoked and that he or she would attempt to discourage these habits in others.

My mother worked on my father until he finally gave up the parties. He wanted my mother to wear western clothes but never convinced her to do so. In the villages she remained in her traditional dress. When she went out she always wore a *habarah*, black flowing robes over her house dress and a scarf over her head.

When my mother was young, she had loved her paternal first cousin. My father, who was her maternal first cousin, however took a liking to her and offered himself in marriage. Her family refused my father initially, although he was better educated than other prospects. He spoke French.

When they refused, he married his boss's daughter who died in childbirth not long after. The child was born dead also. It seemed they were ill fated.

Soon after, my father came again and asked for my mother's hand. By that time my grandfather had died, and her mother said to her, "It must be God's will that you should have your cousin." My mother was against this marriage. She said, "I don't want him, I don't want him, I don't want him." The family turned a deaf ear. Her uncle said to her, "We have no girls who say 'I want and I don't want.' This man has presented himself twice. You shall have him."

She married him against her will. But my father was very kind and patient with her. He loved her and wanted her to care for him in return. She was dead set against him. She would run away every two months or so and go back to her mother's house.

My father took it all in his stride it seems. But my grandmother would scold her daughter and say, "This is your lot, my girl. There is no room for caprice in a woman's life. You must accept your lot and bear your burden."

My mother was twenty-two years old when she married. This meant she was an old bride by the standards of the day. She continued to run away at the beginning of her married life. She would spend a month or two with her mother, then my father would come along and fetch her. He would say, "All right, is it all over now? Have you recovered enough to come home?" Then he would take her back. She would stay a month or two and run away again. Nothing particular happened to cause these explosions, it seems. She just didn't like him. She would cry and complain to her mother, saying, "I can't stand him. I can't bear to be with him. I don't love him."

On his part he treated her with the utmost patience, and in the end he won out. He was gentle and tried to make life easy for her. He hired a servant girl who called my mother "wife of my uncle." She cleaned and cooked for them. He rented a small house with a garden to please her. In the end my mother resigned herself and stayed home. I think she even grew fond of him. But he lived only three years more after that time.

When she remembered him these last years, she was sorry and wept. My eldest brother had been born during these restless years. By the time I came along, she had stopped running away.

As a result of her experience, however, my mother never forced any of us into marriage. She consulted each of us when the time came to make a choice.

When Saad came along, he used to visit us at my maternal aunt's house. I took a liking to him but of course remained silent about my feelings. A girl must never reveal her true feelings. We were neighbors and saw a lot of him. When he came to my mother and spoke for me, I was pleased but said nothing.

At that same time, another man had spoken for me. My mother took me aside and presented me with the options. She said, "Come, Alice, which one of these two would you prefer? Eskandar is a relative of your father's. He works for the railroads. The advantage of Eskandar as a husband is that he is a government employee and has a stable, permanent position and a pension when he retires. Saad works in a shop, and his prospects are less secure." She preferred Eskandar, but I had fallen in love with Saad and chose him.

I thought at that time that marriage was an easy matter: the end of the road, peace, and security. Saad was twenty-five. I was sixteen. As my father had died when I was a baby, I had no knowledge of what men were or what a husband would be like. My mother had never remarried. Men were a mystery to me.

I was shocked by much of what I discovered after marriage. Saad was hot blooded and had a violent temper, which I never saw until after the wedding. When I married him, we had no household help. I had to do everything. I had no idea that there were specific duties and restrictions incumbent on a married woman. In one's father's house one eats and sleeps when one pleases, and one feels free. Saad shouted at the slightest provocation, argued about the smallest thing, and was ready to strike when I answered back. This all came as a shock to me, but nothing to equal the shock I had when I discovered he had fallen in love with a younger cousin who came to live with my mother after I married. I had had two children by then. It's true that she was fair skinned, not dark like me, but she was no beauty. You never know what it is in a woman which inspires a man's desire.

It happened this way. He started to give her money behind my back, a sign of his affection for her. One day I caught him kissing her. I wept bitterly.

This event left me permanently scarred. Even forty years later it still affects me. I grew to mistrust all men as a result. I dislike and disrespect them all intensely and until now cannot tolerate a single man.

Saad has long since repented. He now adores me. But the damage is done. I would have been better off never marrying. He has tried to make amends, but such wounds never heal. I live with him. I give him his due in every way, and I no longer hate him as I did when the matter was still fresh, but my illusions about men have been permanently shattered. Not one of them can be trusted. Not even my own sons.

Saad contrived to marry his brother to my cousin in order to keep matters in the family. This was no solution, but I could say nothing about it. One day I was looking out of the window with my back to the room. My brother-in-law came in and put his arm around me. I turned and flung his arm off and twisted it hard behind his back and left the room without a word. To this day he has his face glued to the ground when we meet. Men are all the same!

My problem is that I am basically open and friendly. I laugh and talk easily with people. This men mistake for an invitation to licentiousness. One has to remain like an owl to be respected.

One night a friend of my husband came to visit. Saad was out. I received him cordially. No sooner was he seated than he said to me, "I love you." I answered, "Yes, we love each other as brothers and sisters must." But he persisted, saying, "This is a different kind of love." So I stood up and showed him the door. I've never told Saad about this. What good would it do?

Another night when he was out another friend came to see him. My youngest son was asleep in the next room. I asked the guest to sit down, telling him my husband would be back soon. As he sat, he looked at me and smoked, blowing smoke towards me in a suggestive way. I was again taken aback. This time I was better prepared. I got up and woke my son and kept him beside me for protection until my husband returned.

My dislike for men does not stem from nothing. I hate them. My hopes for what they would be like have been disappointed by my experiences with them. I was loyal and devoted to my husband, and I supposed he would reciprocate.

When we were first married, I brought him his food right to bed. I knew he was tired after a long day at work. Women are moved to serve a man when they love him. I prepared hot water when he came home and washed his feet and dried them. In winter I would put clean socks on his feet myself to keep them warm. I adored him, and this led to my serving him in this way.

After I found him with my cousin, I continued to perform my duties, but I stopped being at his beck and call in this special way. In the end men don't respect a woman who serves them. They want a woman who makes herself attractive and is good in bed.

On the day of my wedding, the women cleaned my body of all hair. We do this with a soft toffee made of sugar and lemon called halaawa. We work it well between our fingers, spread it on the arms, legs, and pubic area until it adheres to the hairs, and then pull it off vigorously. When my whole body was clean, they bathed me. I was dressed in a pink satin dressing gown. I sat in my mother's house. Saad had moved our furniture upstairs already. When he came down and saw me he began to cheer for joy. He was happy. We would live upstairs. His brother and sisters would live with us.

For the wedding he had hired four taxis to get the guests and family to the church. My sister and maternal first cousin rode with me.

After church we went to the photographer's to have pictures taken as man and wife. Then we took a little drive around the town and came home. My mother had made dinner for us. It is usually the groom's mother's duty to make the wedding supper. But my mother took it upon herself to offer it since Saad's mother was dead. We ate and slept until morning.

I was happy. I loved him, and he was young and handsome. I was not bad looking myself, not like now, with my gray hair and half my teeth gone.

In the morning people came to give us money and see what had happened during the night. We had to show them the blood-stained sheets which prove to all that the bride was a virgin. This is still the custom today.

With the money given us as wedding gifts we went out and bought some gold bracelets for me. They cost about E£2 at the time, the equivalent of about E£20 now. Saad bought me three pairs of gold bracelets.

Although men were a mystery to me, my mother hadn't sent me to my marriage bed without an explanation. She said, "He will do such and such." But of course when you love, this comes easily. If you don't and you have been forced to marry, then sex is hateful, and a girl approaches it with fear.

When a girl loves, she will do anything for a man. She will do anything to please him. But later on, what with all the difficulties of day-to-day life, we came to hate this business of sex.

I was sore for about ten days after my wedding night. When a woman has no problems in her life and she loves the man she is married to, then sex is a pleasure. But if there is struggle or daily hardship connected with any part of her life, she resists it. It becomes intolerable to her. There is no sweetness in loving if you are in financial straits.

I was not married long before the problems were upon me. And then there was the morning sickness. I was pregnant almost immediately, and my eldest daughter was born exactly nine months after I married. Tongues wagged, of course. People knew ours had been a love marriage, and they said I was pregnant before the wedding. Egyptians will talk that way!

Saad's sisters and brother lived in one room of our apartment. We lived in the other. There was a sitting room in between, and my mother lived below.

Saad gave me E£6 a month housekeeping money. I budgeted pretty carefully, but it just wasn't enough. By the time the children came and we were four plus his brother and sisters, I had a hard time making ends meet. Penny pinching puts a strain on marriage. Ours was no exception.

When I ran short of money, I would tell Saad. He would beat me and shout, "Why didn't the money last? I earn only so much. Where am I going to get more?" But there were many mouths to feed. At the beginning I would take whatever gold I had and sell it to have a little extra each month. I would cut off bits from a gold chain and sell it for an extra pound here and an extra pound there.

When money ran short, he accused me of giving some to my mother on the sly. When I had a little extra, he would be equally suspicious. It was a frightful round of problems.

We ate almost no meat. I would buy a bone with very little meat on it. I'd cook it and serve him the meat so that he would not feel the bind we were in. He would eat the meat, and the children and I would go without.

I became angry.

I wanted to find a way out. But without a father or any means of support, no skill or property a woman becomes a slave. She has no options. I had to be patient. I also had the children to think about.

It was perhaps this feeling of all doors being closed to me that pushed me to learn to sew. I had to help myself and when I did, Saad became more respectful. He knew then I was not absolutely dependent on him, and he showed me greater consideration.

That was later. In the early years of marriage, however, things went from bad to worse. If Saad insulted me, I'd insult him back. If he beat me, I resisted. Our life was an endless series of battles. But now this has changed. He throws me all the money to show he worships and respects me. I think he finally realizes just to what extent I stood by him.

A profession for a woman means not only self-support but a chance to have a say in things that matter to her. It's what I try to teach the women I work with now. If a husband is a woman's only support, then sooner or later he'll break her spirit. She'll be no more than a slave in every way.

Men cannot do without sex. When Saad treated me badly, it made sex with him intolerable for me. I think it's so with most women. It was torture.

When the urge was upon him, he would come around and ask my forgiveness. Once it was over, he went back to his old ways.

A woman likes a man who has money in his hand and is open handed with it. Saad complained about my spending, and yet he had money put aside. I spent my youngest and best years in bitterness and perpetual conflict over money. Saad was not only bad tempered but stingy.

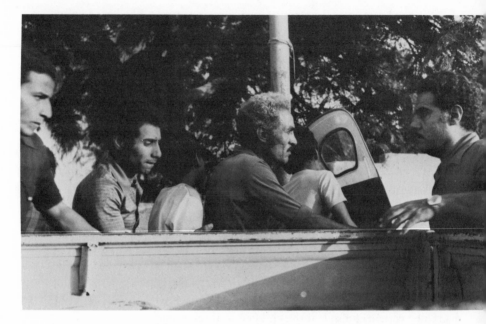

Four men on a motorbike try to squeeze through the intolerable crowds of a Cairo street. Photograph by Asma el-Bakry.

Because of my experience, I am sympathetic to the plight of others. I was not sensitive to the problems of others until I had tasted the bitterness of married life. Now, I feel for every woman I come into contact with.

It is true that I married a man I loved. But that love was soon crushed. Now I have a blind hatred for men in general although I don't show it. They are nothing, mean nothing to me, and I dislike them with all the energy which I possess.

Man is without fail disloyal. I have faith in no man. The experiences of others, as well as my own, serve to reinforce this opinion.

Despite hardship and bitterness, Egyptian women are generally very loyal to their husbands. I have learned though that a woman must not care for her husband like a slave. A woman who makes herself personally attractive forces a man to respect her in spite of himself. If all of her efforts are directed toward house and children, he will treat her like a servant.

Most Egyptian men like a woman who "cooperates" with them at night. In other words, sex is the most important aspect of marriage. Circumcision of girls in our country does not help in this respect. When I was a girl, it was still the custom among Christians to circumcise girls. This continued through to my eldest daughter's generation. She was born in 1940. After that ideas changed, and most Christians stopped circumcising girls.

I remember the time when I was circumcised very clearly. I was eight years old. I was to be circumcised along with my maternal first cousin and my sister. The night before the operation they brought us together and stained our hands orange with henna. All evening the family celebrated with flutes and drums. We were terrified. We knew what to expect. Each would ask the other, "Are you afraid?" and each would answer, "I'm very afraid." This went on all night like a refrain. We couldn't sleep.

I heard the midwife come in about five o'clock the next morning. I was to be the first because I was the eldest. They did the operation and then pounded an onion and salt mixture to put on the wound to cauterize it. When it was all over, they carried me and put me to bed. They told me to keep my legs straight in front of me and my thighs apart to keep the wound from healing over.

Next came my cousin and then my sister. They were put to bed in the same room. We were fed copiously. They brought us chickens and pomegranates. We had to eat. Chickens were cheap then, less than 10 piasters the pair. We each had to eat at least one whole chicken. Pomegranates are important, we were told, because the fruit has a beneficial astringent quality. They told us eating quantities of it would help heal our wounds. They brought us plates full of the juicy pink grains. We had to eat. I think they gave it to us because it is constipating and would keep us from moving our bowels too soon after the operation.

On the seventh day we got up. They had new dresses made for us. Mine was shiny red, my sister's shiny green, and my cousin's yellow. We were pleased with the dresses. Our mothers told us to tie our severed clitorises in the hems of our dresses. The family then paraded us through the streets like brides and took us for a picnic by the river. We were told to throw our clitorises to the Nile. This would bring us happiness. Words!

At sunset we went home. It was all over.

This operation makes it harder for a girl to enjoy sex, and as sex is all important to men, then where is the happiness this custom brings?

If for women sex is not all important, there are factors which help to make it tolerable. How a man treats a woman, for example, and the financial state of a household. And third is love.

If a man insults, offends, or beats his wife then comes to sleep with her at night, the act is repulsive to her. I suffered in my marriage on all three counts. I said to my husband, "I regret that I ever got married." He has never forgotten this. He answered, "Is this something to say?" But I persisted and said, "I had expected life to be different. Now when I hear you coming up the stairs, the sound of your footsteps strikes terror in my heart." This was said a long time ago, but he still remembers it. My words cut him deeply, it seems.

Not all women are reluctant about sex, however. My brother was married to a woman who wanted him day and night. But this too is an illness. It's not normal. If he moved, she desired him, if he stayed put, she would reach out for him. He was quickly worn out. Thinking that all women were this way, he lost hope, and his health failed. His arms and legs became paralyzed. They had no children. He divorced his wife. If she'd had children, she might have been cured. She was unlucky.

When I was first married and grew unhappy, I would go to my mother for solace. When something went wrong, I wept on her shoulder. She would be angry with Saad, and she would take my side against him. This made matters worse. It made her unhappy and made him more violent. So I stopped. I soon realized that I had to stand by him, do my duty, and accept my lot. When he saw how other women behaved toward their husbands, he began to appreciate my steadfastness.

When I was pregnant with my first child, he was happy. He had a good quality which is unusual in most Egyptians. He liked daughters. In fact, he preferred them to sons. As our first child was a girl, he was very happy. He rejoiced at the birth of all our daughters. This is something to be said in his favor. I prefer boys.

My deliveries were all easy. With the first child I had taken a bath when I began to feel a slight pain. It was afternoon. I went to my mother and said to her, "I feel a little discomfort in my stomach." My mother answered, "O Lord, that means you're going to do it."

All evening and night the pain came and went. At ten o'clock in the morning the pain was sharp, and my mother called the midwife. It was the same one who had circumcised me. She came and said, "Heat up some water." My mother did, and the child was born very quickly. It was a girl. I was a bit torn up because she was the first, but she was very pretty, and that pleased me.

Her father was in Cairo at the time. He came back running and saying, "She can't have a child while I'm gone. I'm coming now!" When he arrived, he was happy and took the child in his arms and kissed her. She was very dear to him.

A year and three months later I had a boy. We were having lunch, and he came very quickly, too. I felt the pain, and less than two hours later he was born with the help of the midwife. So it went with the others.

Perhaps I gave birth easily because I was always very active. I used to

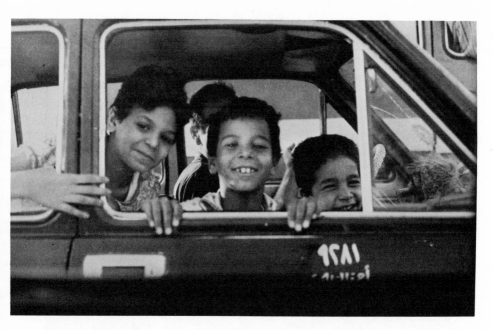

Taking a ride in dad's taxi. Photograph by Asma el-Bakry.

clean the house myself. I went up and down stairs. I did the washing and scrubbed the floors and so on. This strengthened my stomach muscles and served me well in the end.

I was initially happy with my children. But later on when they were grown, I had quite a shocking time with the boys. My eldest son has been a disappointment to me.

Because Mariam was pretty she married quickly. Her husband cherished her. He was a math teacher, and although they didn't have much money, he refused to let her work. She stayed home. Later, when he had saved up some money, he opened a shop. They have done very well. She helps him in the shop and stands by him firmly. They're a happy couple.

Youssef is my eldest boy. I loved him above the girls and treated him better than any of the others. Everything to me was Youssef, Youssef, Youssef. When he did well in school and entered the College of Engineering, I was overjoyed. Whatever he wanted, I gave him. Trips paid for in full, good clothes, pocket money—I gave him twenty-five piasters a day which was a lot twelve years ago—about equal to E£2.50 now. He seemed quite the gentleman!

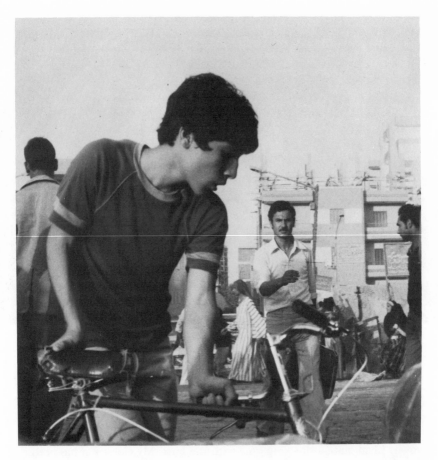

"In his second year of engineering he suddenly changed. He was no longer the loving son I cherished."—Alice. Photograph by Asma el-Bakry.

In his second year of engineering he suddenly changed. He was no longer the loving son I cherished. He was in the habit of letting me know his schedule. He would write it down for me so that I knew his comings and goings. I had it up in the kitchen and could prepare what he liked to eat for him before he got home.

During that year he started to come and go without a word. He would not even pronounce the word "Mother." I had invested great hopes in him. This is wrong. One must never put all of one's hopes in another person.

I tried to inquire as to what was ailing him. I would say, "What's wrong, Youssef?" He would answer, "Nothing." I was confused and wept bitterly.

People said to me, "Could it be that someone has given him the evil eye?" I answered that I didn't believe in such things. But when I wept, his father said to me, "There you are. There's the idol you've created. You kept saying you wanted boys. Here is your son. You favored him above the others, and here is how he treats you now. So accept your lot."

One night when he was having dinner, I suddenly had a thought. He was silent and gloomy as usual. I said to him, "Could it be that you're in love?" He said, "Yes." I tried to guess who the girl was. I said to him, "Could it be so and so? So and so?" until I hit on the right person. He said, "What do you think of her?" I answered, "She comes from a good family, and she's a good girl." I knew her as she was from our town. Then I said, "You can't consider marriage now. I can't support you and a wife as well. I just haven't the means." So he answered, "But I want at least to become engaged." I said, "I can't let you do it now. Engagements too cost money which I haven't got at the moment." There are visits to be made between the families of engaged couples, presents to be exchanged, and a variety of duties which one has to be ready to perform. Everything costs money. He looked disappointed, so I said, "Why don't you agree between you now. We can take care of the formalities later. In the meantime you can finish university. If she is really meant for you, my son, you will know and you can take her when you graduate in two years time."

Youssef was of another mind though. He became even more disgruntled and harsh with me—that is to say he ignored me. If he needed something, he would write it on a scrap of paper and throw it somewhere where I would find it. Nothing more.

The girl he loved was dark complexioned but quite pretty. I wept when I thought of how hard he had become. When he saw me he would sometimes taunt me, saying, "She'll be gone, Lady, by the time we're ready to ask for her." She did in fact become engaged to a relative of her mother's.

Youssef graduated two years later and wanted to be appointed by the government as an engineer. He needed thirty pounds to cover the cost of the necessary formalities. He asked me for it. I said to him, "I haven't got that sum of money." We could barely make ends meet. "You can have it taken out of your salary little by little every month until it's covered." He persisted, "I want it now." I spoke to his father, and his father gave him the money. He presented his papers and was appointed and went to work in Alexandria.

Do you think he would send a letter to me, reassuring me about himself? Not a word. His hardness made me lose confidence in myself. I felt

like a failure. When people saw the sad state I was in, they suggested I resort
to magic to bring my son back to me. I was desperate so I accepted. People
said, "There is a wise man about one and a half hours away from here by bus
in a small town. His father is a priest, and he's a priest and possesses old
books. He'll know how to bring Youssef back to you. When you get to the
village, ask for Am Botros."

I put aside my rational mind, put on a black dress, covered my head,
and set out to find him with a friend.

The village was at the foot of a mountain. We looked for Am Botros
and went through the streets asking for him. When we found him, he asked
my name. I said I was Om Youssef and told him my problem. "The girl my son
wants to marry," I said, "has become engaged to someone else, and this has
turned my son against me. He holds me responsible."

Am Botros looked at me then and said, "Do you want your son back?
Do you want to hear the word 'mother' on his lips again?" I eagerly said,
"Yes." So he said, "I will need eight pounds. Come back and see me next
week at this time." I hesitated then struck a bargain with him. "Here are
three pounds. I'll give you the rest when I see results."

When I came back the following week, he gave me two bits of paper.
One he told me to put out on the balcony, "Let it fly away by itself." The
other he instructed me to grind up, put in some water, and pour this water on
the threshhold of the girl's house.

I did what he told me to do. I don't know whether there really is
something to this magic, but the result was that the girl threw the engagement present back to her cousin, who was then her fiancé, and Youssef wrote
me a long letter of apology. It's all very strange, the work of the devil surely.
I don't know what to make of it.

The girl wrote to him telling him she had broken her engagement
and asking him if he still wanted her. "What do you say?" he wrote to me. O
Lord, the happiness I felt then! The world was not big enough to contain me.

We sent a letter back saying we approved, and he answered by return
of mail, "On such and such a day, you and my father must go to her family and
speak for her." We agreed.

I was worried about her mother's attitude at this point, and I decided
to go visit her informally to test the waters first. If all was well, I would take
the boy's father along on the appointed day.

When I arrived, Samia opened the door and welcomed me very
warmly saying, "Welcome, welcome, Auntie. Come in." So we went in, and
I said to her, "There have been misunderstandings between us. If I stood in
the way of your marriage to Youssef before, it's because I didn't have the
means to come and ask for your hand properly. If you like, let's let bygones by
bygones." So she agreed.

Abu Youssef and I went then to pay the family a formal visit. We went there and said, "It pleases us to be here with you and to offer our son Youssef in marriage to your daughter Samia. Do you have any objections?" If the families know each other, the answer will be, "No, we have none." But if they don't know each other well, the bride's people will say, "Give us a week or so to think and check out the boy's name, reputation, address, and financial status." So once they agree, the two families begin a pattern of visits and exchanging of gifts. The mothers especially visit each other.

After all of this Youssef and Samia were married. And do you think they were happy? No. They quarrelled constantly. He'd made an enemy of his own mother on account of this girl, and now that they were married he didn't seem happy.

Why is there so much unhappiness in marriage? I've often thought about it. In the case of Samia and Youssef, it started in this way. She considered herself richer and better than him. She made him feel it right from the start. He couldn't accept this and began to argue with her. "How dare you say such and such or do this or that?" He's hot tempered like his father, ready to strike out at the slightest provocation.

She would needle him, and he would strike her. She would run away, and we would take her in and take her side because to do otherwise would be shameful. She would calm down, and we would take her back to him. They would patch things up for a time, and then it would start all over again. We took her side because she's a woman and she came running to us when there was trouble. But I feel it's wrong to put on superior airs.

Somehow in the midst of all this I lost my son's love. He treats me like a stranger. All of these conflicts have made bad blood between us, and his wife is partly to blame. When they were first married, she did her best to alienate our son from us. She's better now, but the damage is done.

Before Abu Youssef retired and we came to live in Cairo, we used to have four weeks holiday every year. We spent three in Alexandria and one in Cairo with Samia and Youssef. At this time they were both working. She did her utmost to make us feel unwelcome for some reason. We made every effort to be as unobtrusive as possible. We wanted to be with our son. She made it difficult. When she left for work, for example she would unplug the refrigerator. It was summertime, and we had to drink warm water from the faucet all day. At five o'clock she would plug it in again and put a bottle of water in to cool for Youssef when he came home. These gestures humiliated us.

When her mother came to visit them she and her mother would put on a little play for our benefit. This play between them was designed to embarrass us. It centered around the difference in rank between Samia and Youssef at work. The mother would say to Samia, "What rank have you reached now at work?" The girl would answer, "The seventh or eighth." Her

mother would then say proudly, "And what about your husband?" Samia
would say, "The sixth or seventh." Her mother would then look at us know-
ingly and say, "So there is no difference between your salary and his?" This
was meant to belittle our son in our eyes. They would try to make us feel that
they had married beneath them.

When we came to spend a week with our son we always offered to
pay for our keep. We never came empty handed. We brought with us upper
Egyptian bread and food. Samia ignored these presents. She was bent on
making us feel that we were a burden. Yet our visits were short compared with
her mother's, who often stayed three or four months with them.

One time during a visit Samia offered Abu Youssef food which had
already been served to someone else. It was a stew, and it had traces of
someone else's breadcrumbs in it. This was a shock to me. It showed a
complete lack of respect for her father-in-law.

I think she was afraid all these years that a generous gesture from her
would inspire us to outstay our welcome. But Abu Youssef and I would not
think of being a burden to any of our children.

If my son had been a man, and I consider him not to be, he would
have put her in her place. But even now that we live in Cairo, he barely
comes to ask after us. He visits at the most once a month.

When Samia had children, she mellowed. She said to me one day,
"Auntie, I may have acted improperly toward you. No one taught me what to
do. But I see that you've never criticized me, and I'm grateful. I've also
watched your behavior toward others. I've learned from it because it's unusual. You seem more interested in the problems of others and in helping to
solve them than most people I know. You are healthy and full of energy.
Perhaps this is how God rewards you for your kindness. So I've thought that I
must pattern myself after you." I answered, "No one is better than you,
Samia." She said, "That's not so." She tries now to make amends.

My son, on the other hand, lives only for himself. She started him
off this way, and her early influence has stuck. He didn't think of his youngest
brother, for example, when the boy was a student and could have used the
help and support of an older brother. He hardly asks after his married sisters,
which is his duty. The consequences of this may not be as serious as they
would have been years ago. Times have changed, and women don't depend
on their husbands or brothers as they used to. They can work and be somewhat independent.

If a woman is totally dependent on her husband as I was in the early
years of marriage, then she longs for sons. She prefers them to daughters
because she feels they'll stand by her in time of need—they have the means to
stand by her. My hopes were disappointed in the case of my eldest son and it is

my youngest daughter who asks after me and insists on sending me E£5 from her paycheck every month. This is unusual because custom dictates that a daughter's allegiance will be to her husband's family when she marries.

Boys are expected to give money to their parents once they're employed. They support their parents in their old age and look after the well-being of their married sisters. This is important because a girl who has menfolk behind her is better cared for and respected by her husband than one without men at her back.

The question of happiness in life and in marriage goes back to one thing—money.

People say this is not so, but I believe it's true. Money gives people room for love and hope. The lack of it occupies their minds completely and leaves room for nothing else.

If a woman has money in her hand, she is more tolerant. Her nerves are calmer. She can eat, drink, dress comfortably, and not feel trapped. She can think of love.

If a woman has no money, then her life is one of misery. Her nerves are on fire. She grows intolerant. Where can you look for love in the midst of misery?

It would help, in my opinion, if there were schools where girls could learn about housekeeping, husbands, and how to best manage the business of married life.

So many of the problems which a bride faces here are based on ignorance. She enters into marriage raw, blind, and fearful. By the time experience has taught her the essential lessons of life, her youth is gone, her beauty has faded, and the years have disfigured her hopes.

When I was at school, we were taught budgeting. We divided our money into envelopes. One was for yearly and summer clothes. One was for winter clothes, one for electricity, one for rent, one for daily expenses, and so on. We were shown how to take money from one fund to cover extra expenses in another and how to replace it.

I benefited from this teaching. But because pressures on me in the early years of marriage were extreme, even budgeting could not put money where there was none.

Girls should be schooled in how to deal with husbands. Sex, for example, is so important that the education of a girl in this domain should not be left to chance. I see the wisdom of our Muslim sisters who give their husbands their due so that they may not seek for their needs outside the home. Among the Christians because divorce is so difficult, women don't make enough of an effort. They neglect themselves and the sexual aspects of their marriages.

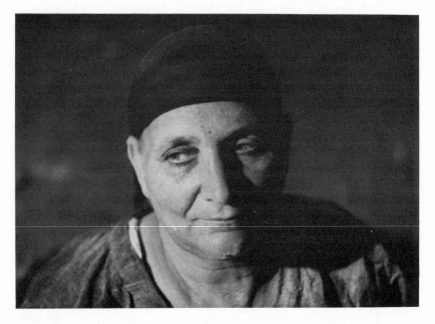

"By the time experience has taught her the essential lessons of life, her youth is gone."—Alice. Photograph by Asma el-Bakry.

Men talk among themselves, and one knows from the other if he's not sexually satisfied. This creates bitterness and jealousy. One will say, "Well, why is he better off than I am?" A woman must know that a man's thoughts revolve around one thing only—sex and how to get it. She must learn to deal with this.

My youngest daughter Salwa married for love, but this didn't save her from the usual problems. Like so many women, she was more interested in her home than in sex. Her sister-in-law, by contrast, leaves her house in a state of chaos and spends her time making herself attractive. Her husband adores her.

Salwa's husband was a friend of her youngest brother, Amin. One day he rang the doorbell and, as no one else was home, she answered. He was bringing a letter for Amin. They were at university together. She received him coldly as is only becoming for a girl when she's faced with a man she doesn't know. He left, but her stern reception stirred him. He came up a second time to ask, "Where can I find Amin?" "At church," she answered and promptly shut the door.

One day he saw her at the university and greeted her. She greeted him back and smiled. He was transported by her smile because it was such a change from her curt behavior at the door before.

He started to come to our house. He also started to bring her home from university. She is very straightforward and would invite him to come up. When he was reluctant, she would say to him, "My father knows we meet at school and that you bring me home." So he was satisfied.

After four years of courtship they were engaged and married. She's a little high strung but very clever.

Before Labib, her husband, she had fallen in love with a Muslim boy. He was a neighbor and the son of a village dignitary who had settled in Cairo. He was married. What made her love him was this. She had seen him on the street one day. He had come across an old man carrying a heavy burden. He stopped and took the burden from the man and walked him to where he was going. This went straight to Salwa's heart.

She watched him from the window as he came and went. We didn't know. They began to speak to each other, and he began to send her greeting cards at feast times. This rang the alarm for us. When we realized what was happening, I beat her and made her stop short. Marriage between a Muslim and a Christian with us is absolutely taboo. She must marry a Christian, and in Minya news of this sort of thing would have soon caused a scandal. We are very attached to our church, and I would not agree to one of my children marrying outside it.

Time went by, and she married Labib. They have three children. But Salwa, being like me, only fulfils one part of marriage successfully. She is a meticulous housekeeper and a devoted mother. As a result she gets the short end of the stick. Although she's not circumcised, this has not helped fire up her enthusiasm in the physical side of marriage. When Mariam, my eldest, came of age, I had had second thoughts about the custom of circumcision. But I had no choice. It was our custom, and it had to be done. I wanted to make it less painful for her, remembering my own experience. I took her to a doctor. He said it was illegal and would not perform the operation. So I had to resort to the services of a midwife. My daughter had a very hard time. Despite being circumcised though, Mariam tries hard to please her husband in this area. She dresses up and makes herself pretty and makes a point of satisfying her husband's sexual desires.

This is not so with Salwa. At the end of a day at work and after her housekeeping chores are done if she's too tired, she says "no." And with her "no" means no. She is inflexible and cannot force herself to do anything she doesn't want to do.

This is among the most fundamental problems in her marriage. It annoys her husband, who feels this is one of her duties as a wife. He had taken her to Kuwait with him when he was offered a good job there but sent her home after a year when he saw that she would only respond to him one night out of ten. He sent her to live with us, and he stayed on.

In Kuwait, he made the acquaintance of another girl who became his mistress. When he came back to Egypt, he brought this girl with him and asked us to put her up at our place, saying she was a friend and that he had brought her here as a tourist. We accepted this and said nothing. One must never doubt another's word without reason.

The two of them began to go out in the morning though and not come back until night. Salwa grew jealous. We grew suspicious, and matters got worse. They went to the Cairo Tower and other sights around the city. Salwa would question them. When their stories didn't match, she began to be upset. There was violent quarrelling, and my son went back to Kuwait with the girl. Salwa stayed with us. The family kept writing though and reminding him of his responsibilities as a husband and a father. He finally returned alone.

Perhaps fatigue makes many women uninterested in sex. One has to be comfortable and relaxed and not overworked to want it or enjoy it.

I regret circumcising Mariam. I've changed a lot, and my ideas have changed over the years. Experience teaches one a great deal and meeting people even more.

I have come to know people of different classes in the years since my marriage. I fell into a trap once which made me lose faith in people. Once again it had to do with money. I had put some money aside to buy a sewing machine. Someone cheated me, and I lost the money and had to start saving all over again.

I discovered then that not a soul was willing to help me. All of my acquaintances then were from among the middle or rich classes. They, surprisingly, are least willing to help one another in a tight spot. Not so poor people.

Now after years of studying people, I have come to the conclusion that by and large it's only the poor who will remember a good deed done for them. They'll recall it over and over again, gratefully. Now I make my acquaintances only among the poor, and I avoid the people of my own class. The poor are loyal. The middle classes are mostly selfish. The poor have more love and give it more freely.

Another change in me came about twenty years after marriage. I was broken and miserable during those first twenty years. When I started to work and go out, my feelings about myself and others changed. My outlook on life became more positive, and I began to mend. I enjoy my life as it is now.

But I still believe that all men are disloyal, and that every man alive is unfaithful to his wife. I don't trust a single man, not even my own sons.

My eldest son, Youssef, was disloyal to his wife. He had been sent to Germany for professional training. There he fell in love with a German. He saw in her a different sort of woman. He saw freer intercourse between men and women which made him turn against what he had left behind. He wanted to divorce his Egyptian wife and marry the German. We stopped him of course and reminded him that he had a small son. His father intervened and put him straight.

Perhaps our youngest son is different and will remain loyal to his wife because he is intensely religious. Religion has a strong influence on people and keeps them from going astray. It's a very important factor in how people behave. Religion is love, and love builds loyalty and good faith.

My own husband has changed through the years. He now realizes his mistakes and confesses to me that he regrets them. He wants me to take all the money I need, come and go as I please, and please myself. So I'm satisfied. Surprisingly though, the old story between him and my cousin still affects me.

Women are more loyal than men. As to being equal with men, this is another matter. Men don't like strong women. Any woman who takes on man's work is permeated with a masculinity which repels men. They like a woman to be weak. What's the point in a masculine woman? It would be as if a man were married to another man. A woman lawyer, for example, assumes masculine qualities, and a man's appetite is closed for this kind of woman.

A woman has to be fine and weak. No man likes a he-she. A man loves a woman's tears. He loves to see her helpless, and he loves her tears.

God created men to be lawyers and engineers and doctors, although some women can be doctors. But I feel there is man's work and women's work, and the two should remain separate, although women should not be entirely dependent on men.

The formula for happiness, as I see it, is based on health and money. To be in good health and to have enough money makes room for love.

My life now has taken a turn for the better. I enjoy working with the poor. I love my grandchildren and feel great pleasure when they are with me and call me *Teta*, Grandma. This is my greatest happiness. My goal in life now is to serve God through helping the poor.

3

~~Suda~~

THE HOUSEKEEPER

"I would not choose to marry a white man. If you choose one of your own kind, you feel that he will put up with anything you do more easily than someone who is different."

MY MOTHER has been ill off and on lately. She likes those who know and is inclined to consult them.

I sometimes believe in magic and other times not. When we are ill and have come to the end of our ropes, or some loved one, like my mother, is ill and we have tried everything to help her to no avail, I turn to these.

When my mother was ill, I took her to three doctors in one day. We have a couple who live in our building, a doctor and his wife, who is also an M.D. The man checked on her in the morning and his wife at night, and I took her to a third doctor at one in the morning, near where we live, in Embaba.

People said maybe when she fell down and injured herself that she was under some spell. In Embaba the streets are badly pockmarked and uneven. She fell in a ditch one day, and her leg was badly injured.

We went to the hospital at night, and she had stitches put in there, but the accident seems to have weakened her. The doctors gave her some pills, and she insisted they stopped in her throat and would not go further.

So a friend took her to a woman who knows in Boulac, another part of Cairo.

This woman said to my mother, "What you need is a pair of male ducks, a chicken, a rabbit, and a pigeon. Incense must be burned around them. You then must wear a white dress and have the animals slaughtered

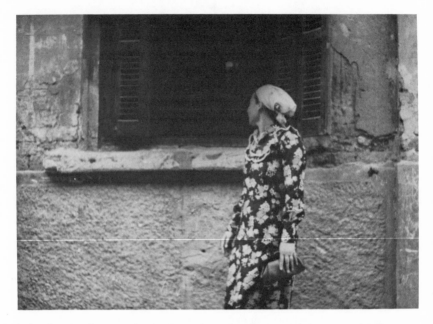

Suda's friend calling to ask after her sick mother. Photograph by Asma el-Bakry.

above your head so that their blood runs over your entire body." My mother then came home and told us this.

Another woman in our neighborhood, however, said she thought this wise woman, *Sheika*, whose name was Faransa, "France," was a liar and did not know anything at all. We said we wanted to do something of the sort because we knew it would make Mother better. So the woman said she would take us to a more knowledgeable *Sheikha* who would help us. And so we went. This one was in Sakkiet Mekkee, on the river.

This woman then said to my mother, "Don't worry. You are all right. Bring me two chickens. A black one and a red one. We'll kill one and not kill the other."

So we took them, and the woman said, "Get hold of three candles which you will light near the place where you sleep, one at a time." So my mother then said, "Do I need to sleep alone?" because she and my sister sleep in one bed and I sleep in another, and our rooms are small.

So we did as she said. The first two mornings we woke up to find the candles half burned and gone out. But on the third morning we woke up and found no trace at all of the candle—not a trace. I was afraid. We thought that in getting up we might have carried it accidentally off in one of our slippers. We searched them but found nothing.

It was then that my mother took the chickens to the *Sheikha* and told her what had happened. She said, "You will now get well. Don't worry." She killed the red chicken and daubed my mother's head and her chest with blood and her tongue telling her to swallow it. So she did.

She then took the black hen and washed her face and extremities as if she were a person performing ablution before praying. She then told my mother, "Take the hen and at night when it is dark take her out, away from houses and people, and let her go. But don't look behind you."

So my mother and I got up at night and took the chicken out to a nearby field and let her go.

I still took my mother to the doctor after that. It's been nearly five months since her accident. She has relapses but can get around.

My mother is about fifty years old. We call her old. She's not like all mothers—she really stuck with us and cared for us even though our father died when we were quite young. He had been married before and was older than my mother.

Most Egyptian women, when they lose their husbands, think nothing of leaving behind two and three children and marrying again. Why should they stay? Not so our mother, who in spite of her youth, tolerated us and looked after and supported us as we grew up.

I suffered very much when my father died. We still lived in the village. My brother didn't worry—well, he's a boy and can take care of himself. My sister was young and cried a little then forgot. But I had a hard time of it. I was seven years old. He died on a feast day, *El 'Eed el Kebeer.* He was the foreman on a wheat and corn grinding machine—and that day was a holiday. He showed no sign of illness. No one works on this day. It is said to be a sin to do so.

On the day of the feast he suddenly died. He said to us in the house, "I'm a bit tired," and by the time we had called a doctor he was dead. So they took us children to an uncle's house nearby, and the baby who was still nursing to a neighbor, who had a child the same age and could nurse her while my mother recovered from the shock.

On the day of the funeral people said that we must be brought out to walk behind our father's casket in the funeral cortège. My brother, who was about four years old then, claims he remembers his father. I don't believe this is true. I myself have forgotten his face.

I remember that my eyes hurt the day after he died. I must have cried. Behind my father's coffin I walked quietly. People said to me, "No use crying because the one who dies doesn't return."

When they took him to the mosque to be prayed on, his coffin suddenly got very heavy. He didn't want to move from the mosque. So they had a *zikr*, a ceremony, on his behalf and read the Koran over him. He was dead, but he seemed to have a will of his own. I don't understand exactly what it's all about. The men said, "Let's go. Let's lift him up and take him to the cemetery." But the coffin remained riveted there.

My father was a good and kind man—perhaps that is why he wanted to remain in the mosque, a holy place. So my maternal grandfather interceded and said quickly to my dead father, "Come on now, Ahmad. The men are tired out, and they want to get on with their work! It's hot. Stop showing off. We know you were a good man. Come along now. Do you want to pretend to be a *Sheikh?*" My grandfather spoke to him in this way. Does a dead man hear what the living say? And then my grandfather said to the men, "Come on, lift him up. I'll lift up with you." And so they went, and the casket fairly flew. It was as if it was self-propelled, and those carrying it could hardly keep up.

People were surprised because he had the reputation of being a womanizer. His job as foreman on the grinding machine brought him into contact mostly with women. People said he pinched the women and was cheeky. But when his coffin "ran" to its final resting place, like a good man's often does, not fearing judgment day, people changed their minds about him.

Until today when we go back to the village, people call us "the children of that good man."

So then they erected a mourning tent, a *seewan*, with the men on one side to receive the men and the women on the other. The Koran is read over a loudspeaker, and black coffee is served. The coffee on this occasion has no sugar in it to show a time of sadness.

If the man has an older brother, it is he who receives the condolences. If he had only a nephew, he receives the men of the family and others.

The following Thursday the family and the neighborhood women go to the cemetery. They take along a special round bread made with milk and butter and whatever fruit is in season. They give a big share, along with 50 piasters or so [about U.S. $1], to the man who reads the Koran and distribute the rest among whoever happens to be there. There are usually a lot of children. It's a kind of charity for the sake of the dead one. Then fifteen days later another *seewan* is erected, like the one for the fortieth day after the man's death here in Cairo, and a visit to the cemetery but without food this time. There is just Koran reading, for which the *Sheikh* is given money.

Certain people cry of course. I cried because he was my father and I remembered him. My mother cried for her lost husband. My paternal cousin cried because he had lost an uncle. But there are no professional mourners among our villagers. We are believers, thank heaven, and do not put any stock by that sort of thing.

In our village a woman who slaps her face in mourning is considered a heathen, *kafra*. We are very religious in our village. Other neighboring villages indulge in this and hire professional mourners to weep at funerals.

We also don't wear black for a year, as is the custom among other Egyptians. After the fortieth day we take it off, not like in Cairo. A woman in her own home does not keep to black after the first or second day. It's unreasonable to expect anyone to wear black to bed. It's too depressing.

We, the women of the family, go to the mosque every Saturday morning for lessons in religion. The lessons deal with marriage, illness, death, and how to deal with them. They give us a feeling for what is right and wrong. They are a comfort.

When we came to Cairo, my mother continued to go to lessons, but then they were on Sundays. As I have to work that day, I would ask my mother, "What did Sheikh Ahmad say to you today?" and so I would profit this way from the lesson she had heard. She would tell me, "He said that a woman must care for her husband, that she must wear clean clothes before going to bed, that she should smell good. A woman before she drifts off to sleep should ask her husband three times, 'Is there anything you desire?' And if not, then she can sleep." So this would be the lesson for one day. Another day he might tell us about fasting and prayer.

Last Ramadan, that is the small fast, I still was going to the mosque. But this year, since my engagement to Salah, I find it hard to do. I am working, and I like to spend my spare time with my fiancé. But at this time last year I would usually break the fast at sunset, them perform my ablutions, then go to the mosque to pray, or pray and go to the mosque. I stayed there until about 10 P.M. I prayed the *Maghreb* and the *Esha*. Then I listened to a lesson for half an hour. Later I prayed the *Taraaweeh* and twenty-two *Rak'as*. These prayers take place during different parts of the day.

Now my fiancé goes home from work and breaks the fast with his own family. He comes to visit me or sometimes comes directly from work and breaks the fast with us. If I go to the mosque, then there is no time for him to sit with me, so now I stay with him.

After my father died we continued to live in the village in my paternal grandfather's house. My father gave his two brothers each their share of the house in cash and lived there himself.

My mother's father and her brother asked her if she would marry again. She said, "No, I'll stay alone and raise my children."

We had an acre and a half which we rented for about E£60 a year. It belonged to my father. My father's sister had half acre that she also rented.

My mother was given the rest. We also had half share in the pro-
ceeds from the grinding machine, and we lived free in the family house.

When my grandfather saw that my mother was intent on staying
unmarried, he would bring us a share of whatever he was growing: rice, corn,
and wheat. So we had stocks for the entire year put away. It was as if we
were planting our own fields and reaping their fruits. My grandfather looked
after us.

My sister and I went to school for six years then decided to stay
home. My brother decided not to go to high school. His mind was closed to
studying. My mother pressed him to continue and hired a teacher to coach
him at E£5 [about U.S. $8] per month which was a lot then. The Arabic
teacher took E£1.50, the English teacher E£2, and so on. She wanted him
to go to university and become a teacher. It didn't work that way. He thought
to himself, "What for?" or something of the sort. Maybe he was just not
inclined or able. He repeated his last year of school three times, three con-
secutive years to no avail. He was not meant for high school. So he quit.

My mother and brother then said, "It's not reasonable that my sister
should continue to live in the village." My maternal grandfather, who lived in
a village near us, had died in the meantime. My uncle was then living in
Cairo. He was next in succession of those responsible for us. He came and
asked my brother what he wanted to do. He said, "You've tried school, and
you're not good at it. What is it you want to do? What do you think would
interest you? Would you like to be a driver or learn to be a car mechanic? Or
would you like to take over your maternal grandfather's three acres and plant
them and take your mother and sisters with you? You could work the land and
feed them and care for them."

My brother said, "I don't want to be a farmer. I want to be a driver."
So my uncle took him to Cairo to driving school. My uncle is also a driver.

When we first came to Cairo, my uncle put my brother to work in a
gas station belonging to a man from our village. The man said, "I'll give you
E£18 a month" [about U.S. $25], and my brother accepted, especially as the
tips were good. When he was established in this job, he went and fetched his
mother from the village to live with him.

In the house where my uncle lives, in Embaba, a flat became available, and so he reserved it for us. We stayed with my uncle the three months
that it took for the flat to become vacant, and then we moved in. Before that
time I went to stay with my older sister who was married. My younger sister
came for periods of two or three weeks to visit, then she would go back to
the village.

I was then about eighteen years old. I knew how to get around.
Getting home was easy. I rode the train to near our village. Then I took two
buses home. The buses cost four piasters [about U.S. 40¢] each to the village.

When we all moved to Cairo, my brother's expenses increased. The man for whom he worked said to him, "Learn to drive and come work for me as a driver. Since you are in the service station business, it will not be hard." So he did and got his driver's license within a month.

But the man he went to work for gave him a hard time. He raised his voice and was unpleasant, so after two months my brother said to him, "Here are your car keys. I'm leaving. Why should you humiliate us?" By humiliating my brother he was humiliating the whole family. My brother was getting E£ 30 per month then.

He left and went to work for someone else, a minister who gave him E£ 50 per month [about U.S. $80–90]. He stayed there one year. The minister's wife turned out to be impossible. Nothing pleased her. My brother had to drive her around. She would say, "Abdo, go slowly." When he did, she would say, "Abdo, you are going too slowly, hurry up," or "Abdo, why don't you clean the car?" He would answer, "Yes, Madam" to all of this, adding, "Although it's not my job to clean the car, I'll do it. I am clean, and I don't like to drive around in a dirty car."

The man also had to go to meetings late at night, and as he did not live far from us, he would say, "Abdo, take the car home. Rest a while and come back." So it was the wife in the daytime and the husband at night. Abdo said, "To hell with the E£ 50. I'll find something else."

He then went to work for a man who had an import-export business at E£ 70 a month. The man had a lot of work, and Abdo was not comfortable there either. He stayed just a year and left. Before he ever leaves one job he makes sure he has another one lined up. He has a mother and two sisters to support!

He took up with a man who gave him E£ 3 a day plus tips, all of which come to E£ 5 a day. He stayed with him a month. Then a man called Saad came along. He had a pharmacy and a factory for cosmetics, things like that red stuff they put on their mouths.

He got my brother a car and pays him E£ 80 to travel with a representative of the company to show samples and deliver goods. With that plus tips, his salary now comes to E£ 130 a month, which is adequate to live on. This man is a Christian. My brother has been with him over a month.

Abdo is pleased as long as he doesn't have to drive for ladies or for the boss himself. He's satisfied making deliveries.

Before taking this job where I am now, I worked for a woman called Nahed whom I didn't like very much. She had a reputation in the building for not being able to keep a servant.

It was not a bad place to be, though. She had a cook and a little boy of thirteen or fourteen who did much of the cleaning. He cleaned the children's room and the living room. I had to clean her room and the dining room. I had nothing to do with the kitchen, although I did some of the shopping. This lady would say to me, "Suda, you do the shopping on your way. I trust you most. The cook doesn't come in until ten in the morning, and by that time the freshest produce is already gone from the market." So I did the shopping. But there was a misunderstanding between us, and this is what caused me to leave. She had agreed to pay me E£25, and I had accepted. She came and said to me very nicely one day, she was very smooth, "Suda, after all, what are your responsibilities? Your work is really very light. Why don't you just take E£20 for your salary? That seems fair for the work you do."

So I said, "Sure, why not, I'll accept E£20." I don't like to argue or make trouble. But I decided I would get my own back, quietly.

I came to work for her the fifteenth of one month. She paid me half the month's salary at E£25, and then I worked half the following month at E£20. She tried to smooth this over saying, "After all, we mostly keep the living room closed, and we eat on a table in the entrance hall. Every week you only do one extra room." This was true, but I was upset by the change. She had given me E£13, and now it had dwindled to E£10. I said nothing at the time, as I had no back-up job. I discussed this with my girlfriend and asked her advice.

My friend said, "Doesn't she have a husband you can talk to?" "Yes, but Egyptian women don't allow their husbands to interfere or have anything to do with the help," I said. "He comes for lunch at 4 P.M., but I have nothing to do with him."

My friend knew that my present employers needed someone. She introduced me to them, and I agreed to come to work for them. "But I cannot start until five days after the feast," I told them. They agreed.

So on the eve of the feast, I took the work clothes I kept in the house of this lady, Nahed. I used to dress very chic even while working, unlike now. I took my clothes and my slippers and wrapped them in a piece of newspaper. When the lady saw this, she said to me, "What are you doing, Suda? Haven't you washed your clothes this week?" So I answered, "They've become very dirty. You don't boil the clothes here as we do at home, so I'm taking them to wash them properly with soap and potassium."

I lied of course. But she hadn't been fair or true to her word. I took my salary and the E£2, the present she gave me for the feast, and an extra pound she gave me to buy vegetables on my return, and I didn't go back.

I felt this money was due to me. I didn't feel guilty taking it. I said to myself, "I've been working for you two months and have lost E£10 to you. So why shouldn't I make up for it?"

My present employer said to me when I came, "My wife cooks and makes her own cup of tea during the day, so your work load will not be heavy." He said this in front of my friend. So I asked, "So what is my job?" He said, "You'll just clean and shop." So I agreed. I discovered then his wife was abroad, and I was worried about being alone in the house with him. To reassure me he said, "Don't be afraid. Don't think I am here alone. My wife is coming." I wanted to show him it didn't matter. So I answered, "Even if you were, I have my job and that's all." But I had been a bit uneasy.

I always take five days off at feast time to go to our village. And as the months passed, I kept getting raises until I reached my present salary of E£ 30.

My life story is a simple one. It might have been different had my father lived.

I stayed in school until I was twelve years old. My sister was married to a paternal cousin of my mother, *Ibn 'Am Ummi*. I addressed him as *Ya Khali*, maternal uncle, and also as *Gooz Okhti*, husband of my sister. After my father died and after I left school, I spent some of my time in the village and some time with them. I didn't need to work. My sister's husband provided for me, and I was content. But one day he died. I felt then that I needed to work. I was about twenty years old.

At this time we became acquainted with a man who was employed as a clerk in a factory for packing and selling fish. He was married, but he kept this a secret for a whole year because he wanted me to marry him. He asked for my hand from my sister, because my mother was still in the village.

I was still inexperienced, and I fell in love with this man. I thought, "So I'll marry him and settle down in my own home. What more can one ask for?" But when I found out he was married, I was upset. He said to me, "Of course you must be upset." I said to him, "Don't come back. Neither come to the village nor to my sister's house again."

I was hurt and unhappy. I returned to our village, and there I fell ill. It's perhaps the only time in my life when I have felt really down. I was so ill that I shuttered my window and closed tight my door. I stayed in bed and neither wanted to eat nor drink. It was a first blow in an otherwise happy life.

The man waited awhile then came around again and said, "What is it you want? Don't you want me?" I answered him rudely, "Yes, of course I want you. You told me you loved me, and I loved you. How could you deceive me?" So he said, "Well, let it be then. I'll provide you with an apartment, and we'll be together, and I'll see my children at night. I was forced to marry this woman who's my wife, and we had two children. But I never loved her, and I don't love her now."

I was not convinced. After all, each woman wants a man all to herself. "What business have I with your wife and your children?" I said to him. At that time he earned E£ 35 a month. So what? What good would that do? It would neither benefit me, nor his wife. He couldn't keep us both on such a salary.

He was originally from the Sudan. He said to me, "Well, if that doesn't meet with your approval, I'll find a way. I'll look for work abroad. My brother at home is well off. I'll sell what I own here and get you what you want and build you a house, or whatever you require. I'll provide you with whatever you need, and you'll not have to worry about this matter of my salary not being enough. I don't want my children to accuse me one day of having 'sold' them."

I heard him out, but I went back to the village. He called me on the telephone all the time from work. Near our house there is a telephone. It's in the mayor's house. Every now and then I would get called to the phone. It was him. I'd be polite and ask after him and after my sister who was in Cairo. He still went to visit her. After I felt better, I used to go back and forth between the village and Cairo. I was two months in the village and two in Cairo. I had not said "no" to him. I was thinking over what he proposed.

As time went on, I realized that, practically speaking, he would not be able to keep me and his family. I then said to myself, "Why should I get married? Of course to be comfortable and stay in my own home and not go out to work." I had not worked yet, and the idea frightened me a little. I talked to myself in this way. One day it occurred to me, "Well, why am I sitting here like a bump on a log? Why don't I go to work, and if I decide to marry this human being, I can help him out, and we can settle down in our own house. If I decide against him, I'll find another man to marry me." I knew by then just how one came by each piaster one earned.

So having made up my mind, I went to work and earned a good, clean piaster. As long as the penny I made was clean, so what? But of course if my paternal cousins, Welaad 'Ammee, found out I was working as a servant in a house, it would be a scandal, a shame. So I hid this from them. I don't know why working in a house is a shame. But I knew that I couldn't have it known back in the village that I worked as a servant. My father's family would be up in arms and say I'd shamed them.

I finally talked to my maternal uncle. I told him that the people I worked for were respectable, and that he could come and meet them any time. This way I took him into my confidence and put myself under his protection. So the year before last he came. He didn't come into the apartment. He stood at the door and talked to the family. My employers then came to our house for a courtesy call, and everyone was satisfied.

Although my maternal uncle knows I work now, my uncle's wife doesn't know what I do. Only my mother, my brother, my younger sister, and my uncle know. Only we five know. I have their approval, and that's enough.

If anyone else asks, we say that I work in the office of an engineer. After all, I do read and write. Half of our village lives in our neighborhood here. They've all built houses. So they can see me go and come, but they don't really know what I do.

Our family is very mixed. We have white and black members. My paternal first cousins are white and all shades in between, dark, light, tan, and black. When I became a conscious human being, I saw that they were this way. It seemed natural, and I didn't question it. It was only in Cairo that color seemed to make a difference. In the village we were known by our name not our color.

Anyway, when I went to work and became aware of how each penny was earned, I said to myself, "My word, I was going to get married for financial security, to be in my own home and let some man support me. But here I am now. I can provide for myself. So there's no need to rush into marriage."

But this married man was madly in love with me and would not give up. He came to my maternal uncle, *Khali*, and cried just like a woman. I've never seen a man cry like that for a woman or a girl. What could I do? I wanted him to stop coming and leave me alone. I had to find a way to make him stop.

He lived in Giza. One day I said to him, "Can you give me your address at home. I have a maternal cousin, *Bint Khaal Ommi*, who lives there. I think she's your neighbor. My cousin had told me one day, "I was going to market yesterday and met this man. He lives around here somewhere." This happened by chance. I decided to find a way to shame him into staying away.

He used to follow me around. He wanted to know all my movements. He wanted to get in tight with my people. I no longer wanted him. I'd grown up. But he would not let go. I had to find a way to make him stop coming. Here's what I did.

One day I said to him, "I don't want you. Why do you insist on coming?" He answered, "You don't know what you're saying now. You're just proud, and you'll change your mind." I said, "I'm older now, and I know my mind." But he wouldn't listen. Every day I'd find him waiting at a bus stop, at a train crossing, just to look at me. First I insulted him, then I ignored him, but he persisted.

He had told his wife that he had a cousin living in Giza, meaning my cousin, and that he went to visit her. One day my cousin and I contrived to come to his house to have tea. We met his seven-year old son outside the building and said to him, "Ibrahim, is your father home?" He said, "Yes." So we went up. My cousin introduced me and told me this was Om Ibrahim, the man's wife and the mother of the boy outside. She told Om Ibrahim that I was going to be married and that we were looking for an empty flat to rent and had come to consult her. "We happened to come past your building," my cousin said, "So I said to my cousin, 'Come on, Suda, we'll go ask Om Ibrahim if there is a flat in her building.'" It was all a trick. He was there. He was embarrassed. When we were ready to leave, he walked us downstairs. So I said to him, "Do you know why I've come? I've neither been engaged nor am I getting married. So if you ever show up at our house again, I'll come and tell your wife, and she'll kick you out and humiliate you. So stay away from me and don't meddle in my affairs any longer." He said at first, "Do you think this will stop me?" But then the light dawned on him, and he said, "You really mean you don't want me?" So I said, "That's right. You have three children to look after. Do you think that I'll marry you and go begging? Or do you think I'd get married and go out to work?" I was still hurt but decided to have nothing more to do with him. I was sure it would come to no good.

This is the one incident in my life which really gave me a hard time. I'd really fallen in love with this man, and I'd say to myself at first, "Well, what if he is married? He'll come to me one day and to her the other." It seemed possible, and love made me try hard to overlook the disadvantages of the situation. But when I was able to feed myself and provide for my own needs, I had a change of heart and had the courage to reject him. Working and being free affected me not only economically but emotionally. I felt a great sense of release. After a time I stopped loving him. I said to myself, "What do I want from him? I'm well now and can take care of myself. Tomorrow I'll marry someone better." I haven't regretted my decision.

After him others came to marry me. But I was no longer in a hurry. I'd put it in my head to wait.

One of my friends has a daughter who had married a foreigner, a man from Senegal. This man had a paternal cousin, *Ibn 'Am*, who said to my friend, "I want to marry your friend Suda." So I said to myself one day, "Okay, why not? I'll marry him and live abroad. After all, what more do I want? I'm tired of Egypt." So I told my uncle and my mother, and they refused. "We'd rather see you married to an Egyptian who sweeps the streets than a foreigner whom we know nothing about. Do we know what he'll do with you once he's taken you away? Supposing our countries become enemies, and we can no longer see you? Supposing you have children there and you become unhappy with this man. What would you do? Is it possible that you'll bring your children and come back here? How would you support yourself and them?" They came up with a lot of arguments against this marriage. I listened and thought about them, and in the end I was persuaded.

My friend's husband has taken out Senegalese nationality for her now. She will stay in Egypt one more year until he establishes himself, and then join him there. Those who marry Egyptian women have them stay here at least two years because air fare is expensive. When they have children, they leave them awhile with their mothers, then take them away saying, "We don't want our children to be brought up in Egypt. We want them to be raised properly in Senegal."

I thought to myself, "I want to be able to see my mother at least once a month." And even if I live far away in another city, I can still come to her once a month and see my sister and brothers. Then, I decided against marrying a foreigner.

After the experience with this first man, I was wary of men. I put an end to thoughts of love. This experience had made me very cautious. I decided, "I'll love the man I marry after he's my husband." But to love someone then think of marriage, no. I'd been "pinched" once, that was enough.

I began to ask the opinion of this one and that one on the matter and when Salah, my fiancé, presented himself, I was ready for him. I've known him well for a year, and I've know the family longer, not with marriage in mind, though. We were acquaintances.

When he came to ask for me in marriage, I consulted relatives and friends, listening carefully to each one's opinion. They would invariably say, "Well, how do you feel?" I'd say, "Well, I think I could marry him." My family was pleased because I'd refused several prospects before him, saying, "No, I don't want any men." I was afraid that all men were like the first one I'd known. That one would lie to me and another would deceive me, and so on. But I'm pleased with Salah because I see him just as he is. His truth is clearly before me.

When considering his suit, I asked him if he'd finished military service. We couldn't live on the three or four pounds a month a soldier gets. He said he had. So I said, "Show me your release papers." I had to be sure. His papers had to be laid out on the table. I had to see what was right and what was wrong, how he was going to get a driver's license, for example, and so on. I would say to him, "Today you must go get your license. Tomorrow you must do this and that." All of this was worked out in detail. Everything I want, he does. For this reason I feel this is a man with whom there can be give and take, a man I can marry. He listens to me, and I listen to him. He'll say to me, for example, "This dress is a bit too transparent. You must not wear it. It's not modest enough." So I reply, "All right, I won't wear it." He'll say, "Suda, I don't want you to speak to this man or this woman, because when women sit together they will say to one another, 'My fiancé bought me this or did this for me,' and if, for example, I don't have the means to get you the same, there will be problems. So there is no need for you to go out with this woman or to tell her your secrets or your thoughts, no need for you to repeat to this friend or that what I've told you. It could bring problems." He is persuasive. Or he'll say to me, for example, "My basic salary as a driver is E£45, and if I work overtime until 5 P.M., I'll get an extra E£15. Here is the money I earn. You keep it." He gives me his salary, and I give him whatever he needs from it, spending money, and save the rest. He'll say, I need to spend such and such on something today." I give it to him. He doesn't smoke cigarettes or have any other bad habits. This pleases me. He is responsible and serious as a good husband should be.

After a few months I found that I had a sum of money saved up from his salary. So I said to him, "How much do you want to spend on my engagement present?" So he answered, "If it were up to me, I'd like to spend E£500 on your present. I want to get you something very big." I said, "No. I want just a pair of gold bracelets and a ring for each of us." I was counting on gold being reasonably priced and getting the engagement present, a *shabka* for 130, 150, or 160, pounds. Among the best of us today, the *shabka* is not as important as it was in the past. The modern couple just gets rings, and that's it, not even bracelets. We prefer to save for other things.

When Salah insisted on getting a *shabka* to show how much he cared for me, I watched for the price of gold in the newspaper. I'd come to him and say, "Can you believe the price of gold is such and such now?" So I'd say, "Never mind, Salah, forget it. Let's just get wedding rings like people are doing now. We'll wear these and take the rest of the money and put a down payment on a refrigerator. By the time we consummate our marriage, it will be ready for us." He'd answer, "No, no. This gold is the woman's present from the man. I want to give you a gift. I must get you something which will give you the feeling that I cherish you."

This jewelry now and all of the necessary accoutrements for the wedding ceremony can be rented by the day from the hairdresser's. I suggested doing that, as so many others do. But he said, "No, let me buy you everything you need to wear for the wedding. I'd like it to be your own." He goes on this way, and I've discovered that he is very decent and considerate.

I might say to him, "It's enough for you to spend E£10 a month," and he'll respond, "All right that's enough. What do I need more for?" And, in fact, what would he spend more money on? He can give his mother five or ten pounds a month from his salary and have some pocket money on the side. A son must support his mother. If I get E£40 of his monthly salary, it adds up. In a year we can save and buy something useful for the house.

Every now and then he comes and says to me, "Don't ever let any woman say to you, Salah is such and such, Suda, and believe her. Or, Salah used to go around with me." So I say to him, "You mean you haven't been around with any girls?" He answers, "Yes, I have, with many during my time in the army. But I wasn't serious about any of them. If you are worried about something, come and ask me. Don't jump to conclusions. People always want to make trouble."

Salah is black like me. I would not choose to marry a white man. If you choose one of your own kind, you feel that he will put up with anything you do more easily than someone who is different. Supposing I were to have a caprice or made a mistake sometime? I feel he'd let it pass more easily if he's one of us. But if I'm black and I'm married to a white man and I do anything to displease him, he might say, "Do you think you can carry on this way on the strength of your blackness? I could have taken a white woman!" So I spare myself this sort of injury by taking a man of my own kind.

There are a lot of these mixed marriages though. My aunt, my father's sister, married a white man, and their children are all white.

My maternal uncle, *Khali,* is married to a white woman, a beauty with a face like the moon. They are expecting a child. When I see her I say to her, "What have you done? Fie on you! If I were in your place, I would never have looked at this black man!" Honestly, she's white and pretty, so why should she marry this black man? But she answers, "I love him."

My paternal cousin, *Ibn Ammi,* in the village, is also married to a moon-faced beauty. She's as sweet as a piece of sugar! And the son of my paternal cousin, *Ibn bint 'Ammi,* who lives near the native village of the famous Egyptian singer Abd el Halim Hafez, is married to a white woman.

I felt no problems with differences in color until I came to Cairo. In the village I am known, I am from a known family, and everyone knows who my father was, who my uncles are, and no one can say to me, "O black woman!" They wouldn't dare.

But here if I'm walking in the street, a kid might come up to me an say, "You *Barbariyya!* O black woman!" I snap back at him, "You bastard, you son of a dirty woman!" These comments make one answer rudely. I walk very rarely with a white girl. Most of my girl friends are dark. But it happens from time to time. One day my friend Laila and I—she's dark too—were walking with a white friend of hers. The white girl was between us. A couple of boys saw us and began to laugh and hold on to each other and say to the white girl, "Move away from them, girl! Their color might run onto you," and words of that nature.

I'm laughing now, and really it doesn't hurt me. I'm one of God's creatures, and God made me this way. These comments annoy me though, and I answer, "You son of a whore! Did you create me? Why don't you look at yourself?" The ones who usually comment have something wrong with them, either they're too tall, or too short, or have a limp. I give them back as good as I get. I'll say, for example, "Why don't you right yourself? Why don't you fix that broken leg of yours!" and so on. Someone like that then becomes embarrassed and walks away.

Another might come up behind me and say to his friend, "O Brother, your deed is before you," in other words, yours is a black deed. So my friend and I laugh. Another will call out, "O white one!" So I answer, "Improve your eyesight, you blind dog, you son of a bald woman!" And so it goes as we walk down the street. I insult them and laugh! We have to walk quite a distance so there is a lot of banter. Mostly this happens in the popular quarters of town. A fellow might follow us and say, "O Lord, if only all this beauty were in a white woman, I'd never leave you, I'd follow you to the ends of the earth!" They don't mean anything serious by it. It's just street talk. They have nothing better to do. There's nothing I can do. Another man will come up behind the one teasing and answer the first and say, "In any case, O white one, half of beauty is darkness." So I say to him, "Honestly, you're a moon-faced beauty yourself, nothing short of a piece of sugar. Your head is an illuminated light bulb," and so it continues down the street. We end up answering, sometimes without realizing what we're saying.

This is not so in the village. It's known that you're the daughter of so and so. The village is divided up into families. Ours is called the Asad family. There is another family called the Hasheesh in the village, and they give us a bit of trouble. Our family is extremely religious. The members of the other family are a bit like sons of bitches. They have no manners or morals. A boy may covet his father's wife, for example, or the wife of his paternal cousin, Ibn Ammo. We say to them, "You immoral and low creatures," and they say to us, "You black slaves." It's the only family with whom we don't get along in the village.

The mayor of the village is from our family.

Originally of course our people came from the Sudan. One of our grandfathers came to Egypt first. There came a time when the urge to marry was upon him. So his family married him to a white girl. They had children, and he began to buy bits of land. He married his children in the village and gave each some land. I don't know much about the history of the family, but those of us in the village just know that it all started with our grandfather whose name was Bkheet Asad.

We are all on good terms with each other in the family. When I was a child in the village, feasts were important to me. They still are. Until today I must have one or two new dresses on the occasion of a feast. My mother taught me to be this way, to care for the way I looked.

My mother would always have a street dress and a house dress each made for me and my sister every year for the big feast. For my brother she

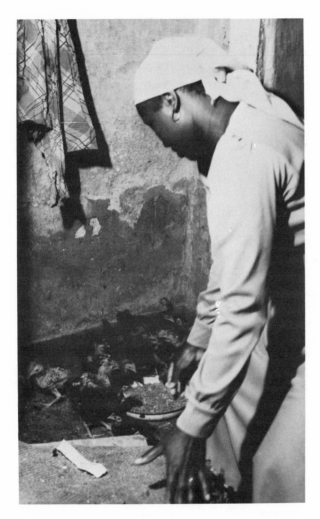

Suda feeding the chicks kept in a small room off the kitchen. Photograph by Asma
el-Bakry.

prepared new trousers and a shirt and a pair of pajamas. Each of us must have
two new pieces of clothing. That's how it was and still is.

On the eve of a feast, *yom el wakfa,* we bathed and put on the new
clean clothes. On the day of the feast itself, at about four o'clock in the
morning, we washed our faces and dressed and went out on the street. There

was no noise, and the village was quiet. As the morning progressed, people began to set up stalls and sell whistles and hats and sweets. One man might put bunches of grapes in a basket to sell. It's like a market day. Our relatives would give us some money, and we'd go out and buy candies or swing on the swings shaped like little boats set up for the occasion.

The men went to dawn prayers on that day and came out together from the mosque at about six o'clock in the morning. Then they walked all over the village greeting one another and wishing each other "happy feast." This happens every feast. The women stay at home, and the men make the rounds. Then they go back to perform feast prayers at the mosque. They don't return home until after noon. We eat *kahk* at Ramadan, sweet cakes powdered with sugar and stuffed with a honey mixture. We must always have these or the feast would not be a feast.

The women exchange visits in the late afternoon. The second day of the feast always is a market day. We buy fish and broil it on that day. By then we are tired of meat because during the fast, before the feast when we don't eat or drink all day, we break fast at dusk and often eat meat. Before daybreak, the time called *sohoor,* we eat beans or cheese, yogurt, milk, hard-boiled eggs, or buttermilk. We eat no cooked food, *tabeekh,* at that point because everyone is weary. My mother used to fast all day and cook for us. It was tiring for her. But we often ate meat at sunset, at our first meal of the day.

On feast day we do no cooking. We just reserve that day for rest and visiting. Sometimes we would prepare sardines, salted sardines which they sell in the market, and eat these. They're broiled, then salted and sold ready to eat in our village. We call them *fihliyya.* I don't know whether people make them in Cairo! They're a long, thin fish, stacked in woven baskets, one layer of fish and one of salt. People prepare them this way, keep them for a week or two until they're nicely salted, and then sell them.

After the feast we eat regular food.

People's stomachs after the fast are sensitive. When we eat sweet cakes made with lots of fat and sugar, we end up with diarrhea and upset stomachs. But we do it anyway. It's an important custom.

People who are well off might slaughter a sheep or a ram and give away a quarter of it to the less fortunate, about half a kilo to each family. You might give a quarter of the animal to a married daughter, for example. You'll say to your daughter-in-law or an unmarried daughter, "Here, carry her share of the feast to your sister." You might also include twenty kilos of rice or wheat and some *ro'a',* thin crisp country bread, and also some soap. These gifts are expected. They're important because they keep a family going for some time.

A married sister's share of the feast from her father's house shows her husband and his family that she is well cared for and protected by her own people. It adds to her stature with her in-laws. People who can might take a whole sheep or lamb to a married daughter.

Young children get money, twenty-five or fifty piasters each, according to people's means.

Grown children don't usually have to give anything to their parents. But if I have the means, and if my husband says to me, "You give this thing or this sum of money to your mother," then I do. But to take something behind my husband's back and give it to my mother would be a sin. The *Sheikh* tells us so in our weekly lessons.

He says, "When a woman gets married and has left her father's house and come to her husband's house, then it's a sin for her to give as much as a glass of water to her parents without her husband's knowledge." Even if I lend my neighbor a handful of salt, I should tell my husband, "My neighbor has borrowed a little salt from me." It's his right to know, and telling him is my way of showing my respect for him. This of course applies to people who interpret religion to the letter. For us, it's a lesson we hear, and then life goes on as before.

One way I learn my responsibilities toward the man I marry is by listening to the problems of other women. I like to sit with women who are older than myself. This one is my neighbor, for example. This other one is my friend's neighbor. I sit and listen to their talk. This one has left her husband. Why did she leave him? It's an embarrassing question, and some people don't like to reveal the truth about themselves. Mostly I don't ask questions, but I sit and listen. They see me sitting quietly, and sometimes one of them will come up to me and say, "Suda, don't ever get married." So I ask, "Why, what's happened?" When I hear her say, "Don't get married," I'm pleased because she's given me an opening. I can draw her out and gain some insights on marriage. Why should I not marry? What is troublesome in marriage? She might say to me, for example, "A man always says I love and adore you. I worship you. I'll get you whatever you ask for, then after he's taken his pleasure with you, he forgets what he's said." This is one of the problems in marriage, and one the women discuss constantly.

One of our neighbors is married to a man who came and asked for her hand. They were married. She had three children by this man. All this time it appeared that she didn't love him at all. I ask myself, "If I don't like my husband, why should I have children with him?" I know perhaps that I'll leave him or that I don't want to stay with him. So I would take birth control pills so as not to bring children into this world and make them suffer. Not everyone thinks this way though.

A man I know married a woman and had a daughter by her. Then he went into the army and stayed three years. Then on returning, he had another daughter and later on a son. When he finished military service, he went back to his job in a sporting club. He's the type of man who never says to his wife, "What have you been up to today?" or "What have the children been doing?" When she asks him, "What do you want to eat today?" he answers, "See what the children want to eat, and I'll eat with them." If she came to my house, for example, and stayed all day and he came home and found her gone, he'd never ask, "Where have you been or what have you been doing?" To ask these questions is a man's right. And after all, he is an Egyptian! I don't know how foreigners are, but among Egyptians the man will say to his wife, "Where have you been? Where did you go? What were you doing? Why did you stay out so long? Don't go out today." It's his right. Our religious teachers tell us it must be so. I don't know if this is the truth or not. If he doesn't do this, it shows he doesn't love his wife, doesn't care.

If I said to this neighbor, for example, "I'm going to run such and such an errand. Come with me," she'd say, "Yes, let's go." So I'd say, "Aren't you going to tell your husband? Or leave word for him?" She'd answer, "O Sister, why bother? Does he ever bother to ask me where I've been or what I'm doing?" The problem here is that he doesn't make her feel he's a man. He doesn't ask after her. In the case of these two, it's gone so far that they even sleep in separate rooms. He sleeps alone in one room, and she sleeps with the children. So she tells me.

I was puzzled by all this for a time and would say to her, "Well, then, how did you ever have these children? They must not be his children." She answered, "They are. I felt when we were first married that if I had children from him, he would change, improve." His problem is a strange one. When you ask him about it, he'll say, "She doesn't care for me or look after me. She leaves me and sleeps with the children." But then I think to myself, "Is she, a woman, going to ask you to come to her?" "Is she going to say, 'I must sleep with you by hook or by crook' and spend the night in your room?"

When she talked to her women friends about her problem, we advised her to be more aggressive. We said, "Yes, a woman must do this. A woman must go to her man." He's proud and says, "I'm not going to demand that she comes and sleeps with me." And she says, "I'm not going to annoy him by insisting that I want to sleep with him in his room." The two of them have made a mountain of this matter. So we say to her, "Be patient and tolerant." They have a couch in their bedroom, and so we said to her, "Go and lie down on the couch at night and sleep there. See if he does anything. See if he comes to you at night or if he avoids you."

So she did as we told her to, and he continued to ignore her. She would say to him, "Is there anything you desire?" He would answer, "No." So she would resign herself and go to sleep.

She comes and tells us and cries, "What can I do? Am I to sell myself? Do you think I can stoop so low as to say 'Come to me I want you?'"

She's greatly annoyed by this situation, and she says, "Why am I married to him? Am I his wife only in order to serve his children? Am I his servant?" She goes on in this way and feels very badly.

The womenfolk then said to her one day, "Look here, go to his bed and lie down on the side of the bed which is against the wall and sleep there. Even turn your face to the wall. You don't need to be so obvious as to come face to face with him. But don't let him get away so easily."

We lived across the landing from her, and we couldn't avoid being involved in her affairs. She was nervous and angry.

My maternal uncle who lives upstairs is a good talker, and he was constantly involved in their affairs. Her husband would complain to my uncle, and she would come and tell him her problems. We liked her very much, and we admitted to her that she was not being given her due. But to give her patience we would say, "But of course you must tolerate him because of your children."

One day she finally said, "I won't tolerate him any longer. As far as my children are concerned I'll stay with them in my apartment, and I want him to leave."

We tried to mediate between them. He would shout, "I can't stand her. I don't like her, and I don't want her. She's not a good woman."

So when Ramadan came, he said, "I'm spending the feast days with the children and then leaving. I'm going back to my father's house." So he did. He stayed fifteen days. One night, when everyone was asleep, he made a bundle of his belongings and left. She said, "I woke up when I heard the door shut, and he had left."

When this happened, she got up and came to wake us. Her father lived above her on the second floor. So we went up and told him, "Such and such has happened." She was there, and God only knows whether she was miserable or happy.

In the meantime she had set her eye on my uncle. It was obvious she liked him. My uncle had been married seventeen years. His wife was barren. People always say, "Get married so that you can be blessed with children." My uncle was childless and not happy. In our part of the world, a woman has to have children and a man must have children, otherwise what will he leave behind him when he dies?

This woman stayed alone for a short time, then went up and stayed in her father's flat. A woman can't stay in a house alone. By and by her husband sent for the three children and took them to live with his parents.

At this point my uncle's wife said something to him which angered him. They quarrelled, and he told her to leave, saying, "I'm going to get married again." He wanted the other woman. So now there was a problem in my uncle's house, too.

This neighbor is pretty, and I said to her, "How can you look at this rotten man?" meaning my uncle. She laughed and said, "I love him." So I answered, "Love him then to your heart's content, you fool."

My uncle divorced his wife, who was a respectable black woman from our own village. He stayed alone for three months or so until the other woman received her divorce papers and then, after a couple of months, they got married. She had two miscarriages, and she's pregnant a third time now in her fourth or fifth month.

My uncle likes his home. He watches over his woman properly. She had noticed this quality in him and liked it. She used to complain to me, saying, "How can it be that God blessed this childless woman with such an attentive husband, and I who have three am neglected?" She went on in this way, and perhaps she had it in the back of her mind all the while to marry my uncle. I don't know.

He had his flat painted before the wedding. She had her furniture refurbished and gave her apartment back to her father, who rented it to a doctor. She married my uncle and moved in with him. She seems happy. My uncle orders her around.

The reason for the break-up between this woman and her first husband was probably sex. I'm nearly sure because she used to complain to us, saying, "Can you imagine that he only sleeps with me every seven or eight months?" We didn't believe her at the beginning. How can a man with a wife like a jasmine blossom just ignore her? We thought she was a liar. We didn't know what his point of view was. But when we got to know him better, he began to talk. He became so intimate with our family that he would come home from work and say to his wife, "Om Aziz, bring our food here to Om Abdo's house. We'll all eat together." He hated being alone with his wife. So he brought his wife and three children and their food, and we'd set out the low table, *tabliyya*, in the entrance hall and sit on the floor and eat together, just like in the village. We would have lunch together, dinner together, and even at Ramadan when everyone is supposed to eat in his own house, he came and sat with us at meal times. He would say, "I feel you've made it easier for me to tolerate the shit she makes me live with." She would needle him, and they would not talk to each other for two or three months sometimes. They were constantly quarrelling. But he never failed her where money was concerned.

I don't know whether he had something troubling him, or whether something she had done made him dislike her, or whether he was just tired of her. He's now remarried, and his second wife has a two-year old son.

I learn about life from observing. I think to myself, for example, "If my husband should give me a hard time or if there are differences between us, then I will know enough not to have too many children so that I don't suffer having to bring them up alone." I'm a bit hard perhaps. I want to know a lot about the man I'll marry before I marry him. Listening to women talking of their problems has made me wary. But of course since my father died when I was a little girl, my maternal uncle took on my education. He taught me right from wrong. He would say to me, "If someone were to do something to you, the results would not be good." In this way he tried to warn me of the problems which I might face. This made me strong and unlike many young women. He helped me be cautious and patient.

My mother never spoke to me about relationships between men and women. But my uncle would take me aside and tell me a story, even if he made it up, to illustrate a point. He would say, for example, "Look. There was once a girl who fell in love with a man. He said he would marry her, but after he had taken his pleasure with her, he abandoned her. This is a calamity because a girl lives for the day when she can be properly married. Remember, we are peasant folk, conservative, just like Upper Egyptians. You must guard your honor at all cost." And he would go on explaining this way until I understood.

A woman's honor is her most important asset. Even when I was in love that first time, I made the man keep his distance. Although we spent two and three hours alone, he never tried to touch me. That was one of the things which made me love him. But supposing I were to hug and kiss a man, he could hold this against me. If I were to be angry and insult him one day, he could say, "Now look here. Remember what happened between us?" He could embarrass me. Even if I were to give him a photo of myself, he could use it to humiliate me if there was disagreement between us. Egyptians are no good in this way and are always trying to get the better of each other. A woman must be very careful.

If we were photographed together in a public place, for example, and I took one copy of the picture and he the other, he might use that to blackmail me. If we disagreed, he'd say, "I'll show it to your mother. I'll show it to your brother." I might say, "Well, go right ahead," but then if I become engaged to someone like Salah and he showed him such a picture, then Salah would say, "Well, I'm sorry. I can't marry you. You've been such and such and done this and that. You're unworthy." The way things go here, even if nothing happened between two people, at least nothing of great importance, if you've held hands with a man or kissed him, then all the other men assume that you will do the same with them. You spoil your reputation.

So I've been very careful. One sees people's problems and learns from them.

When I was a little girl, there were two families in the village who hated each other. The son and daughter from the families were in school together and loved one another. He came to ask for her hand, and her family refused. So he said to her, "You sleep with me, and we'll force them to let us get married." So she did and became pregnant. The families said they had to kill them both, but people intervened and said, "Are we Upper Egyptians, that we should act in this beastly fashion? Marry them and be done." The boy said he had done this thing because he wanted the girl and there was no other way to get her, and so the families married them. That was a happy ending, but it's not always this way. They had to live outside the village for three years because of their behavior but then moved back. They now have five children, they're respectable, and the whole story is forgotten.

In the old days we used to marry the whites. Now it's become less and less frequent. We don't really want to any more. Supposing I were married to a white man and I saw him speaking to a white woman, I'd say to myself, "Well, she's white like him, why shouldn't he speak to her? Why, after all, should he want to stay with a black woman like myself?" I might be jealous and upset.

If my husband and I are the same, then he's never going to say to me "black woman," nor am I going to say to him "black man." Of course not everyone thinks this way. My brother-in-law is engaged to a white woman. They quarrel all the time, and his color is always held up to him as a bone of contention. People say, "If she'd been a black like him, she'd have been respectful, and her family would be mindful of his feelings." He'd like to get out of this engagement now.

We joke among ourselves sometimes, saying, "O white woman, why don't you marry one of your own kind? They're many of you but few of us, and why should you take one of the few black men? If you marry one, then whom shall I marry?" and so on. These are problems. My paternal niece, *Bint ibn 'Amee*, calls her father "black man." She's four years old. She has a little sister who is dark, and this girl calls her "black Maha" and says, "You're black like your father Maha."

Her father laughs and says her attitude will change when she grows up. But it never does. So I prefer not to mix.

My uncle of course married this white woman, but she said to all of us before she married him, "I'm at his feet. If I ever do anything wrong, he can do what he wants with me." Which means she respects us.

I had no objection to my uncle marrying that woman because they love each other, but I said to her, "If you love him, marry him, but then don't complain," because my uncle is rather difficult. He does not like to leave even a penny in a woman's hand. He gets everything she wants for her. He goes to the market for her every three days or so but doesn't give her an allowance or allow her to go out to the market at all. She stays home. That's how he wants it. That's how it was with his first wife. If he should give her any money, he keeps a written record of it. He believes women should be provided for but not given money. I say to him, "By God, if my husband were like you, I wouldn't live with him a single day." His wife says she prefers it that way, but I don't think it's really true. He gives her all she wants but doesn't give her the freedom to choose anything.

If she says, "I want a dress," he'll say, "Of course," and he'll go and buy her one according to his own taste and give it to her. Will she be able to say anything? No, because before he married her he warned her, saying, "No woman of mine will tell me what to do or say to me I want a dress this color or this shape. What I like I do. I give her what pleases me." And indeed this is how it goes with them. He'll bring her what she wants and will say to her, "You'll do this and that. You'll have this material made into a dress this way." So she has to obey. He also says, "No woman of mine is allowed to go out. So if you come and say, 'I want to go see my friend or go to the market,' you must know now the answer is 'no.'" She agreed to all of these conditions and so she can't complain now. She came crying to me one day, saying, "Your uncle doesn't let me go anywhere." So I said to her, "You knew what you were getting into, and you agreed to it." She put the noose around her own neck, now she has to accept her life as it is.

Money and sex are the problems most often discussed among Egyptian women. One woman will complain, like my uncle's wife did about her first husband, that her husband gives her all the money she needs but neglects her. For another it's the reverse. Sex and money, money and sex. Even circumcision does not lessen a woman's desire for attention from her husband.

Every Muslim girl must be circumcised of course, otherwise she would not be considered Muslim. Only Christian girls in our village are not circumcised.

It's a must. It's the first taste of suffering a girl ever has.

I cried for a week before I was circumcised. I was twelve, but I knew what to expect from the time I was eight years old. I learned from the talk of the older girls.

People say that the older a girl is when she's circumcised, the less chance there is of these parts growing back. I don't know if that's really true. But that's why some people keep this ordeal until a girl is twelve or thirteen.

I was told it would hurt a little, but it was hell. The midwife puts alcohol on you afterward, and you're on fire. I knew I had to go through this operation. I knew there was no getting around it. It's as sure a thing as having to get married or give birth. People would say to the girls, "Marriage is just like circumcision only better," or "You have to be circumcised, otherwise you can't get married." And when we are little of course the thing we want most in the world is to get married.

I wasn't terrified before it happened. The older girls had said it didn't hurt much more than a pin prick. Our mothers would say to them, "Don't tell the little girls about it. Don't talk to them about it hurting so that they don't grow afraid." The women of course know what it's all about. But they want to encourage not frighten us.

When my time came, we were about five girls: me, two of my paternal cousins, *Banaat Ammee*, another girl, and her maternal cousin. It was after Ramadan. The Nile water was red. It was the season of the flood. The Nile still flooded then, not like now.

We bathed the night before the operation and went to bed. The next morning was scorchingly hot weather. So my mother said, "Get up girls and go bathe in some cold water." They say you have to cool the body before this operation. All the girls came to our house. Meanwhile, the women had prepared sugar and lemons to make lemonade for us after the operation. I've hated lemonade every since. They give the same thing to a girl after she has consummated her marriage.

So that morning they took the oldest girl and spread a straw mat on the floor for her and put a piece of sacking under her so that the blood wouldn't stain the mat. The women started to hold and undress her. I was astonished. I didn't think anyone would hold us down. One women held one leg and another the other leg, and the midwife was in front of the girl. We were standing there, and one of us said, "What are they going to do to her?" So the women told us to get out of the room, to go fetch something or other. I felt faint. I was shaking, then I heard the scream. My cousin wailed the loudest. Then the next girl was taken in and the next and the next. It was my turn. They locked each girl in a room away from the rest and left her to cry there. We asked why she was crying, and they said, "It's nothing. She's a little coward. She's just afraid. She's badly brought up," and words of that nature.

When it came my turn, I said to them, "Look here, I don't want anyone to hold me." So they said, "Well, sit down then." So I did. The midwife put flour on this thing [the clitoris] to keep it from slipping between her fingers. When she took hold of it, I objected, "What are you doing, woman?" She answered, "Don't you want to get married?" and then told the others to hold me. I cried and shouted, "What are you doing to me you bitch? Did I tell you I wanted to get married? Leave me alone." She used a very sharp barber's razor. Then it was over. I felt nothing until she put alcohol on. Then it stung.

I cried, and my mother said to me, "Have some lemonade. It will cool down the stinging." So I said pointing to my head, "I drink lemonade

from up here, what has that got to do with me down there?" I've hated
lemonade ever since.

At noon the women wanted to feed us. People said, "Don't give
them meat. It will give them a fever." So they fed us eggs and milk. By night
time we could get up and walk around a little, and each girl went home.

The midwife warned us to keep our legs apart to keep the wound
from shutting. She said if it did, she'd have to come and open it up again with
her razor. She struck terror in our hearts. My mother put pillows between my
legs, and my paternal cousins stayed with us.

The second day this woman, the midwife, came and put a piece of
cotton dipped in oil on the wound. On the third day, we went down to the
river to bathe, and we were healed.

The midwife, *Daya*, gave us each the bit she cut from our bodies.
She said, "Take this. Keep it with you all the time for a month." This is to
prevent us from becoming sterile should an ill-wisher put the evil eye on us.
My mother put mine in a piece of cloth and pinned it to my dress. After a
month, I went to the river with my cousins and threw it out.

After I was circumcised, I knew I'd grown up. I knew I would be
married soon. I was going into sixth grade at school. I was tall and strong and
said to my people, "I don't want to go to school any more. I'll learn to sew."
So my mother sent me to a number of seamstresses to learn. Each one would
say though, "Suda, sweep the floor, clean this, do that." I went back to my
mother and said, "This woman wants to use me as a servant." So my mother
said, "To hell with sewing. Why should you be exploited? Stay home. We
have no girls in our family who work as servants. You'll soon be married."

I got to know my fiancé through his mother. We were walking past a
government co-operative one day when we saw people queueing up there as
they usually do to buy food. We asked the women, "What are you queueing
up to buy?" They said sugar, lentils, or something like that. So I said to my
mother, "Let's stand in line and get some, too." I hadn't started to work yet
and had time on my hands. My fiancé's mother was standing there that day.
She had with her her youngest son who was about six or seven. So I started to
banter with him and said, "Sweet little black boy, you're as sweet as a piece of
sugar. By God, I'll marry you to my daughter. Be an angel and queue up for
me, and get me a couple of sacks of lentils. Get me some black lentils and
some red lentils." We talked and joked.

Soon his mother turned to me and said, "What do you want to get,
Sugar?" So I said to her, "By God, Granny, I want a couple of sacks of lentils."
So she said to her son, "Stand in line, my boy, and get some lentils for your
sister. We'll sit here at the edge of the sidewalk and wait." So he did.

We didn't know each other, but we were black like them, and people
of like color are drawn to each other. There was instant sympathy. So the

mother said to me, "Sugar, you're pretty. You have a sweet disposition and you're lighthearted. Is this your mother?" I said it was. So she said, "Our house is just here behind the co-op. You would be welcome to visit us at any time." So I thanked her. We got our lentils and went our way.

Another time I met her again in the market, and she said, "Come, come brave one, how are you?" I said I was fine and asked after her little son. She said he was fine. She then said to me, "You know I have two daughters. Come and make their acquaintance, and you can go about together. My daughters like having friends." So I said, "Yes, God willing." She said, "On the twenty-ninth of January my little son is having a birthday. Come and celebrate it with us then." So I said all right and told her where we lived. I was reluctant to go to their house, so she said she'd send her daughters to me. And then she said, "Better yet, why don't you come up with me now? We live on the fifth floor." I said I couldn't. I was afraid to go up. After all, I didn't know her. One has to be cautious. So she told her son to go call his sisters instead, and he went. It was toward the end of the day. By and by one of the sisters came down, and I took her to our house. I didn't want to go to their house first.

I got to know this sister. We became friends over two or three months. One day I said to her, "I'm going to make meat balls today for lunch." So she said, "I'll come and make them with you." So I said she was welcome. She visited me often and then came to invite me to her brother's birthday party. I said, "Come and fetch me because I don't know the house." I didn't want to go there alone. So it was agreed. That was my first visit to their house. I felt strange and didn't know anyone. I asked who this person was and that one until we were all acquainted.

After that we exchanged visits regularly and began to study one another carefully. There was no question of marriage or anything of the sort. Salah, my fiancé, was in the army then, but his older brother had finished military service and was home.

I'm the sort of person who does not like to exchange too many words with men. I'm straightforward but reserved. Salah's brother tried to draw me into conversations. I was reluctant. I thought to myself, "Why bother, why would he be better than any other men?"

This brother then took a liking to me, and when I came to visit, he would be there and would walk me home at night. He was a bit of a playboy and liked to talk and joke. He would say to me, "What harm is there in letting me go out with you?" I would answer him, "Sorry, I'm not the girl for you. I'm not the type who goes out. Go find someone else." The same happened with a younger brother. He would say to me, "Why are you walking so far from me? Come close. Do you think I'm going to eat you?"

I would get angry and answer, "What business is it of yours? You've offered to see me home. That's all. There's no need for you to walk beside me."

We were going down the stairs of their house one night when the younger brother tried to hold my hand. I insulted him, saying, "May God curse you, you disgusting beast. Are you a child acting this way? Get out of my sight."

Of course it would be shameful to hold his hand, and I wasn't brought up to allow this sort of thing. If I gave in, I would get a reputation for being "easy" and then that would lessen my chances for a good marriage. I was constantly on my guard as every girl should be.

This brother soon gave up taking me home. But it seems he said to others, Suda is the cleanest girl to enter our house yet." The other brother was angry with me though and would say, "She's ill mannered and always ready with an insulting word." So one of the sisters would answer, "Is she ill mannered, or did you want to feel her up and she would not agree?" He'd say, "She's not a good girl. She's capable of insulting one in public!" He said this in front of me one day, so I answered, "If I wanted someone, it wouldn't be a pipsqueak like you!" That resolved it, and he left me alone.

Salah, when he came out of the army, heard about me. When we got to know each other, I told him what his brothers had done. A girl must always tell her fiancé her past history so that if someone confronts him one day with, "Did you know your fiancé was going around with another man before you?" he would be armed and could answer, "Yes, I know." So of course I told him about the man I'd loved, saying, "I loved this man. He turned out to be married, and I put miles between us for such and such a reason."

When Salah began to court me, his father was upset. His folks had wanted to marry him to the sister of one of his sisters-in-law. He refused. He told them, "I love this girl," meaning me, "and I'll marry no one else." This caused a rift between him and his father. His father said, "I'll not come with you to ask for her hand." Salah answered, "I want nothing. I don't want a penny from you." And a cold war was declared between them. Neither spoke to the other for about three months on my account.

After a time I said to Salah, "This situation is no good, Salah. I'm going to speak to your father myself." By this time we were legally married, but the marriage was not yet consummated. I still lived at home.

Ramadan came, and I said, "This is a feast time. This rift between you and your father is a shame and a sin. We've got to clear up any misunderstanding before the feast." So we went to see the father, and he welcomed us. I think he realized he was in the wrong.

I said to him, "Are you upset because you don't want me to marry your son? If that's so, there's no need for me to marry him." But I added, "I think though that each man chooses the woman he wants to live with, and this should not upset you." He answered, "No, my child, I'm not upset, it's just that I'm afraid Salah will get me into trouble because he's just come out of the army and has no money." So Salah said, "No, Father, I'll not get you in trouble. I do have some money of my own and will not say to you 'give me anything.'" Then I said, "And also I would not have a man whose father had to give him money to get married. If you were to give him money today, who would provide for him tomorrow? If I wasn't sure that this human being could take care of me, then I would not marry him."

So everything was settled. I get along well with my in-laws. Even my brothers-in-law have repented. Now they say, "We were just testing you to see what you'd do." It might be true. As I was a friend of their sisters, they had to be sure I was not loose. A brother has to protect his sister from bad influences. Yet even now I never go to their house without Salah. He's very careful on that score. He says, "When you want to visit my people, I'll take you and bring you home. Don't go when I'm not there." It's just the way he is. He's right. It's best to avoid problems.

When Salah decided he wanted to marry me, he sent his mother to speak for me. She came two or three times. We didn't accept right away. We wanted her feet to ache a little before giving her an answer.

The first time she spoke to me, she said, "Suda, I've noticed that Salah treasures and loves you and wants to marry you." So I answered, "Who told you so? Did he send you or are you coming to tell me this of your own accord?" She said, "He told me. I agreed, and we discussed it yesterday. He wanted me to come and ask you and said to me, 'Mother, I still don't know what Suda's opinion on this is,' so I've come to speak on his behalf." In fact I had not expressed my feelings to him when he began courting me. I'd simply said to him, "Your mother is the one to come and speak to me first. She has to be willing before we consider the question further. Then I'll say 'yes' or 'no' after that." It's very important to get along with your mother-in-law. If you don't, she can make life hard for you.

His mother then said, "He told me of his desire yesterday but said 'Suda is mature and has her own ideas, and perhaps she would object to someone who is just starting out because I may not be able to give her all she wants.' But he's a good boy. He listens to what one has to say, and if you could see your way clear to waiting for him, you'd have a winner."

Before all of this and before the engagement even, Salah used to come and say to me, "Suda, please keep my salary for me. When I need something, I'll come and ask you for it." There was understanding and good-will between us from the start. He'd come and say to me sometimes, "I want to get myself a pair of trousers, come and choose them for me." So I would. He would say, "How amazing. It's just what I like. We have similar tastes." I don't know if he was just humoring me. I try to pick things which suit the taste of the person they are for. He has an image to maintain, and I would pick something for him which was appropriate. Some men don't care. They'll appear in a pair of red trousers or a green shirt. They don't look respectable.

We go shopping together. At home they would know I was with him, and after all our families visited back and forth. But for the sake of appearances before we were engaged, I'd say to him, "Look, Salah, for the sake of appearances in my neighborhood, please wait for me at the bus-stop. I'll meet you there." So we would go where he wanted and get him what he needed, and that way we got to know each other better.

One time he said to me, "Suda, I want to get a present for my sister." So I said to him, "What would you like to get? Is it her birthday or some special occasion?" So he answered, "No, nothing special." I knew then that he wanted to get me a present and was using his sister as an excuse. So I answered, "Look here, don't lie to me. I don't like lies." So he confessed. He said, "I really want to get you a present. You've gone to a lot of trouble on my behalf. I want to get you something." So I said, "Thank you very much, when I need something, I'll tell you." I really didn't want to accept anything from him. I didn't want to feel under any obligation to him. So I said, "Presents can come later. This is not the time."

When his mother came to speak to me, I said to her, "Salah is kind. He's a good man, and being your son he'd be forthright and honest." So she answered, "Well then, don't embarrass me and my son by refusing us. Salah likes you very much." So I agreed, saying, "May God set us on the right path. I'll tell my people, and then you can speak to them."

So when I broached the subject with my uncle, he said "Yes, why not. I know him, and he's fine." Later on I went and told his mother, "Granny, you can go to my people now." So she came. Then we thought it would be a good idea to have the children from both families present and ask them what they thought of their brother's choice, what the bride price should be, and what sort of an engagement present would be required. The family has to live together, so it's best if everyone takes part in important decisions. When we were gathered, my uncle said, "Salah is just beginning his life, and he should stand on his feet before anyone makes any demands on him. When he's ready to give something, then there will be no objection to his having Suda. But since these two love each other, then let the marriage take place with no strings attached." No one raised any objections, and so they agreed we would marry the following week but wait for the consummation.

Salah waited a week and then took me and bought me some light blue chiffon for a long dress and a pair of sandals to go with it. Everyone wanted me to buy white or silver sandals. But I said "no" and chose some blue ones, the color of the outer leaves of cabbage. I chose something I could use easily later on. Later he bought me a pair of earrings and then some material for a dress and a pair of shoes for the feast. The fabric is a good jersey, the sort which costs E£3.50 a meter. Now he's waiting for me to set the day of the wedding.

We'll wait a year to consummate our marriage. We both decide on the time. We don't have E£700 or E£800 with which to set up a house now. We need at least E£300 to put down for key money on an apartment in this area. The bride price will also be E£300. This my uncle will use to buy us furniture for two rooms. The family will add some for other necessities, and Salah will save as much from his salary as he can to start us out properly. I'll go on working for another year. I have to have a washing machine.

I'll stop working once I'm married and living with my husband. I couldn't run my house and work as well. As it is now, I go to work, come home, eat, and sleep. All I do now is wash my own clothes, nothing more. When I'm married, my home will require my full attention.

4

Dunya

"This is my story with its sad times and its tears and nothing added and nothing taken away."

I WAS BORN in El-Hussaneyya, which is one of the old quarters of Cairo between Sayyedna el-Hussein and Abbaseyya. I have a brother, Yehia, who is two years younger than I am and my sister Lolla who is the eldest.

We moved from El-Hussaneyya to Boulac when I was young, but still my understanding was broad. It's so with human beings. Their potential for understanding doesn't increase with time but is born into them from the beginning. We say that God gives each breadth of spirit and understanding according to his individual makeup and constitution.

When we went to Boulac, the woman who is now my mother-in-law, Om Fouad, lived there. She was in good standing with her husband, who was my father's first cousin, and she was good to us.

We were children, and we spent most of our time playing in the street. I played there with Ezzo, my present and second husband, and with his sisters, and my sister Lolla. We all lived in the same house. Ezzo's mother gave birth to him in that house in the summer of 1950, and three days later my mother gave birth to me in El-Hussaneyya. So we are the same age, and we grew up together. I used to call his father uncle, and his mother, wife of my uncle.

When there was misunderstanding between the two families, my mother would say to us, "You children go and play together." She didn't believe that we should be included in arguments or family feuds. And so it

87

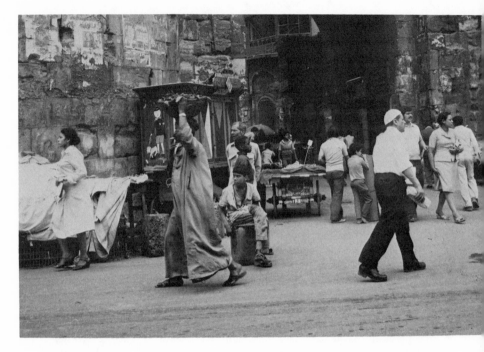

Historic Cairo quarter near where Dunya was born. Photograph by Asma el-Bakry.

was that Ezzo and I were close during those first years and shared everything. I gave him what I had, a sandwich, for example. And he gave me what he had, a sandwich also.

When Ezzo went to school, he would bring home the sweet wheat porridge which they gave him there, and we would stake out a little corner of the house, apart from the other children, and eat it together. We were exclusively devoted to each other, and he would often prefer to sleep with us rather than his own family. As we lived in the same house, in two rooms facing each other across a hallway, this was easily done. His family is still in that house.

When we got older, my father said, "Dunya will marry Ezzo, and Lolla will marry Fouad." We began at that time to understand more of life as does the human being the older he gets. But circumstances conspired to separate us, and I was to marry once before my marriage to Ezzo in 1974.

It happened that my father's cousin died when we were still young, and when he died, he left behind four children: two boys, Fouad and Ezz el-Din, "Ezzo," and two girls, Aliyya and Soheir. As there were three of us, we were seven children altogether.

Om Fouad then went to work as a maid for some foreigners in Heliopolis in order to support her four children. My father felt sorry for this woman who had neither worked before nor ever faced the push and shove of public transportation. Without telling my mother, he decided to marry her thus taking on the responsibility of a second family.

One day, he took the seven children to Ataba to buy sandals for the summer as he had done every year. Om Fouad came with him, and at one point they left us in the shop and said to wait there as they had an errand to run in the district. As it was they had actually gone to get married. When they came back, they were looking happy, and it wasn't until later that I understood what had happened.

My father used to beat my mother. At that time his violence toward her increased, and it would seem that Om Fouad was the cause. She would whimper and complain about my mother, saying Om Yehia had done this and that to her, and my father would believe her and beat my mother. My mother suffered badly because she had a rheumatic heart, and although she looked strong and healthy, she wasn't.

People of my parents' generation used to eat better than we do today because food was cheap and plentiful, and so illness didn't show as much on them as it does now on us. Food is more expensive now, and we have to eat more sparingly. So my mother suffered, and any time there is more than one wife they vie for the man's time, this one wanting him to sleep more with her and the other the same.

Seeing that problems between the two women would not cease, people said to my father, "It's best to separate them, and then you can administer justly between the two. You sleep one night here and one night there." So my father found a house for us in Embaba, which is popular district like Boulac, and we moved. I was about eight years old, and Ezzo was in the second grade.

Until his father died we used to play in the alley together, and as we were children we had no feeling for what death was and no sense of what suffering meant. Until now when someone dies or is in pain, I think to myself looking at the children playing, "We used to play like them on the street, and it's the adults who are sad and who realize what death is, what life is, and what companionship means."

So my father separated his two wives and rented a house for our family which consisted of one room above and one room below. He likes plants very much and started a little garden for us in tin cans. I fetched dirt from across the river in Zamalek, and he got a start from someone and planted

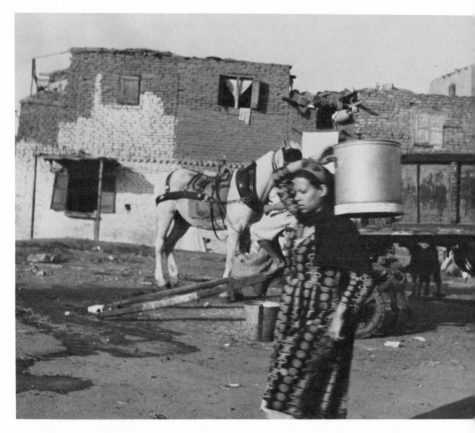

In many popular quarters in Cairo, people have to rely on the neighborhood public
water pump for their supply of water. Photograph by Asma el-Bakry.

basil and cactus. You might live in a chicken coop, but if you take care of it, it
can be nice.

    So we divided up the work there between us in order to keep it that
way. I used to fetch water, as we had no running water in the house, and care
for the plants and do the shopping. No, my mother did the shopping, and I
fetched water and threw out the dirty water for Lolla who washed. We took
water from a neighbor who had a tap, but if there were rugs to wash, I did
them in the river. When we had someone over for a meal, I used to scrub the
pots and pans in the river and shine them up well. I was clever in that way.

    As the plants grew, they provided a special touch in the house. I

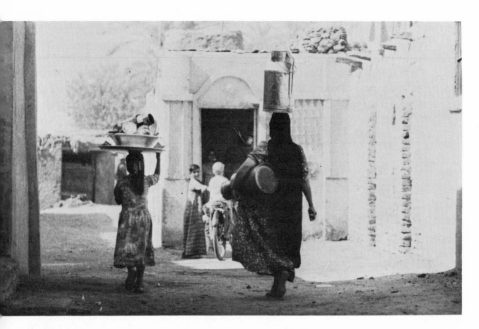

Walking home with clean pots and pans after washing them in the river. Photograph by Asma el-Bakry.

liked the basil especially, and at the end of the day I would tap its leaves between my hands to release their perfume. I would dust and spray the plants then too in order to keep them green and healthy. It was my father who taught me. Each person in this world performs as well as he is taught.

When we moved to that house, my father said, "I'll do something new here." He could see that the house squatted close to the ground, and he felt that we were easy prey to thieves. The second floor was really the ground floor, and the first floor was below ground level, and you had to go down some stairs to reach it. We did the cooking in the room below and used it for storage and slept on a rug in the room above. So my father, seeing the way the house was, said, "The plants will form a wall which will serve as a deterrent to thieves, and they will be something that is at once beautiful and protects." We would transplant any time we salvaged an extra tin or bucket, and with it we would elevate the wall around us. Above the second floor room we had a creeper growing to provide shade as that room had no roof and was open to the sky. So I used to fill the buckets with water while my sister washed, but I didn't like anyone to tell me what to do. I was stubborn and liked to follow my own mind.

My father had a violent temper, and when we sat before him we were never at ease. He's still this way, and until this day I dare not appear before him with bare arms or wearing makeup or anything but the traditional costume of our people. We act as we have been accustomed to do. A disapproving glance from my father can make one feel like urinating. He is very strict and conservative. When we girls asked him about going to school, he replied that girls who went to school didn't learn to mind their homes properly and were subject to the attentions of men on the street to and from school, and so he refused to send us. My brother Yehia and Fouad and Ezzo all went.

My father is from Upper Egypt from a village near Sohag. He is a God-fearing man, however, and taught us right from wrong. He used to say to us that if we were dishonest or didn't mind, that we would go to hell. He believed that those who didn't lie and were honest were loved by God and man alike, and that the stones of the earth themselves regarded them kindly. My father is about sixty years old, and my mother is fifty. She was born and grew up in El-Hussaneyya.

When we moved to Embaba, on the nights when my father was not there, I would ask my mother about him. Everyone asks after his father when he's late. So my mother would tell me, "Your father is spending the night at work." My paternal cousin opened my eyes, however. She would say, "Your father? Your father is married to Om Fouad and sleeps there." When I finally asked my mother about it, she said it was so, adding that these things are all a matter of luck and individual fate.

My mother wasn't easy about Fouad as a prospective groom for Lolla, perhaps because she knew that Lolla herself didn't want him. Ezzo and I, as we got older, used to go out together, and she did not seem to mind that.

We didn't go out in the sense that couples who are engaged do, getting dressed up and going somewhere special. No. Ezzo would come and visit us and would say, "Would you like to go out to buy sunflower seeds to nibble on?" "Please, Mama," I would say, "could we go out to buy sunflower seeds?" And she would say, "All right, go." So I would put on the *melaya* over my dress or the *tarha* over my head and we would go. Sometimes we would go out for roast corn along the river when the weather got warm, and as we were going to buy something anyway, we would take a turn and come home. They all knew I cared for Ezzo and he for me.

At some point my maternal cousin came to ask my father for Lolla's hand. My father refused. But, as he is cunning, he didn't tell Lolla but wanted to test her waters and then impose his will on her. So one day he called her and said, "Your cousin wants to marry you, as well as another cousin and Fouad. Whom would you prefer?"

Lolla was most inclined toward her maternal cousin. The family was well off, and her uncle had gone on more than one pilgrimage. My uncle had a factory for primus stoves and a commercial passport to export them to Syria and Lebanon.

Lolla was pretty. She is a little short but had a nice figure, and everyone called her *el-batta* which means duck, and indicates that she is pleasingly plump. I, on the other hand was referred to at that time as *dakkar*, which means male, because I was tall and had no bosom.

So anyway, my father asked Lolla to name her choice, and although at first she had said that she didn't wish to marry anyone, she reconsidered and said, "To tell you the truth, Father, I would prefer Waleed my maternal cousin." My father repeated, "You would prefer Waleed your maternal cousin?" and then began to strike her. He wanted to bring her to her knees and, after knowing what was in her mind, show her who was boss.

My mother was there, but she could never fend off my father, and if he insulted her, she would cower, and if he beat her, she would take it without uttering a sound. So she couldn't help Lolla and ran instead to a neighbor for help.

Everyone has those who wish him well and those who wish him ill, and this neighbor was good and was a friend. As it was summer she was in her housedress and grabbed what she thought was her *melaya* to go over it. In her haste, however, she had taken a bed sheet instead, and that is how she arrived with my mother at our doorstep. My father was shouting, "She will marry Fouad, and her shoes up over her head," which means that Lolla would do as he wished and not be able to move a muscle any more than an animal bound for slaughter. So, brought to her knees, Lolla said, "All right, Father, I'll take Fouad. It's all the same."

So Lolla was engaged, and her cousin came to wish her well. He brought her cakes and candies, and he wept as he had wanted her himself. All those assembled knew of course that Lolla had preferred this cousin and, while there was no question of love between them, there had been mutual sympathy. After a while, Waleed wiped away his tears and left, and Lolla forgot about him and we began to prepare her for marriage.

But the engagement lasted five years, as Fouad's earnings as a day laborer were small and erratic. After all that fuss, that's how long they kept her in a state of suspense until they built Fouad up enough to enter into housekeeping. In the meantime we bought Lolla a dress here, a shirt there, undergarments one day, and china and other necessities the next, until she was married.

One day I went to the big vegetable market in Rod el-Farag to buy mangoes. I said something about the price to the merchant, and he insulted me. So I replied, "God forgive you," and he answered in a rude way. So I put

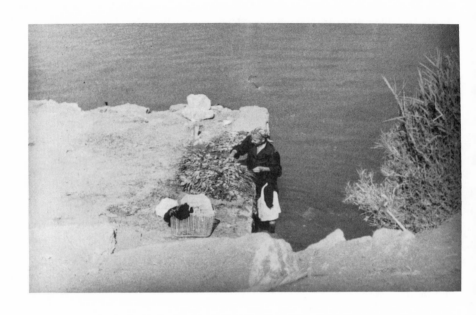

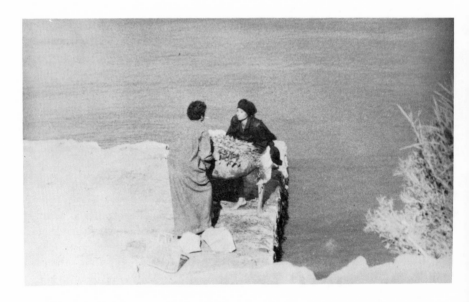

Washing *mollokhiyya* in the river before wrapping it in wet burlap sacking to take to

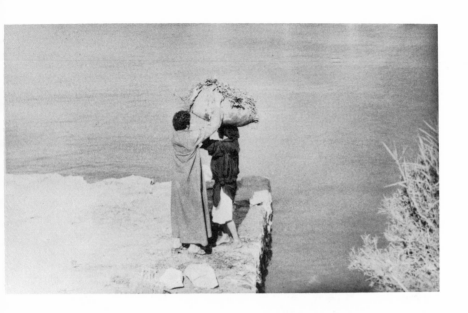

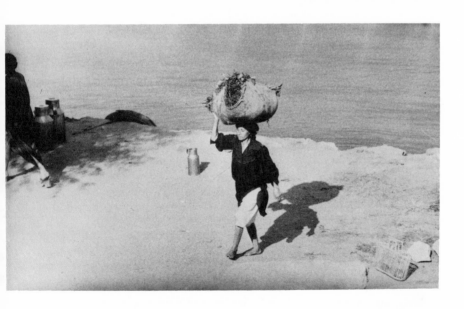

the vegetable market. Photographs by Asma el-Bakry.

away my polite manner and my pretense at meekness and lit into him as I know how to do. I said, "Who do you think you are, you bastard? You low creature, you coward!" And I took my mangoes and left on board a donkey cart. These carts cross the Embaba bridge, and so I could get off close to home. It seems that a young man standing there watched me through all of this and then followed me home.

On the street I met the friend who had come to Lolla's rescue one day, and she asked me where I had been and when I told her, she said, "Did you get taken?" and I answered, "Get taken? No indeed, I am Dunya!" I have always been confident of myself. So she laughed, and I went on home.

This young man, it seems, then asked her who I was, and she pretended I was her sister's daughter and asked him if I had done or said anything to him. He answered that I had not but that he wanted to marry me. So she told him that my father was home on Tuesdays, to come speak to him then. But he wanted to meet my mother first, and one day he appeared at our doorstep. He said to my mother, "I would like to marry this young lady." My mother replied, "Young lady? My boy, you will be struck with a calamity!" But he answered, "I know everything about her, and I know her tongue." So my mother asked, "And how did you come to know it?" So he told her about the incident at the vegetable market and said that he liked a girl with spunk.

His name was Omar, and he was a student at Cairo University. His father was a big wholesaler in the market. My mother said to him at one point, "My son, this girl is not for you. She is illiterate and doesn't know an *alef* from an ear of corn." He answered, "My lady, I know this, but I want her."

But my mother didn't agree, and my father likewise refused him, saying that it was a mistake for me to marry a rich man's son as I would always feel out of my element. My father added, "And don't think that because you are clever with words that you are anything special. Everyone knows how to talk. And animals, if God had given them the power of speech, would have done as well." But I didn't agree and said so, and my father stopped me short by ordering me not to philosophize to him as he was not fooled by my glibness. So the matter was dropped, and Omar did not come back.

Another young man came after Omar. His name was Magdi, and he was a stranger who followed me home also. He asked the neighbors about me, and they told him I was a very good girl but quick with words and sharp tongued. That didn't seem to discourage him, and so one Tuesday he brought with him a go-between and came to see my father.

My father liked this one because he was poor. His family lived in Tanta, and he had come along to the city and had rented a room in Mounira. Magdi had a face as beautiful as a full moon, but for some reason my heart wasn't easy about him. I am guided by my heart when it comes to people, however, and not by my eyes, so I had to find a way of getting rid of him. He would drop in sometimes in the evening, and I would say to him, "Have you chosen to come now in order to get some dinner?" and my mother would be mortified and say, "You have shamed us." I would say to her, "Shut up, you bitch!" I was terrible, but my mother always spoiled me.

When we were young, I would beat Lolla and Yehia and then tell my mother that I had done it because they wouldn't let me play in the street, and she would beat them also. She spoiled me. But in spite of this Lolla loves me very much. I beat her son and rough him up when he deserves it and say to him in the presence of his parents, "Do you see that bastard Fouad? Do you think I'm afraid of him and of your mother?"

The kids mind me and their uncle Ezzo much more than they do their parents. Fouad spoils them and doesn't believe in beating them, but how can they survive in our kind of neighborhood and among our people unless they're brought up like the rest of the children? Ezzo and I are firm with them when it's necessary and soft when it's time. There's a time for everything, and for everything there are limits and traditional boundaries.

So my father liked this fellow Magdi. I don't know why my father likes poor people! Finally I told my father that I didn't want this fellow, but I had to find a reason. So I decided to make up a tale to disgrace him.

We used to put a big pan of water in the upstairs room of the house and bathe there. We would go in and shut the door behind us and bathe. So I told my father that Magdi had come one day and looked in on me through the keyhole as I was bathing. May God account with me for this, because of course it never happened! I said to my father, "Would it please you to see that one who has spoken for me should come to the door and tap on it and when I have said I was bathing, put his eye to the keyhole and look at me?" So my father said, "And how did you see him?" So I said, "I heard him knock and then looked at the door and saw his little finger wiggle in the keyhole and then I saw his eye glistening there and going back and forth, coming and going."

So my father said, "Let it be," and spoke to Magdi, saying that what he had done was shameful. Magdi swore that he had in fact come up, and when I had told him I was bathing, he had not hesitated but left immediately.

So then my father asked me why I had done this, and I told him I loved Ezzo and didn't want Magdi. He was pleased and soon after told Magdi that my cousin had come and asked for me and that we were engaged. Om Fouad had been very keen on seeing me married to Magdi because she knew of Ezzo's attachment to me and that didn't please her. Until today and tomorrow, she holds a grudge against me, and I don't know the reason why.

One time, when I was about ten and Lolla was twelve, my mother

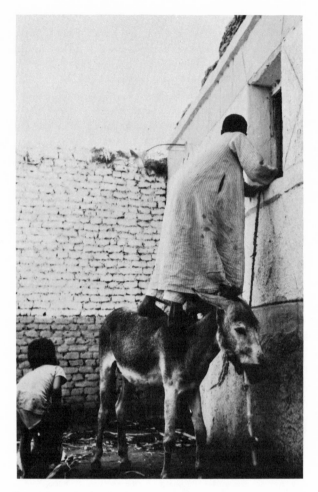

Visiting on donkey back. Photograph by Asma el-Bakry.

went into the hospital for an operation. During that time Ezzo's older sister came to stay with us. She would tear up the place and make a mess then blame it on us, and when my father came home she would whine and whimper to him, and he would beat us. We have a saying that if you turn the water jug over on its mouth, the daughter will come out just like the mother. In my mother's absence we had a rough time. Lolla washed and cooked for us as much as she could, but it was difficult.

When my mother came home, she had had two ribs removed in order to have her rheumatic heart operated on. We were hard up, and she decided to go to work without telling my father in order to supplement our income. She would go out and come back quietly and without much ado. People wondered where she went. They always suspect the worst.

I have the same problem, but if you allow people's talk and gossip to affect you, you would never step out of your room even for a moment. Among our people it's not a shame to work in a store; it is to work in a home. They call servants "plate lickers," which means that after the household has eaten, we come around and lick the plates or eat the leftovers. These are small-minded people, and that's how they think.

On our street I am referred to as *al-khawagayya*, which means the foreigner. It is because I dress well and keep to myself and because I hold different opinions on many things from those of the people of the neighborhood, and I speak my mind. I don't know how to pretend and, this is a flaw in my character which causes me no end of trouble. Only those who are as forthright as I am like me.

Even now with my own husband, I don't know how to pretend. The womenfolk fault me with this, saying, "A man needs this and a man needs that, and men are like children and have to be cajoled and babied." I answer them, "Do you have to whine and pine after your man this way, you women, because you're not sure where your next meal is coming from?" They laugh and cannot answer me because they know that while they sit and gossip and chatter, I mind my house and my business above all. So they laugh, and I say to them, "O women, you low creatures, the only thing you know how to do is to sit sprawled in the hallways of your houses with your bottoms spread out like great loaves of flat bread! But me? I am energetic and lithe, and I see to my house and my husband's needs with action not with words." They cannot say anything. Each one of these women leaves her house and her chores and calls out to her neighbor, "O so and so, what did you cook today? O so and so, what did your husband do to you today?" And so on with this sort of nonsense which breeds nothing but more nonsense like itself.

There exists a kind of banter when our women congregate that we call "hallway conversation" because it takes place in the hallway of the houses where they sit as most of us have no living rooms. One woman will say to another, "So and so, has your husband slept with you tonight?" But they say it in a dirty way, "O so and so, did your husband fuck you tonight?" When I hear them, I answer, "You ill-mannered bitches, hold your tongues." This talk embarrasses me.

When one of these women sleeps with her husband, she tries to cajole him with words and make him love her. She will say to him, "Again,"

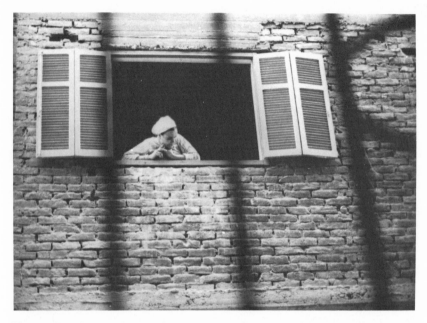

Visiting from her window overlooking one of Cairo's typically crowded alleys, this woman is seen through the prisonlike bars of a neighbor's window on the ground floor. Photograph by Asma el-Bakry.

meaning to sleep with her again as she thinks this will please him and make him love her. She will call him "my love, my heart, my soul, my mind," and with these words try to attach him to her.

But my husband loves me already, and I see no need for this sort of pretense. Then after they have done this, they try to upstage one another by saying, "O so and so, my husband gave me such a one tonight; it reached my head. My husband because he loves me slept with me tonight." So they sidle up to one another and prod and say, "So and so, your husband, because he doesn't sleep with you, doesn't want you. But my husband, because he wants me, slept with me last night." Or one will call to another and say, "O so and so, my husband lifted the hood of the car tonight," meaning her legs, "and he came in with a 'peace be upon you, how do you do, and fare thee well!'" And it goes on this way. These hallway conversations are terrible!

I think, on the contrary, that if a woman is going to have intercourse with her husband one day, it will last a half hour, an hour, two hours, in other words a matter of moments that pass. What's important is what follows, the day to day business of living and companionship. It's true that these are necessary things, but they have their proper time and their proper value.

When these women speak to me about such things, I say to them, "A plague carry you off! Is a woman not disgusted with herself after such an act? Can she hardly stand herself? She gets up right after and washes and splashes to rid herself of the messy traces of the man that are left upon her."

I find it impossible to sleep right after intercourse. Impossible. I get up and wash. We don't use toilet paper, and we share a bathroom space with our neighbors. So I try to be discreet (this is where I've lived with Ezzo since our marriage in 1974). So as we don't use toilet paper, there are special towels reserved for these purposes. After I have washed and used them, I scrub them over with scented soap because it's difficult to get rid of those substances. Then I hang them up to dry on a hanger in the bedroom so that they may be concealed from others. These towels are recognized, and I don't like anyone else to see mine or know them.

In the morning I bathe fully and wash my hair, and then he gets up and says, "Good morning." I respond, "Good morning about what? Good morning about our foolishness!" he answers, laughing, "Foolishness?" and I say, "Yes, foolishness. Isn't it enough that you have dirtied me and that I had to get up in the middle of the night and remove your crud from me? It was your crud, was it not?" And so he says, "Hush, woman. Have you heated some water for me to bathe in?" And I give it to him, and he goes out and bathes and is pleased when I speak to him this way.

So, my mother went to work for an Italian woman in Tewfikiyya, that is where all the foreigners live. At that time my maternal uncle came to see us and said to her, "Why do you work to help him out? Throw him back his children, and I'll marry you to someone far better." My mother had a lovely figure and is a beautiful woman. Her foot is like a cube of sugar. She tried to do what was right by my father and take problems in on herself, but my father is not grateful by nature and overlooked all of that in his treatment of my mother.

Before Lolla's marriage Ezzo was drafted into the army and stationed in Alexandria. He used to come on home leave every fifteen days or so. My mother and Om Fouad began to quarrel about Lolla's engagement and the preparations being made for her marriage. We finally rented a room for Lolla at two and one half pounds a month, and she didn't move into her present apartment until later. The rent for that is four and a half pounds a month, and Fouad's salary then was six and a half a month. Lolla managed, however, as she had a good sense of budget and would buy an eighth of a kilo of meat to cook with vegetables for her and her husband, and in this way they entered housekeeping, and the real troubles began.

At that time I was working at a shirtmaking establishment on Abdel Khalek Sarwat street called El Borai, and Lolla was married. Fouad used to shout at her, insult her, and beat her, and his mother forbade my mother from coming into the couple's home. She was really playing the role of the mother-in-law to the best of her ability. When my mother wanted to see Lolla, she would come to a neighbor's, and the neighbor would send word to my sister who came, and they would visit there. While my mother took things on herself, my mother-in-law was exactly the opposite. She would circle and circle and then strike and blame my mother for any troubles that arose.

Some time after Lolla's wedding, my mother opened a butcher shop with my brother Yehia who was getting tired of working for someone else. He said that he would use some money he had saved to go into business for himself and that if he was successful, the profits would be his and if not, at least it would be his own responsibility.

My father was working as a butcher in a restaurant near the Cinema Rivoli. He would prepare the meat and chicken and shrimp for the cooks. There is a bank now in its place. It wasn't the sort of place our kind of people went into, but a fancy restaurant for upper-class folk. Ezzo, when he came back from Alexandria, would take me to and from work, but problems began to pile up, what with his mother's cunning maneuvers, my father's violent temper, and Lolla's suffering at the hands of her husband. Life seemed like a non-ending struggle.

We had a neighbor in Embaba who cared for us very much and who looked in on us regularly. He worked as a cook for someone in the building where Mohammad Hassanein Heikal lived, near the Sheraton. When my brother opened his butcher shop, Zain used to put in an order for meat each night on his way home, and I would deliver it on my way to work each morning.

I would work from nine-thirty each morning until about two, then go visit Zain and have lunch with him, and return to the shop at four and work until eight o'clock in the evening. I earned two pounds a week. At the end of the day, I took a bus home and got off at the stop we call "Kit Kat," which is the name of a shop on that corner. There is also a mosque there, and we call it by that same name.

When my mother started minding the butcher shop, the house began to be neglected, and my father told me I had to stay home and take care of it. I agreed. He had had no objection to my working until then because he has confidence in my good sense and knows that no one can easily steer me into trouble. He would say that he could trust me to walk home alone at three o'clock in the morning but would worry about Lolla on the street in broad daylight. A father knows just how balanced each of his daughters is, and he knew that I couldn't be deceived easily.

Yehia began, at that time, to lose money on the market, and he was obliged to go back to working for someone else. My mother said that the big butchers at the wholesale places cheated him on the weight of the meat he bought. So she decided to stay in the shop herself while my brother went to work outside. In this way they would try to make ends meet.

I was home, my sister was married, and I would hear from time to time that Ezzo was in Cairo, yet he didn't come to see me. I was perplexed and hurt and would ask myself, "Why didn't he come?" and my heart would throb and pain me. I would wonder, "Doesn't he have even a penny for bus fare?" and I would feel badly. His neglect worried me and I fell ill. I was feverish and vomited and my face went yellow, and I had to be taken to the Embaba fever hospital.

Ezzo was in Cairo at that moment, and he came to see me. He sat for ten minutes or so, and then his mother said to him, "Get up and go visit your sister." This is the sister who used to tear up the plants. I was very ill and nearly dead and was being fed glucose. His mother came to see me every day, but his neglect was surely her doing and she wasn't sincere.

At that time, I was wearing the ring and bracelets Ezzo had given me as engagement presents. When his mother spoke to him, he got up and said, "Well, Dunya, I will be going now." So I replied, "May you go in safety." I was very cool. In these situations I am very cool. It's possible for me to desire someone and yet to lead him to think that in fact I can't tolerate him. I am proud. Very, very, proud! So after his mother left I took off the ring and the bracelets and gave them to my mother. She looked puzzled and said, "Why are you doing this, Dunya?" But I refused to give an explanation, saying, "Not a word. I don't wish to speak about it." And so my mother let it be.

I got well and left the hospital. At that time my mother was about to stay home from work at the butcher shop as it got to be too much for her to cope with. There are jobs for women and jobs for men. And there are women who cannot handle a man's job. Commerce requires a tough man, not a mere woman.

So I left the hospital, and my mother stayed home, and we liquidated the butcher shop and sold the scales and the ice box. Then I turned to my mother and said, "Now, Mother, am I just going to sit here with my hands idle? Who is going to take meat to Zain, and where are we going to get it from?"

We decided to charge a butcher of our acquaintance with the responsibility. I would deliver it as usual. Zain would have his vegetables bought and cleaned and, by eleven o'clock, I would arrive with the meat, and he would prepare it. I entered the building from the front and not from the service staircase as I was still very young and used to dress in the modern fashion, not in the traditional *gallabiyya* and head covering. Sometimes Zain would open the door to me and sometimes it was the lady of the house. She liked me and let me play with her children and gave me chocolates. I was about eighteen years old. After a time I was tired of staying home and, as my father agreed, I went back to the shirtmaker and Zain began to get his own meat.

So Yehia worked for another butcher, and Ezzo got back to Cairo and asked me where my ring was. I said, "It's only on my mother's hand." He said nothing further. I had complained to people about his neglect of me, and it seems that they had reported this to Om Fouad who had answered, "No matter what we do to her, she can't leave us." My mother heard those words, and I heard those words. As my mother is kind, she said nothing, but I was furious and said, "Me not leave them no matter what they do to me?"

I put Ezzo's ring and the bracelets in a box, and I handed them to my mother and said to her, "Please take these and give them back to the one who first brought them to me." My mother said, "My child, Ezzo is a good boy," and words of that nature, but I answered, "It's over!" When once I spit something out, I never lick it up again, even if the spittle should turn into something more precious and brilliant than a diamond and twinkle up enticingly at me. Once I have said "no," it means no. My mind is like an old shoe.

What did his mother mean by saying I couldn't leave her son? She was imputing that I had been dishonored and was therefore no good to anyone else. This sort of statement means one thing and one thing only which is that I had lost my virginity.

We have a proverb which says: "The one who loves you, return his love and his pleasure becomes your own; whereas the one who hates you, return his hate and never seek his company." My mother tried to reason with me, saying, "Why and why not?" and I replied that it was finished. My father came and said, "You must marry Ezzo," and when I refused, he left and went back to his wife in Boulac. He discussed the matter with her, and she must have persuaded him not to let me have my way so easily, and so he came back and said, "I don't see that Ezzo has done anything to warrant such a stand on your part. What if he failed to come and wish you well at feast time? What if his mother didn't come in his stead?"

So many problems arise from people talking and striking hate in the hearts of others! Some people didn't wish me well and wanted it believed that Dunya was sulky and quick tempered and stubborn. But my father woke me up with his reasoning.

It's customary among my people to visit back and forth at feast time and to do so is expected. As Ezzo was in the army, it was his mother's duty to come and see me and to ease my heart with kind words of concern to show their good faith. Normally either the groom comes or his mother comes bringing a gift to the bride. But as we were one family, and I knew of their financial difficulties, I didn't expect anything from them. But to me, inquiring after one another is worth the world. As the proverb says, "Find me, do not feed me."

So she didn't come, and I perceived that these were the manners and mannerisms of people who had already sold their wares. When I heard in addition what they had said about my not leaving them whatever they did to me, I felt humiliated and shocked. A shock went through my whole body, and I thought, "How could she say such a thing about me whose actions have been constantly blameless?"

I knew myself, and there was nothing between her son and me save a few outings to the movies. Ezzo had never been allowed to touch me. I made up my mind at that point to have nothing to do with them, saying to myself, "By God, even if this person were someone I worshipped next to the almighty, nothing would induce me to go to him now." It was over, and from that time on I put pressure on my heart to keep it from overflowing with feeling for him. But it was hard to do. I was in torment, and I couldn't keep myself from thinking about Ezzo and about what his family had done.

One day my father came to me and said, "You must have him." I responded that I wouldn't, and he left and returned to his other wife in a sulk but not until he had vented his anger on me. The beating he gave me that day nearly crippled one of my arms, and it was my mother who had to bathe and dress me for some time after. I thought that he had given me this beating thinking that, like my poor sister Lolla, I would be brought to my knees and say, "All right, I'll have him." But I wouldn't concede. Lolla had said, "yes," but I would say "no." When my father saw that it was no use, he left us.

I was still working at the shirtmaker at that time. I wept a great deal. People whispered and talked, saying that I must have someone else, someone at work whom I liked better than Ezzo and who had captured my imagination. But in fact there was no one at all, and the men at work were all married. It's true that they all liked and respected me because I was helpful to them, answering, "with pleasure," when they requested that I pass them a pair of scissors or a bobbin of thread, though this was not my job, as I was there to do finishing work and not to wait on others. But people never stop talking.

One day I was weeping at the home of an elderly neighbor when she said to me, "Would you like to marry the father-in-law of my daughter?" Her daughter is older than me by far, and so I asked, "What do you mean?" She said, "You can marry this man and cut yourself loose from Egypt altogether and leave your problems behind you." Her daughter had married a Libyan. She then said to me, "By the time the news being circulated reaches Ezzo, since people will not stop talking, you will be married to an elderly man, and Ezzo will see clearly that you didn't betray him, because this man is old and you have never seen him before." I thought about this and felt that the woman, because she was older, must have some special wisdom in what she advised me to do. I was still a child. I agreed to see the man but wept and lived a tormented existence at that time.

At the time people came to me and said, "Your father is out to kill you," and as he is a butcher, the holding of a knife in his hand is natural and easy. So people continued to tell me that my father was going to intercept me in the street one day and that I had better be on the lookout.

So, I thought to myself, "Dear God, it's a fact that when a woman marries, her husband must protect her, and her father can't say a word against her." Everyone thinks in her own way and according to her own capacity, not someone else's.

So one day the old man, the Libyan that neighbor of ours had spoken to me about, came. He saw me, and I was still a mere child, and he said, "Yes, I will marry her." My friends and well wishers said to me, "Dunya, think before you throw yourself away," but I replied, "There is good in whatever God chooses." I was like a person drowning and reaching for a straw. I agreed to marry this man. His name was Hagg Ali. He then said, "I will marry her and come back later to complete the marriage contract." We call this *katb el kitaab* or "writing the book." But, fool that I was, I said hastily, "No, no, write it now, write it now." And so he did.

Sometimes at night when I sit and ponder, I don't know how I could have acted in this way, or said what I said then. But it happened. Hagg Ali then said that he didn't have money for the dowry, and I replied that it was of no consequence at that moment. We registered the marriage and in three days the papers were ready, and he left for Libya, saying he would find a place for me to live and then would come back in a year to consummate the marriage. This is called the *dokhla*, the entry. Before he left the Libyan said, "Now that you are married it wouldn't be proper for you to go on working." I replied that when I was in his house, he could then give me orders. But as he insisted, I agreed, but only after giving my employer a chance to find a replacement. So he was satisfied.

But before actually leaving work one day the boss sent me to have button holes made, and it was on the way there that I met my father on the street. As soon as I saw him, my heavenly days, I felt as if the world were spinning with me on it, and I was propelled upward and pulled down again. I felt as if I were on a boat on the high seas, and it was spinning and I couldn't stop it.

My father called to me and asked me where I was going. At that moment I felt the urine rise up in my body as if it would come jumping out of me, so I clamped my legs together. I was afraid. He had obviously heard the news of my marriage, as no one keeps quiet about anyone else.

At work I wore a coat with buttons and that is what I had on at the time. My father then said, "Come back to your workshop with me." I answered that I was on my way to make button holes and began to stutter and get confused. He shouted, "Get going in front of me now," and he raised up his hand and BAM! hit me right then and there, in the middle downtown Cairo, right at the corner of Abdel Khalek Sarwat Street and Sherif Street. At that point he looked around him to make sure that none of the passersby were getting ready to come to my defense, else he would lay hands on them also. My father is very difficult! He shouted to me to get going in front of him and do as he said.

I had told my boss about my problems, and he had said that I had acted in haste and without thinking. I ran to him at that point with my father on my heels, and when he saw my face he said, "What is the matter, Dunya?" I answered, "Nothing, but my father is behind me," and so he understood. I said, "What shall I do? This trouble is all his fault. If he had only been patient!"

Parents provoke their daughters. If they would only give them a chance to accept or refuse someone at their ease, none of this would happen. If he had been reasonable, I would have probably waited until things quieted down and either followed my destiny or gone back to Ezzo. When I'm stirred up and my spirit is in a state of revolt, no matter what anyone says to persuade me, I don't budge. So until my inner and outer voices have had a chance to converse and I have been able to think things out quietly, I can't be moved.

As my father arrived, the boss told me to run and take shelter among the girls in the back room. My father was getting ready at that point to pick up a pair of scissors that were on the counter and stab me with them. He began to shout about taking me home, and the boss said that he would bring me himself by car at the end of the day. My father stubbornly insisted, and the boss finally said to him, "When your daughter came to work for me, she came of her own free will. You didn't bring her. She can't leave now, but I will drive her home when the day is over." So my father made him swear on his word of honor that he would drive me home, and the man did and so my father left.

The boss did as he had promised, and I was embarrassed to take him to our house because it was so modest. When I expressed these feelings to him, he said, "Dunya, a person is neither judged by his wealth nor by his poverty but by what he is." In this way he put me at ease.

When we came in, my boss asked my father what his pleasure was, and my father said that I must find a way of divorcing. I answered then that I agreed but on one condition, that I not be forced to marry Ezzo. So my father said, "You will marry him and your feet up around your neck." So I replied in anger that I had done all this to protect myself from him and that I was not going to go back to where I started from. I said, "I married this man to protect myself from you." I was at the end of my rope and thought to myself, "Let me die now! After all, we only die once and no more. I shall be done with it."

My boss had left by that time, and my father got up and called to my mother to collect all of his clothes, and he took his knives and personal belongings in a bundle and departed. He was showing us that because of my ways he would have nothing more to do with us and would withdraw all support and leave us to our own devices.

My brother was working at a butcher shop then, my husband had made me quit my job, saying he would send us money but none had come, and our money ran out, and no more seemed to be forthcoming. I remember clearly having seven and a half piasters in my pocket and no more.

I gave my mother five piasters, and I took two and a half piasters for myself and went to visit Sayyeda Zeinab at her mosque. I like to visit the holy tombs. So I went to offer a prayer in hope that she would act on our behalf. When I got home, I found that the man in Libya had sent us twenty pounds, and so I thanked God. But this man, who had said he was not coming until December of the following year, sent word that he was advancing his arrival and coming only four months after he had left, that is, in April of the same year.

During this period I hadn't seen Ezzo, but people had said to him, "Dunya is married, and he is a foreigner, and he has money and is young, and she left you for him," and nonsense of that sort.

It so happened that Ezzo and I met at the birth of Lolla's first child, and he took me aside and said, "Isn't it a pity, Dunya, that you should have betrayed me in this way? Am I not young also?" So I said to him, "Is that what you think happened? Well, let me put your mind at ease. Here, look at his photograph!" So he looked and shrank into himself and was ashamed.

This man was old, and wrinkled, dark and ugly, thin and wiry, and as the photo I showed Ezzo had been retouched, he looked even better there than in real life. So I said to Ezzo, "Here, look at this, it will surely dissolve any illusions you might have had and resolve this problem for you once and for all."

When Hagg Ali was with me and we walked on the street, we met with no end of teasing from passersby. They would say, "What's this old man, why don't you leave your granddaughter alone?" I was so ashamed that I would think, "O earth, be rent asunder and swallow me up!"

I used to straighten my hair and wear it parted in the middle. It was long. With it I covered each side of my face so that when people talked about me, my hair would cover my eyes and cover me almost entirely. I always carry a handkerchief in my hand, and with it I would cover my mouth and nose and as we went down the street, I looked no more than an anonymous mobile structure in the shape of a human being. O goodness, I saw such days as were blacker than the hair on my head, blacker even than he was!

He arrived on a Sunday and said that the marriage had to be consummated the following Thursday. I said, "Thursday?" and then the fog that had until then hovered over my mind began to clear, and I woke up.

We say of a person who is confused that a knife has stolen his senses and likewise that a knife brings them back. And so when he said that the wedding night was less than week away, the shock brought me back to reality. People kept saying to reconsider, to think of my youth and so on, but it was too late. Ezzo could have saved me perhaps, and I think he tried. He could have withdrawn his suit, but he would say he was giving me up on the one hand and would burst into tears the next moment. His tears excited my father's anger and his determination to give me to Ezzo if I was free. For Ezzo, it was God above and Dunya below, and although his head told him to leave me be, his heart refused to obey.

So people continued to pity me, and to give myself courage I would say, "Oh, don't be sorry, I'll marry and be done with this world and go travelling and see Libya!" I am not dazzled by bright colors and adventure, but I felt there was no going back.

The marriage was consummated in the traditional fashion of our people. In the evening we go into the sitting room, and the women clean and depilate our body, legs, underarms, pubic area, and so on. When they did this to me, I was astonished and said, "Why are you depilating me?" I didn't understand anything. I was under the impression that you married a man and that man and woman simply lived companionably. How children were conceived, I didn't know. My mother never spoke of such things or allowed us to be near situations where people would be involved in those things, and even when she went to pluck her eyebrows, she would make us leave the room.

They dressed me in white that night with a veil and a crown, and my sister still has a photograph of me at that time with hands raised and eyes looking to the sky as I say, "O God!"

The Libyan rented a furnished flat in Zamalek for the occasion, and the family took me in taxis along with my mother and an old woman who was to hold me for the defloration ceremony. The men were in another taxi on their way to slaughter a sheep for the festivities.

This old woman was a friend and was chosen because she was big and strong. My mother didn't have the heart to be present in the room with me.

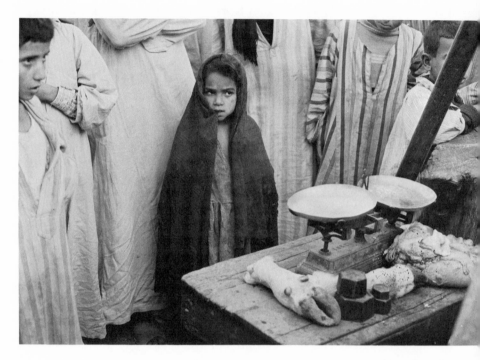

"I was six years old when I was circumcised."—Dunya. Photograph by Asma el-Bakry.

They hold the girl and pull her legs apart. A strong woman sits directly behind, legs stretched on either side of the bride, holding her. She has to be strong because unless she can hold firm, the girl might squirm or move and this way be injured by the thrust of the man's finger into her vagina. So they held me, and at that moment I recalled that this sort of thing had happened to me once before. I said to myself, "But they held me in this way when I was a child!" It was of course when I was six years old, two years older than Mouna, Lolla and Fouad's child whom I have adopted, when I was being circumcised.

I remember the circumcision clearly, and when the knife hit, it was as if someone had built a fire under me. They then twist a length of clean sheet or gauze which is soaked in disinfectant and sulpha powder, and they bind the child with it. My heavenly days, it's worse than fire, and you stay in bed, unable to move, with legs apart, for days!

I wouldn't do it to my daughter. I wouldn't want to hurt her. But when they did it to me, I had no choice and no mind of my own. I couldn't discuss or argue or resist. If I had been an adult, I would have opposed it, but a child is still possessed of the mind and thoughts of its parents.

Since I have undertaken to bring up Mouna, I will take a stand on this issue on her behalf. After all, there is such a thing as freedom of speech! If her parents insist on circumcising her, however, they could put me in an embarrassing position. They could aim a word at me that would penetrate me to the bone. They could say, "She's not your child!" I would then be like a dove, flying, flying and feeling expansive in her flight when she is suddenly brought down by a slingshot crippling her wings. They could hurt me, but I realize that they would be in their right.

I've been told that in America an adopted child becomes truly the child of the parents who care and nurture it. It isn't so here. In certain ways foreigners have taken our gentleness of character, and in other ways we have taken their hardness. I have known many foreigners, about four. They always treat one with kindest concern no matter what their station in life might be. But take an Egyptian; if you put an extra ten pounds in his hands, he will puff out his feathers and keep you at bay until the ten pounds are spent, then he will lay his feathers back down and be approachable again.

If God had meant for girls to be circumcised, surely he would not have created us as we are! Witness his wisdom in all things, and observe how he created man with thick hair, for example, in order to affirm his maleness and woman with fine hair all over her body in order that she may easily depilate and be beautiful!

We are told that circumcision is necessary because drinking the water of the Nile as a child makes a girl passionate when she grows up. So this helps her get hold of herself so that she doesn't tire her husband or need these things if she's a widow or divorced. It's rare that an Egyptian woman asks for her husband. It's he who would and must desire her, although it doesn't always happen this way. But I would never ask for Ezzo, even if he were going away for ten years and this was our last night together. A woman has to have pride.

Ezzo and I were married in 1974, after my divorce from the Libyan in 1970. This year he got a job in Saudi Arabia, as many Egyptian men do now, and the night before he left his mother and his aunt came to sleep with us. Usually I have a curtain dividing our two rooms. The curtain happened to be down that day. Ezzo's aunt said to him when it came time to go to bed, "Go sleep in your mother's arms so that she may have her fill of you before you leave." Ezzo answered, "No, you and my mother sleep on the bed and cover yourselves with the blanket. Dunya and I will spread the quilt on the floor and sleep there." So we did, but the whole night was a pushing and shoving match because Ezzo wanted to sleep with me, and I wouldn't do it with his mother and his aunt there.

For these things one must be at ease, and there has to be some give and take. I don't believe in stolen moments or in advertising my intimate relations with my husband. But some people, unless they are side by side and the man's leg is wrapped around his wife and they are embracing each other, can't sleep. I, on the contrary, can't sleep unless I have freedom of movement. And some women, because they pride themselves greatly on how often their husbands sleep with them, walk around in the morning with their heads wrapped in a towel to show that they have bathed and washed their hair, which we must do after intercourse. I can't tolerate this sort of thing and don't like people to know my private life.

When I cook, for example, whether I am going to satisfy my hunger with some fried eggplant or some sharp roasted peppers or a piece of bread and cheese, I like to keep to myself. When I cook I leave the door to the outer room open to allow the smell of cooking and the heat from the primus stove to escape, but as soon as I have finished, I put my food under the wardrobe and cover it and shut my door until it's time to eat or until Ezzo comes home and we sit down to our meal. My mother accustomed us to never eating until my father came home, and I do the same with my husband.

I don't go as far as she did, however, in other things. When my father came home, we would be waiting for him, and my mother would take off his shoes, and we would wash his feet, and one of us would pour while the other was ready with a towel to wipe them, toe by toe and between each one of his toes. He liked me to pour the water. He liked me to pour because I could do it more delicately than Lolla. In the morning my mother would help him dress and have a clean *gallabeyya* ready for him.

This generation doesn't do that any more, but these women in our neighborhood, as I was saying, keep almost nothing of their lives to them-selves. Even if they have some rice or lentils to pick over, they come out of their rooms and station themselves in the hallways where they can see who is coming and who is going and who has a new dress. I cook and then close my door, but if a child should appear on my doorstep, I will give her a sandwich but not invite her in. I'll feed her because she is after all a child, but I'll say to her, "Here is a sandwich, now go eat it at your mother's house."

So that night before his departure Ezzo would come close to me and say, "But I am leaving for a whole year, Dunya, and I would like to have my fill of you. I'll miss you." I would answer, "A plague be upon you, go to sleep. I want you also. There, I've said it, but are these my relatives or yours? Kick them out, and we can do as you please." So he would turn over, but he squirmed and fussed all night, and when the call to prayer sounded at dawn, we had not slept a wink.

When Ezzo left, we hadn't slept together for ten days or more. But all of his intimate friends, knowing that he was about to leave, would say to him, "You must really be cutting the fish by the tail these days," meaning, you must be getting together with your wife every day. But that wasn't true, and when Ezzo and I indulge in this act, it's every fifteen days at the most. Our marriage is one of companionship rather than of love. Even if there was love at the beginning, it got wiped out by the problems that we passed through. But I understand that when two people really love each other, love each other very, very much, that sex can be the most delicious thing in the world. Another world altogether. And even if a woman is circumcised, her heart guides her and allows her to feel pleasure.

I am perplexed by this question of circumcision however, because there is a woman who lives in our house who is circumcised like myself and whom you find together with her husband morning, noon, and night. It's terrible! But it's true that people have different constitutions, and that each of us is hung from his own individual cluster, like grapes on a vine.

Look at me and my sister Lolla, for example. While it was one back that conceived us and one belly that bore us, we are different. Perhaps education plays a role in this; not the sort of education you get in school but by being out in the world and by trying to keep informed. Someone told me that if only I could read and write, I would make quite a stir. So my sister knows only the market, her home, her bed, her children, and her and her husband on their bed. She has not been in touch much with the work-a-day world, whereas I've worked since I was in my teens.

There is another woman in our neighborhood whose husband will beat her on the one hand and who will desire her to sleep with him on the other, and she accepts. How can that be? These are the actions of animals.

My Lord, if Ezzo should only wound me with a word, I will have nothing to do with him. It's he who has to come and make amends and console me. When I feel particularly vexed with something he has said or done, I'll sleep along the width of the bed in the shape of a pretzel. We have a wide bed, 160 centimeters across. When he comes to bed, no matter which way he turns, he runs into me. So he says, "Straighten up!" and I answer, "Go sleep at your mother's house." So he gets up and sleeps on the couch in the other room. Sometimes he stays there five nights, sometimes ten, and sometimes a month. I continue to prepare his meals for him, and I do his laundry as usual, but I say to him, "Just consider me a servant in your house," and it's he who must be the first to make amends.

So I don't see how a woman can be mistreated and still go to her husband. It could be that he smokes *hashish* and that in his passion he gives her no choice. The smoking heightens passion, they say, and can make a man act like an animal. A man doesn't mean to, but he can't feel himself. It's better if a man remains in his natural state. If he's natural, a woman will taste gentleness and kindness at his hands, and sympathy and reciprocity can exist between them.

On the night of the *dokhla* of my first marriage then, with the Libyan, I was positioned in front of him with the old woman friend holding me from behind, and he wrapped the customary gauze around his finger and plunged it into me. At that moment, I felt as if a light had gone out of my eyes, and I went mad. I began to shout and swear at him and at the company gathered, that is, the women who were with me in the room. I said, "You bastard, you dirty son of a dog, may God bring a plague down on your mother's religion," and when I saw the blood, I became even wilder and shouted, "You bastards, let me go, why are you making a hole in me, why are you piercing me, let me go?"

During all of this time, the company standing outside the door banged and sang, as they usually do on these occasions, to drown out the shouting or crying of the bride. They sing a song which begins, "Did you whiten the gauze, O Bride," meaning, "Did you honor your family by showing you were a virgin?"

Did you whiten the gauze, O Bride,
Your husband is a joker, O Bride;

Oh, dates that have bloomed and ripened,
Did you honor your four uncles?

Behold the blood of the peasant girl,
Behold, it's red and bright as an apple.

On an aluminum bed, whether you cry or not,
This is a night worth the world.
On a bed made of brass, whether you cry or not,
Consider it a night among nights:
It will soon be over.

On bedsheets made of silk, O Bride, give me a kiss.
O Bridegroom, the night is long.

On a mat of straw, O Bride, give me a kiss.
O Bridegroom, long live your people!

When it was over they were satisfied that I was indeed a virgin, and they let me go and said, "Get up and insert a lump of sugar into your vagina." My mother was waiting outside, but my father's wife had refused to come. She should have been there to see that I was honorable. Those who don't see the blood-stained gauze the night of the wedding come to see it in the morning. It's as if you had a vase you were proud of, and you brought it out to show the company assembled. But of course you don't show it to everyone. Close female relatives come to see it and male members of the family who are forbidden you by marriage, like your father, brother, father's and mother's brothers, but not male cousins as they would have been prospective mates. My father was not there.

Anyway, I got up and washed and didn't listen to anyone about the sugar. I washed and as I did, blood would flow out. I would wash and more blood would come, and I thought, "Drown now, O Dunya!" How was I to know about these things, if no one had told me what to expect! But then when I finished, I got up and danced. Lord, what stupidity! Can you imagine anything more stupid than this? I got up and danced like an idiot, and my husband was sitting outside looking pleased because he had taken the virginity of the bride.

At this time the festivities began, with music and dancing. Someone sang the part of the bride, saying:

> My dark boy who is so cool and distant,
> My dark fellow who seems so cool and easy,
> Deign to stay in my heart seven minutes at least.
> I craft my words carefully and soften the
>   hardest heart,
> Then I craze the one I love with longing . . .

This means that she throws the bait and then when she catches the fish, she does as she pleases with him. Others joined in the song individually throughout the rest of the evening. They usually make up their own lyrics based on personal experience. Women seeing the happiness of the bride on her wedding night sing of their own misfortunes at the hands of their loved ones or their mates. One who had lost something precious, whose husband had deserted her, sang:

> Between the eyebrow and the pupil of my eye,
> A white pigeon has flown from me.

> It's been seven years, this very year,
> That I've made my back into a ferry for
>   his crossings,
> But the ungrateful coward has bought and sold me.

At one wedding I went to at the time I gave Ezzo back his ring and bracelets I was feeling downcast. I sang these words to show my sadness, and to annoy his mother:

> Come sit beside me and let me tell you
> And wipe my tears on your sleeve;
> All that has befallen me is your mother's doing.

> Come sit beside me and let me tell you
> And wipe my tears on your handkerchief;
> All that has befallen me is from your sweet words.

> You, then, you fellow with the shirt collar,
> My soul hangs on your every word.
> As long as we're both of this world,
> If what separates us is of this world,
> Then one day we shall find each other.

As the festivities continued on my wedding night, I danced, but every time I looked at the groom, I shrank in horror. Every time I glanced in his direction, I shrank. But then the people went home, and he lay down next to me. He wanted to sleep with me. I then said to him, "What is this you have in mind, you son of a dog? Have you gone mad?" He answered, "It's necessary." I said, mimicking his words, "It's necessary? Why don't you just thank God that you have a pretty bride with a face like a moon, you old crone, and go to sleep." So he did, and for one night, two nights, three nights, he didn't touch me, but he began to complain about me to people.

My sister Lolla then came to me and said, "You must submit, Dunya, otherwise why do we get married." So I replied, "O black day, I can't even stand to look at him." So people suggested that when he came beside me I cover my face, but I didn't do that. I turned off the lights so I couldn't see him, and until today and tomorrow I do that. It's become a habit, and Ezzo teases me endlessly about it.

This man came close to me again after a time, and it seemed that I had healed over. When he entered me, I bled again and soaked the bedsheets and the nightgown and slip I was wearing. My mother came to see me the following morning, and I said to her, "In the name of the Prophet, you bitch, if you had married him, would you have had the heart to sleep in his arms, old as you are?" So my mother wept for me, and I wept and struck my face in despair.

We stayed in Egypt seventeen days then got our papers together and left for Libya. Then he said to me, "In your own country, you relied on the protection of your people, but now I can do with you as I please." He would beat me in order to try to sleep with me. But I took these beatings and would tolerate them better than sleeping with him. He had a twisted leather whip like the sort they make in the Sudan which he used. He was like a starved or rabid dog, but I would take one of these beatings and say to him, "The stars in the sky are closer to you than I am."

When I got to Libya I also discovered that he had four other wives, two of whom he had divorced, and two still remained. He also had not prepared a place for me to live but put me up with his son's wife: not the Egyptian but the Libyan one. She was kind and gave me pills to insert in my vagina to prevent pregnancy in case he succeeded in penetrating me. She would say, "Never mind, Dunya, try to be patient and tolerate him, otherwise he'll continue to beat you."

People who saw that I was in an intolerable position suggested sending a letter to my mother, asking her to telegraph me saying she was ill and in danger and would I come. So this is what happened. I had been in Libya forty-three days, and during that time Hagg Ali managed to sleep with me only twice. I remember the exact number of days, one month and thirteen days, because one never forgets bad times.

It seems, however, that the pills which the Libyan woman gave me caused an irritation in me that may be at the root of some of the problems from which I suffer today. Anyway, the telegram from my mother was brought by Hagg Ali's son, and I pleaded and begged to be allowed to leave, but the Libyan said that he didn't have money for a ticket to Egypt. I said to him, "Here are the bracelets you gave me. Take them and sell them and buy the ticket with the money they bring." So he did, and I left by airplane. Of the presents he had given me, there is a gold ring still which my sister Lolla wears.

When I had left Cairo, my brother Yehia was engaged to a woman from Giza. He was to be drafted into the army and was told that if my father divorced my mother, he could be exempted as he would be considerd her sole support. So I came home to find my mother divorced and my brother married and living on her furniture, and my mother sleeping with the woman who owned the building where we rented rooms, and whom we called *Khalti,* or Auntie. There were all these changes, and in the midst of them, I wondered what my mother and I would do with ourselves.

I resented my mother's having let Yehia take her room and furniture, and when I told her so, she said to me, "You were in Libya, your sister is married, and I thought it would be good to have someone to care for and be with your brother." So I said, "You are sleeping with Khalti Om Labib, but I can't, because I don't like to be an imposition on anyone, you know that."

So it happened that we found another room near my brother Yehia, and we ate and drank with him and then went back to our room to sleep. Whatever they cooked, we ate with them, but I was feeling badly from the Libyan experience and knew that I couldn't go on this way. Presently Hagg Ali sent his son to fetch me, but I refused to go with him, saying that if he wanted me, he had to come get me himself.

Not long after, people on our street came running to me, saying, "Hagg Ali is here. Hagg Ali is here." He came and said that as I wouldn't go with his son, he had come to fetch me. He had given me a dowry of a hundred pounds after the initial wedding contract was signed, and we had agreed later on another three hundred that would be forthcoming. He had borrowed the hundred pounds back and left a promissory note to that effect with my mother.

When I heard he was coming, I decided to myself that I would overlook all the money owed me if he would agree to divorce me. When he arrived, I proposed this plan to him, but he refused, saying, "Am I fool to divorce you; can I find another like you now?" So I answered, "Well, if that is the way you feel, why don't you treat me as you should, like a daughter, and let us forget this foolishness on the bed at the close of day."

But he didn't agree, so I tried at first to persuade him, saying, "May God give you wisdom, I am not for you. That has become clear. Why don't you divorce me, and let's separate in good faith. The Koran says that if you join together, do so in good faith and if you separate, do so in good faith also. We consummated our marriage with joy cries, let's not leave each other with wailing." But he was unmoved, and I was at my wit's end. One pinprick at that point and I would have exploded and did when he insisted that the stars were closer to me then than divorce.

I took off my slippers and with one of them gave him a sound thrashing until he was nearly dead. Meanwhile he screamed, "Let me at her, let me at her," and as people gathered to watch, I answered him with another resounding slap of my slipper. My mother was in the middle of all this hubbub, and the neighbors all came to my support. "You dare beat me with your slipper, I'll show you," he screamed, and I responded between smacks, "You son of an old shoe, I've been trying to tell you for an age now, divorce me! Are you ready to come to your senses?" Was it believable that I should sleep in his arms? What madness was this? But neither persuasion nor my slipper would convince him to pronounce the words "I divorce you," that I wanted to hear. So I let him go.

Presently he sent two policemen to the door. They tapped and inquired if Dunya Osman was within, and as they entered, they looked at my mother, thinking of course that she was the wife in question because of the proximity of their ages. But I stepped forward and said, "I am Dunya Osman. May I help you?" They looked at me, astonished, and said "You?" and they explained that I was being summoned to the police station, and so I got dressed and followed them out to the street, with the whole neighborhood in tow. At that point my paternal cousin arrived for a visit and ran after us, as did my brother Yehia whom someone had gone to call from work.

When we emerged from the house, we found the Libyan waiting on the outside with his son's mother-in-law, whom he had rallied to his support. They were on the opposite side of the street, the Nile side. We were on the side of the houses. So we began to walk, they along the one side and we along the other, and I didn't spare him my insults, until we reached the Embaba police station. There is something so comical and sad in all of this! He walking on the one side of the street and I on the other with all the family and neighbors behind me!

The officer in charge at the station was named Tamer, may God watch over him. He had two stars and was working toward a third at the time, and when he got it, he was moved out of the Embaba precinct. I explained my side of the drama to him, and the Libyan had his say. After much discussion and resistance on the part of Hagg Ali, we finally came to an agreement. I would absolve him of his debt to me, and he would divorce me.

So it happened, and we signed a statement to that effect, he with his thumbprint, and I wrote my name. I don't read or write, but I did learn at one time to write my name and that of my brother and my nephew, so that I might not be embarrassed if the need arose to sign a document of any kind.

We went to the courthouse the following day and finalized the divorce. I remember the time clearly because between the day of my divorce and the death of Gamal Abdel Nasser there were barely three or four days. He was buried in October 1970, on a Saturday, and I was divorced the following Wednesday.

So this man left, and my struggles began afresh. How should I live, where shall I go, and how shall I come? He tried to come again and patch things up, sending his son to mediate and his son's mother-in-law, and then came himself. But as far as I was concerned, it was over. So questions of survival were uppermost in my mind.

At that time my old friend Zain had taken a new job in Giza. That was about 1971, and as his wife had died, he had sent his children home to Aswan. Where Zain worked there was room for one extra person to help, so I suggested to my mother that I go and help him, and she agreed. I didn't want to just sit home and have my brother throw me a scrap like any stray dog. My mother decided to work also to help me make ends meet, but she had had four operations by that time, and in the end she really couldn't manage. So I suggested she stop working and stay home, but this coincided with my brother Yehia's beginning to grumble about our taking all of our meals with him and his wife. So I thought to myself, "The money I earn is not sufficient to keep us," and I had to think of a solution.

At this time an acquaintance came to see us and told my mother that a brother of hers had seen my mother and was taken with her and would like to marry her. So we spoke about it, and I said to her that it was not as if she were marrying to satisfy any desires but that instead of working as a servant in someone else's home, she could earn her keep in marriage by putting bread on a table which at least would be her own. My brother Yehia and Lolla didn't approve, because the man was slightly younger than my mother, but then they were settled in their own homes and couldn't know of or feel the difficulties that beset my mother and me. We lived like refugees.

In the end my mother married, we vacated our room, and I was on my own once more, faced with the problem of what to do and how to live. With my mother's marriage, my existence as a migrant began once again. I couldn't stay in the room alone as I was no longer married and that would be improper.

I slept for a time at my brother's but paid for my own keep there. I would say to my sister-in-law, "Are you going to cook today, Nariman? Here is some money, please include me." Or, "Are you going shopping today, Nariman? Here is some money, please include me." I spoke in this way in order to keep her from feeling that she had taken a lodger. Even so, I rarely ate there and stayed out of their way as much as I could. I would spend a couple of nights with my mother and a couple of nights with my sister Lolla, but I never stayed at my father's as they had only one room.

Ezzo came on home leave from time to time, but his salary was not enough in the army to permit him to look around for a wife. He would come to see me and ask after me, and I would return his greeting and his concern and ask him whether he was not planning to get married and settle down. He would answer something about being interested in a woman here or there, but it seems that all this time, unbeknownst to me, he had his sights set in my direction. I had no thoughts of him in that way.

The summer of that same year, Zain's employer went on home leave for two months, and it was apparent that I would have to find another job in order to live. I checked back at the shirtmaker, but they had their full complement of workers. There was an employee there, however, whom I had known and who suggested that I go with him to see his maternal cousin who owned a sort of boutique in Ataba. He knew about my marriage and divorce and thought he could help. It turned out that in fact they did need a shop girl and that I would qualify. The cousins talked over my story but agreed to keep it from the oldest of the two brothers who ran the shop because it is believed among our people that a woman once married becomes greedy and that wouldn't recommend me for the job.

So, I began work there and earned eight pounds a month, and the people were kind to me. If they bought a melon or a watermelon, for example, they would always offer me some, and they insisted that any tip I got from customers was mine to do with as I pleased.

The elder of the brothers gave me the nickname "Sphinx," because I didn't like to joke or banter with the customers, and because I could pick out the customer who was there to fool around or to pass the time of day. If such a person came in, or if another who didn't know what he wanted asked to have this and that brought down off the shelves, I would look him in the eye and say, "I don't believe we have what you require. Come another day." The customer would then say, "Why do you speak to me in this way?" and I would respond, "I don't think we have what you need. Check back with us later." So he would leave, and the owner who was sitting just outside the shop would chuckle and say to me, "You? You're like the Sphinx." He meant that I was immovable, but indeed whether I smiled at the customer or not he would buy or not buy with his own money.

One day, about five years ago, a police officer and an army man got into a fight in the area of the shop and beat each other up in the street. The shops of Ataba were closed up, and the buses stopped running, and people in uniform changed out of them as quickly as they could and put on *gallabeyyas*, in order to avoid a spread of retaliations between army and police.

I couldn't get home, so the owner invited me to stay with his family that night. They lived in a native type of house in the district called Salah Salem, behind the mosque of Sultan Barquq. They had one room below and two above. So he said, "Tonight you can come sleep in the protective arms of Om Salem and with my brother's children." They were all a family, and the children were those of a brother working in Saudi Arabia. They were very kind, and as they were from Upper Egypt, they put a lot of onion in their cooking.

My paternal cousin came at that time and asked me to marry him. My father stubbornly refused, saying, "Dunya, if I give her to anyone, it will be to Ezzo." The cousin would plead that he could make me happy and make up for the hard times I had had. Everyone in the family knew my story. My father, however, said, "No."

Ezzo also came sniffing around at that time. But I was getting weary of this life of one day here and two days there and no place of my own. Ezzo's brother Fouad would tell Lolla, "Your sister stays with us, and yet she refuses to marry my brother," and this would put me in an embarrassing position. I was caught from all sides.

So when this cousin's mother, who is my father's sister, came to speak to my father about having me for her son, I was pleased. But my father wouldn't budge or be persuaded, and the matter even came to blows. My father slapped his sister, and they weren't on speaking terms for a long time afterward. He continued to say, "Dunya is for Ezzo. He was first intended for her, and that is whom she should have married." But my feelings for Ezzo had cooled considerably by that time. It would seem that time makes one forget. Perhaps also the love which I had felt for him was more a brotherly kind of love. Anyway, my heart had forgotten him, and the troubles that one passes through have a way of nesting there which makes it hard to go backward.

I wanted, at that point, to marry my cousin. He had a decent salary, and I was getting tired of barely existing. I was tired of wearing a dress that was too tight. My life was like wearing such a dress. I wanted a little leeway, a dress that was even a fraction larger but which would allow me to fill my lungs to capacity without bursting, even if the enlargement were just an extra patch. For this reason, I was inclined toward my cousin and favored him.

When there wasn't much business in the shop in Ataba, the owner would say to me, "Put on your street clothes and go home." And at such times I went to visit my aunt, my father's sister, in Deir el-Malaak, which is before Kasr el-Goumhoor. My cousin would often accompany me back home. He talked of marriage, saying how much he was touched by all I had suffered and how he wished to spare me the fatigue of standing all day in a shop, and how he would like to make up for my difficult past. He knew that I wasn't susceptible to talk of love and that sort of nonsense, and so he was straightforward with me.

As I wanted my cousin also, I approached my mother's husband, hoping he would intercede on my behalf. But he refused, saying I had a father and it was not his business to get involved in the decision of whom I should marry. My brother approved of this match, and my cousin directed his request to him. But Yehia couldn't convince my father, who said, "My sister is too well off for us and besides, Dunya has a sharp temper and so does her cousin, and they'd never get along. Ezzo, because he loves her, will tolerate her ways."

I said to myself, "Shall I always struggle and suffer this way?" And I went to see my father in a last attempt to persuade him to let me marry my cousin. When he heard me out, he said, "I have only two words to say to you. Take them or leave them, as you please," and he reminded me of what had happened to me when I had acted on my own. He said, "If you act without my consent again, you are neither my daughter nor have I ever known you, nor will I ever intercede in anything on your behalf. But if you take Ezzo, whatever he does, I will stand by you, and my neck will serve as a protective breaker behind which you can feel secure." Words of course are not actions, but it seems that Ezzo and I were meant to end up together. He sat weeping and saying that Dunya should be with him and he with her and so it was, although I would have preferred my cousin at that point.

My cousin married about the same time that I did. He is now a police officer. But I consummated my marriage before he did. He took a girl who had gone to school, as if to say to me, "You see, you wouldn't have me, and now I have someone better than you." But before he married and while I was still engaged, he used to telephone and ask me why I had agreed to Ezzo and say things like, "Even if you marry ten others, I will marry you in the end." I would reply, "It's over. Do you think I'm moved by such threats, you smart aleck!" and I would slam down the receiver in his face.

It was over. What could I do? I was engaged, and I would get on with the business at hand. That's how I am. As long as something is settled and irrevocable, I don't like to look backward. If I look backward, it's I who will trip and fall. So I look straight ahead at the road before me, deal with life as it has presented itself, and try to stick to what is obvious and clearly marked.

So in that spirit Ezzo and I put together some money we had saved and some money from cooperatives we had joined, and we bought a bedroom set. My father paid for the cotton for the upholstering and my mother-in-law for the ticking to cover two comforters, two mattresses, and two pillows. We rented the rooms we now have and were ready to start married life.

These cooperatives are a handy thing. Ten people or so join together and contribute each a certain amount of money every month, and then one of the ten gets the entire amount each month by turn. That's how I bought Mouna her first pair of gold earrings. I don't deprive Mouna of anything, but I can't forget the proverb which says, "Feed me, clothe me, but in the end I shall find the path back to those who bore me." For Mouna, I had joined a cooperative at three piasters a day until my turn came to collect, and then I bought the earrings.

When Ezzo and I entered housekeeping, it was as if I had never been married before. Nothing had been lost except my virginity. But by that time, I began to have problems which are still with me today. My menstrual flow began to lessen, and I suspected that the pills I took in Libya had affected me in some way. My blood became more and more scarce each month until eventually it stopped altogether, and instead of my period I was gripped by terrific cramps which still make me suffer today.

So when I married, I said to Ezzo, "I'm not well, and I can't even bear to insert a little finger into myself, so how are you going to insert your entire member into me?" But Ezzo was very gentle. He took his time, and it wasn't until one or two or three days that he took his ease with me. So until today and tomorrow, when I say "yes" to him, it's yes, and "no" is no. Ezzo is good that way, and I have made him accustomed to doing things my way. The proverb says, "Your husband until you train him and your son until you raise him," which means that with time and perseverance, you can get each of them to do as you please.

I consummated the marriage with Ezzo two months before Ramadan and quit my job in Ataba, but was helping out Zain in Giza twice a week. I couldn't work in the shop from ten until five, help Zain, and also see to my husband's needs.

Lolla at that time was pregnant with Mouna, and in the third month after I married, she gave birth to her. In these three months my period was still very light and irregular, and I began to suspect that I wouldn't be able to have children. So when Lolla gave birth to the little girl, I named her and asked if I could have the child to raise. My sister answered, "Why not? You and I are one and the same." So Lolla would nurse Mouna, and I would sit with her, or she came to my house to nurse the child, and I would sit with her and we continued in this way until she was weaned.

Some people suggested that I go have a checkup to find out what was wrong with me. So I did. It turned out that I had a blockage of the entrance to the womb, perhaps caused by the pills I used in Libya. But I know women who have inserted Egyptian aspirin into their vaginas to prevent pregnancy with no ill effects to themselves. I don't know why the pills I used were harmful. Perhaps it was because they were foreign aspirin. Anyway, I went to a free hospital and was told that I needed an operation. So I stayed in this hospital called Farouk Hospital and had two operations in two weeks and then was discharged.

When the time for my period came, .and I know it because it wakes me up in the dead of night from my deepest dreams, the cramps got hold of me and worked on me until I could hardly stand it. This was after the operations, and people said to me, "Forget these free hospitals and free operations. They are never any good. Go to a paying hospital for help."

I went to a doctor in Bab el Luq who said, "You need an operation, and it will cost you thirty pounds plus one pound for the consultation and one pound for the nurse's fee." So I thought about it and got hold of the money somehow and had the operation right in the doctor's clinic. It was Ramadan in 1976.

After I recovered, my maternal cousin, Ezzo, his maternal cousin, and a girl friend of mine who is now an engineer with Egyptian television, took me home. All of this fuss was in order for my period to come. I went back to this doctor and had every other day a consultation, every other day an examination, and in the end he said to me, "You need an 'oil' X-ray which will cost you another thirty pounds."

I thought to myself at that point that it all sounded like a lot of nonsense, and then I began to feel discouraged. Not all doctors are clever, and some young ones might know more than old ones, but it's difficult to judge who is good and who is not. I felt lost. Other people who had used this doctor had told him their tales of woe, and he had done operations free for them. But I always went to him dressed well, and I was too proud to tell him that I didn't have this sort of money. I said I would come back, but I never did.

When I got home, I began to weep. I had already spent seventy pounds with no apparent result. I said, "My God, is the one who is miserable fated to remain so always?" When the time for my period came, the cramps would grip me, and I would drain vials of Novalgine in order to ease the pain. It was so severe. This liquid Novalgine was intended for injections and was very bitter, but the cramps were far worse.

One day they came on when I was at my mother's house in Matariya. Her husband saw me and said, "Look here, Dunya, although I'm not experiencing the pains you are in, it is as if I could feel them in my own body. I shall take you to the hospital for female diseases in Abassiyya tomorrow and see what they can do for you." No one who saw me when these cramps were upon me could feel anything but pity for me.

So we went. The doctor wrote out a diagnosis which was copied on a typewriter and said, "Let's take a sample from the womb." I replied that it had already been done and gave him the diagnosis of the last doctor. So he said, "Let's do an examination under anesthesia, then, and see what you have inside." He told me that I had half an hour in which to get myself ready. There was no time to lose because I was being squeezed in among the emergency cases as a special favor to an acquaintance of someone whom we knew at the hospital.

It was early morning, but as I am always washed and prepared, I said to the doctor that I was ready. These are sensitive areas in a woman, and they must give her time in case she should want to wash or depilate before being examined. They can't just ask her to walk right into the examination at a moment's notice. But I was prepared because I knew what to expect.

They gave me an injection, and I gave them my name and then I didn't feel anything. As soon as I came to, I felt myself in this place and saw that I was bleeding. So I looked at them and asked, "Did you do an operation?" They said, "No, we did a probe under anesthesia." So I inquired about what they had found, and the doctor said that the entrance to the womb was blocked. He asked when I had had my first period, and I answered, "I had it when I was thirteen years old. It came flowing like honey and without any pain. It lasted three or four days, and its blood was the color of red roses." Then I explained that it had stopped coming after I was married the first time and divorced. So the doctor said they would, God willing, do an operation to enlarge the opening of the womb which would help solve my problem.

I was then admitted to the hospital for the operation and was there one month and five days, which felt more like two years. Most of the people who come to that hospital are poor and have to wear clothes dispensed to them by the hospital and eat hospital food. I didn't have to do either. My mother had made a long white dress with puffy sleeves for me to wear, and sometimes I would wear a white *gallabeyya* belonging to Ezzo. My mother came every day and brought me my meals. I would give her money for meat or chicken, and she would cook and bring it to me.

In the hospital everyone wears white, and I covered my head with a white kerchief which came down over my ears. Although I wore my own clothes and ate my own food, I felt like a prisoner. I would say to the women on the ward, "When will this come to an end? I feel like a buffalo waiting for the butcher's knife at the slaughterhouse!" They would laugh, and I would laugh, but I was worried. I was getting more impatient by the day. The waiting was the hardest part of this ordeal, but they took us in turn, and there was no other way. I would turn to the staff and say, "Aren't you going to open the stable doors and let the buffaloes out?" They laughed, and the women laughed, and we waited.

The doctor finally operated and after they brought me back to my bed I woke up feeling happy. Ezzo had cried with me over this ordeal, but for me the worst, the waiting, was over. I was hopeful of the results but hopeful anticipation was short lived. The doctor came and said that they could do nothing for me. "You are very narrow," he said, "and I was afraid of puncturing the womb if I acted in haste." What this meant, of course, was that if the womb were punctured that I would not be worth an onion. I would be no good and would die. So tears lept out of my eyes even before he finished his sentence, and I wept. The doctor then spoke sternly to me saying, "Did you want me to kill you and send myself to the devil in the process?" I wept, and he left the room.

After the operation people came to visit. They would walk in with "Mabruk" on the tips of their tongues and words of congratulation, and I would reply by striking my face in despair and weeping. I was in physical pain from below and in agony over the failure of the operation. They had given me anesthetic and tried to insert the tool that they use for enlarging but couldn't get it in. I struck my face then and wept, and the family and friends wept with me. I would weep, and they would weep with me, saying, "Never mind, Dunya, God is merciful, God is wise," and all these words with which we give ourselves courage to go on with life.

I then asked to be discharged, as I could see that it was a struggle which came to nothing in the end. But the doctor said that it wasn't time yet and that the senior staff member would come to see me the following day. He came, checked the wound, and began to talk with me about my problem. He said, "Look here, Dunya, I must speak to you frankly. But I will do so in terms which you would understand as of course you have no knowledge of medical science." So I asked him to go ahead.

He said, "I will try to illustrate the problem for you. Supposing you had a zucchini squash which you were preparing to stuff. If you were to insert your coring knife into it all at once to clean it out, what would happen?" I answered, "I would puncture it." So then he said, "Correct. You're a bright girl, and you follow my meaning exactly. But supposing, now, that you were to take your coring knife and clean out the squash little by little. You would have it properly hollowed out without damaging it, and then you could put your rice in it safely and cook it. Isn't that so?" So I agreed, and he continued by saying that like the squash, I had to be enlarged a little at a time in order not to hurt me, and before he left he said that I could come back for the next treatment in three months time.

The bleeding and cramps continued with me for several days after the operation, and then I was discharged. I went to my sister Lolla's house to recover because she has more room than I do and could more easily accommodate the visitors who came to see me. My mother was with us, my father came to see us often, and Ezzo was thoughtful and considerate but never stayed very long.

After a month or so the cramps resumed, and they were so strong that I would bang my head against the wall in desperation and cry out, "Why did I go through all of this pain and expense if this is the result? I had had two free operations at Farouk Hospital and one which I paid for and three more. That makes six operations altogether for which they had plied me with enough anesthetic to kill a donkey. I am not a donkey but a human being. So when the cramps came, I used to drain ampoule after ampoule of Novalgine and punch myself in the belly. I cried out, "My God, you have given me this pain, but I can do even better than you," and I would punch myself. I wasn't well.

People who saw me said I should go have the next enlargement operation. But I was through with operations and answered, "I am neither going or coming." I felt that it was useless and that doctors, especially when they do anything free of charge, have no conscience and fail to see that God is their witness. So now what could I do? My period, if only it would come, would solve a great problem for me. Without it I can't conceive, and if I can't have children, I live in fear of Ezzo's taking a second wife.

Although I live well and have everything I need: a mixer, a television, a radio, and a tape recorder, this problem hangs over me and colors everything else around it. I am clean in my home, and neat in myself. I see to my husband's needs and am generally content, but because I am childless I feel unsettled.

The problem of living without having children of my own is a terrible one. It's like living in the shadow of a curse, something which I can't and am not allowed to forget and which makes everything else in life that much more of a struggle. If only my period would come as it used to and flow out of me instead of these cramps, I would feel blessed and fortunate. So this is my big problem, and this is my story with its sad times and its tears and nothing added and nothing taken away.

5

Om Naeema

FISHERWOMAN

"I was pregnant three times and gave birth to three children. After that God gave me no more. I gave up trying and became resigned to my fate."

*L*IFE IN A FAMILY where there is more than one wife is bitter. A second wife is always subject to the hatred of her stepchildren, and we always say, "May God see fit to cut short her days among the living." Can one wife ever trust her husband's other wife or wives? It is not possible, and they can only wish each other heartbreak and misfortune. I shall tell some stories to illustrate my point.

In a village near our own, a woman has just killed the son of her husband's second wife. She was jealous and could see that her lot in life from the time the child was born would be no other than that of a servant and slave to her husband's second wife and her male child, and so she decided to do away with the baby. She took him one day when no one was looking and placed him in the large earthenware jug which contains our drinking water. The child was found there, drowned. He had not reached the age of one.

The feeling among our people is this: if you are a first wife and have no children and your husband marries again, you will ask yourself, "Shall I let him get away with this? Shall I allow this woman to fill his home with children while I pine alone and barren like a servant to her offspring? Shall I sit back while he looks on her with loving eyes and prides himself on her accomplishments?" It is not easy to do so.

So you will inquire of yourself, "What is the best way I can get back at him? How can I break his heart and singe hers so that she will live in pain for the rest of her days?" The one sure way is through her children. It is the one place where a woman is most vulnerable. If a child is ill, or dies, or disappears, the mother will pine endlessly for it and lose her appetite for life. She will no longer put black *kohl* in her eyes or make herself beautiful. She will no longer desire to laugh and joke or jest with her husband nor wish to sleep in his arms. She will reject him and through this rejection, the first wife will have her revenge. She will hurt the first wife through her children and the man through his wife.

Another woman, also in a neighboring village, took revenge by giving her co-wife's child potassium to drink. This caustic matter is used to whiten the wash. It killed the baby by tearing his guts to shreds when he drank it. It happened in this way. The mother left her child in the care of the first wife for a brief period. The second wife then brought the child to her and said to him, "Here is a glass of milk, dear heart. Drink this." The child, trusting, drank. When the mother returned, the child cried out to her, "Pick me up, Mother, pick me up!" So the mother said, "What is the matter, soul of your mother?" And the child answered, "My stomach hurts."

When the father came back from the fields, the child was in great pain, and so they asked him what he had eaten or drunk, and he answered, "Fathiyya gave me a big glass of milk to drink." The father said he would take him to the doctor, but before he had finished speaking, the child was dead. The mother, suspecting foul play, insisted, "My son will not be buried until an autopsy has been performed." When it was, the mystery was unravelled, and the stepmother was sent to prison. Now she is out of prison, and everyone looks on her with fear and trepidation. No one will have anything to do with her. Only her father will receive her into his home.

There was a mother of three in our village. Her husband succumbed to the charms of another woman and married her. This new wife had surely laid a blue spell on him, otherwise it is not sensible that he should have taken her into his home knowing how these situations separate parents and children. The first wife was then hungry for revenge, egged on by her people, who said to her, "Why should we leave you to suffer? If your husband can marry again, so can you. We will show him. Throw him back his children, and let him shoulder the responsibility of bringing them up."

Her brothers, who were particularly annoyed with the husband, said, "If it is good looks he desired in a wife, she has them. If it is an accomplished housewife, she is one. If it is a clever woman, she is clever. What more did he want? How can he in all good conscience take the daughter of so and so over our sister?" In this way, the atmosphere was poisoned, and the plotting began.

When the divorce proceedings took place, the man said to his first wife, "I will give you so much child support for the three little ones." But she, pushed by her family, refused, telling him to take his children. Her mother cried out, "Load them on your back and carry them off. We want no support and no children. May their necks be broken along with yours." The man took his children and expected his second wife to care for them.

She did so for a time and then began to get tired of them. They were a burden which was neither her flesh nor her blood, especially the youngest who was still a baby and required much care. She was further annoyed by the fact that her husband not only lavished most of his affection and time on his children, but also slept with the youngest cradled in his arms. In the meantime, the first wife's mother said to her daughter, "Just wait and see, the children will occupy so much of his time that he will have no leisure with this woman, and she will eventually flee from him."

One day this man went to the fields and left the baby as usual with his second wife. This time, however, her jealousy got the better of her. She slaughtered the child. She cut him up and put him in a basket and was about to take the body out when one of the older children walked in. He was still too young to understand what he saw. He said to her, "What are you doing, Mother?" His stepmother answered, "I'm cooking for you." So the boy said, "But this is such a lot of meat." So she said to him, "We'll keep some of it for another day." And she took it and buried it in the animal house.

When the father came home and inquired about the baby, she said she didn't know where he was. Perhaps he had wandered off. He was a child of two of three. They looked high and low for him and called out his name over the loudspeaker from the mosque, as they do when a child is missing. The father wept and suspected his first wife of having taken the child. He sent word to her, and at once the mother and grandmother became alarmed and came running, their hearts beating wildly with anticipated grief.

The missing baby's mother then took one of the older children aside and began to ply him with questions. She asked, "Don't you know where your little brother went? How does your stepmother treat you? What does she feed you?" And so on. The child answered, "She brings a lot of meat into the house. But she didn't give us any to eat." So his mother said, "But what does she do with it then?" And the child answered, "She has just buried some in the animal house."

The mother's suspicions were then aroused, and without further hesitation she openly blamed the second wife for the disappearance of the child. The husband, who received the full brunt of her invective, then answered violently, saying, "You and your family are trying to bring ruin on me and wish nothing better than to bring the rest of the house down about my ears. Haven't you done enough harm?" But still he began to inquire and later followed his little son to the animal house where they dug and found the body of the baby. The child's leg came first and then the rest. He called on his second wife's people, and they all tried to hush the matter up, but word reached the dead child's mother, who arrived with her family in time to see what was left of the baby being brought out. Their voices then rang out with grief, filling the village with all their pent-up agony and frustration over the situation they had plunged themselves into.

The police were then called in. And the first wife, who had felt wronged by this second marriage of her husband, sent him and his new wife away in irons. They were sentenced to fifteen years in jail, and neither had time to enjoy their time together nor look forward to anything but heartache and misery. This is how it is with men and women and how they behave toward one another.

The remaining two boys went to live with their paternal uncle, their father having forbidden that they ever set foot in their mother's house again. But this will not be the end. When these boys grow up, they will lie in wait for their stepmother and take revenge with their own hands. They might also kill their maternal uncles, whom they would hold responsible for having talked their mother into leaving them in the first place. They might also blame them for marrying their mother off a second time thus causing a rift between her and her children.

It is believed that a woman with children, when she remarries, cannot feel the same bonds of motherhood with the children she begat with a man other than her present husband. So it is in our countryside. People spread an umbrella of hatred and mistrust over each other, and life becomes a long chain of marriage, divorce, children, jealousy, and death.

My mother was my father's second wife. My father's first wife was living with him then and had born him only two daughters who were in their teens when my father married my mother. People had said to my father, "Why don't you marry again, Ahmad, and give yourself a chance at having a bit of a son to sustain you in your old age?"

My mother before that time was married to a fat man, but they had had no children. In this man's house she was also a second wife. It is said that the man's first wife worked a magic spell which caused my mother to see her husband as a monkey and to grow to hate him and to find his proximity to her intolerable. There is never any love between co-wives. With this spell the first wife caused her husband to divorce my mother, thus eliminating a rival and setting my mother free to marry again.

When my mother married my father, she became pregnant almost immediately. Her stepdaughters, who naturally resented their father's new wife, plotted with their mother to see what could be done to make life hard for my mother. First, as they wanted to know if the child she was carrying was a boy who would surely upstage them, they went to a wise man with some of my mother's belongings and asked him to see what he could read into them.

These wise people are given powers to see beyond those of the average human being. So the stepdaughters stole one of my mother's head scarves and measured a piece of string against one of her dresses which hung out in the sun to dry and which was to represent her height. They presented these things to the wise man and asked him if he could tell them what sort of a child she was carrying in her belly. The wise man said that it was a male child. When the stepdaughters brought this news to their mother, she wept, saying, "Now the mother of the girls is done for, and the mother of the boys is ascending." Her eldest daughter then replied, "By God, Mother, if I let this newcomer inherit what was to be ours from our father, or allow our father to take pleasure in this son, even for a day, then my name is not Fatma!"

Fatma then went to her maternal uncle who was a wise man and asked him to help. She wanted to place a spell on my mother which would make her seem hideous to her new husband, causing him to reject her. This she did by taking some of my mother's hair, her head scarf, a string to represent her height, a piece of her underclothing, and a five pound note in payment for the man's services.

The spell was cast, and soon the magic began to work my father over. One day he got up and announced to all that come what may he did not want this woman who was his new wife. People said to him, "Think, Ahmad, this woman is pregnant with your child and may give you a little son." But he would not listen and answered, "Let her go to hell. I don't want her. When she stands before me, I see a monkey." So he rejected her and sent her back to her father's house. There she gave birth to her first child, my eldest brother. People then came again to my father and said to him, "Be reasonable, Ahmad, take back your wife. You are now father to a son." But he persisted, answering, "I don't want the boy or his mother."

My mother's people then suspected that this mysterious behavior could be none other than the work of the first wife and of her daughters on my father, and they set out to unravel it and counteract it. They went to visit another wise man, who said to them, "This is the result of a magic spell which is pinned to the side of a tomb. It has been put there with a dead man. Give me three pounds, and I shall search it out, bring it to you, and you can dispel it." So they did. The bundle containing the magic writings and my mother's belongings was brought to them and they set out to "star" it in order to be rid of the evil it was working on their daughter. This they did by placing the contents in a bucket of water and putting the bucket on the roof at night, when the stars were out, allowing it to absorb their light. In the morning before the sun was out, they took it down, and this they did for three nights.

On the fourth day they dumped the contents of the bucket in the river, and the spell was broken.

The very next day my father sent a go-between to ask my grandfather to bring my mother back. He had been enlightened on the cause of his distaste for her, and when he discovered that it was Fatma who had cast a spell on him, he tied her up and left her to spend three nights alone in the house where we store the animal feed. He then quarrelled with his first wife and with her brother, accusing him of having been party to this deed. My stepmother's brother denied the charges, and people intervened and patched things up between them. My father's first wife, however, lived in anxious anticipation of what this new son would bring by way of problems to her and to her daughters, and Fatma, although she was temporarily subdued, held a grudge against the little boy, and meant to do away with him as soon as an opportunity presented itself.

One day, my brother was alone with my stepsister. He was about one year old at the time. She, seeing that there was no one around, took him by the neck and began to strangle him. His face had turned the color of mud when my father suddenly walked in on them and rescued his son. He severely chastised Fatma and sent for his first wife. When she came, he said to her, "You must either care for my son as if he were your own or leave. It is essential that you consider this little boy a brother to your daughters." His wife answered, saying, "What you ask of me, Ahmad, is not reasonable. Did I carry this child in my belly and under my belt in order that I should feel for him as one does for a son? How can I consider him as my own and expect him, when he grows older, to walk before me, to fetch and carry for me as a son must for his mother? It will never happen. A boy is brother only to his own sisters and son to the mother who bore him. These girls of mine are without a brother to care for them and will remain so all of their lives. You, in time, will also forget them and have eyes only for your son."

So my stepmother left the house with her daughters, and within forty eight hours she fell ill and died. Fatma remained with her grandfather but never forgave us the loss of her mother and eventually her younger sister came, and fearing a fate like that of her mother's, took care to treat my father's son gently and watch over him.

My mother then was a second wife and married my father when he was already getting on in years. She bore him four boys and three girls. She had a child almost every year and usually had two nursing at her breasts at once. I am next to the youngest, and my youngest brother is the end of the cluster. We were only three or four years old when our father died. Our oldest brother became like a father to us, and my mother in fact often referred to him as our father. It was the year this brother was drafted into the army that

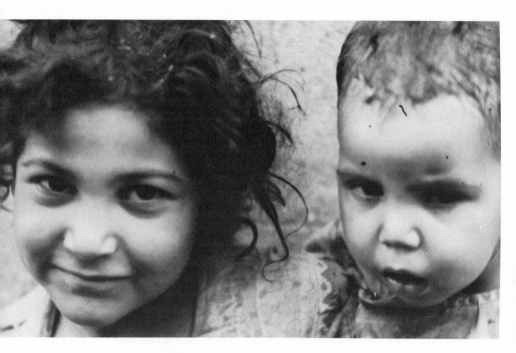

Fatma's younger sister "took great care to treat my father's son gently and take care of him."—Om Naeema. Photograph by Asma el-Bakry.

our father passed away. He was broken hearted at the idea of this son who was the apple of his eye should be taken away from him. He tried to buy his way out of military service, as was possible in those days, but failed to put together the necessary influence and money to do so. This affected him deeply, and shortly after my brother left he died.

When our father died we suddenly found ourselves cast upon the waters like a "band of cripples." The older children comprehended the mean-ing of death and knew just how much of a calamity had befallen us. We would have to struggle from that time forward to keep ourselves alive. I am told that at the time of his death, I sat in the fields playing on a drum and singing while my father's goat romped around me. I do remember the crying and the wailing though as the mourners gathered around my mother, slapping their faces in sympathy with her and sharing her grief.

I recall my mother crying and saying, "O poor one, are you not like a creature drowning now. Where do I go now? To whom have you left me? I have neither brother nor sister to lean on and no shore on which to rest. In whose hands have you commended my fate, O lost one!" To these outcries the mourners responded, "Think of God at this time, Sister." My mother would answer them, "What will become of my children? The poor ones! Life will not spare you its harsh blows, my little ones." And indeed it did not. Neither uncle welcomed us nor did a relative look in on us, and early we learned to work not only in our own fields but as field hands picking sweet potatoes for others at seven or eight piasters a day.

As we were growing up, we would ask our mother, "Where is our father?" She would respond, "God is your father. He will provide for you." We were reminded of our father's absence especially on feast days when other children appeared in new clothes, carrying brightly colored sugar dolls and camels, tokens of the festivities in which we could only share in part because of our impoverished state. Other times when we questioned our mother as to our father's whereabouts she would say, "Your father has gone to a far off market town and will be back tomorrow. Tomorrow." She persisted in this way, trying to spare us, and we could do nothing more than sit in the fields as we had done before and watch enviously those whose fathers sat beside them.

I remember very slightly the way life was before our father died. He would wake us up in the morning and would hold us and pet us and ask us to sit around him. If he had something for us to eat, he would feed it to us, and we sat and ate at his side. After breakfast he would take our farm animals to the fields, and we would follow him and sit in the open air to guard them as he worked on our behalf. We sat near him as he plowed or dug the earth with his spade. Our mother usually stayed home to grind wheat or corn for making bread. She cooked, cleaned, and washed and came to work in the field only if she was needed. By the time we began to wake up to what we were and were old enough to serve our father as he had served us, he had met his maker, and we were left to fend for ourselves.

We rented a small plot of land at the time from a big land owner which we planted in corn or wheat or clover. Generally the crops from these were sufficient to keep us and feed our animals. We had a buffalo, a donkey, and a goat. If we ran short of clover for them, however, we would buy a little extra from our neighbor. This field my mother began to work herself after my father died. We did what we could to help. She would give us a trowel, for example, and show us how to weed while she thinned the corn. On days when we had to irrigate, we would attach our buffalo to the water wheel, and one of us children would drive it around in a circle while our mother directed the flow of water into the fields. If our turn to irrigate fell at night, as it did on occasion, the neighbors would say, "This woman is alone and has small children. She must not be left out in the open alone at night." They would then trade the time allotted to them in the daylight hours for hers at night.

People did show concern for us but not our own families. Occasionally some-one would bring us a basket of oranges, some second-hand clothes, or a bowl of milk with which to make savory pastry or rice pudding. The relatives, however, went about their own business and ignored us.

When I was about seven years old, my mother had me circumcised. We circumcise girls in summer during the months of *Abib* and *Misra* and until the small feast. Girls are circumcised to keep them cool and able to control their sexual urges. Boys are circumcised because it is believed that they cannot copulate or beget children if they are not.

Most often in the villages, a group of girls is circumcised at the same time. Afterward, the women wash them in the river, each in turn. Then they bind them with a clean cloth dipped in oil and iodine. If these girls have been circumcised in the same house, they are not repelled by one another, but if they are circumcised separately and accidentally meet at the river, the one who comes upon the other first must notify the first girl's mother.

The mother will say, "Did the daughter of so and so meet you at the river?" She'll answer, "Yes." So the mother will be silent. After the girl's wound has healed, her mother will say to her, "When you are married, if you can't conceive, go to the daughter of so and so who was circumcised at the same time you were. She met you by accident at the river when washing her wound. Have her make a small cut in one of her fingers and lick up her blood three times. With a piece of cotton you'll have prepared, soak some of her blood and insert this piece of cotton into your vagina. Be sure it's done at a time when you'll not be going out or walking in the street. Do this at night, maybe, when you go to bed." This will break the spell one girl puts on the other accidentally, when she met her at the river when she shouldn't have.

It's important to notify a girl's mother if this ever happens and you don't wish her ill. If you don't do it, you might "block" her forever and prevent her from conceiving or bearing children. Notifying each other like this is considered a favor. Women will then reciprocate if the occasion to return a favor offers itself.

One day, my mother said to her father, who was a sort of male nurse, "We want to circumcise the girl." So my grandfather responded, "Why not. I'll do it." One morning, he came to the house with a razor and sharpened it carefully in order to make the operation as quick and painless as possible. I was afraid. I knew vaguely what was about to take place because I had seen other girls and heard them crying before me. But unlike the midwife who also does circumcision and whose hand is often heavy and whose knife is fre-quently blunt, the male nurse's hand tends to be lighter, his instrument sharper, and he uses something to numb you. This diminishes the shock associated with the operation.

The day of my circumcision, I remember my mother calling in a man from the neighborhood to hold me so that I wouldn't squirm and be injured by the razor. I also remember that when my grandfather came into the house it was still very misty outside, the way it often is early in the morning in the countryside. I didn't feel anything when the knife hit, but later when feeling came back and the medicine wore off, about noon that day, I thought the sky would come crashing down about my head from the pain. I cried. My mother was distressed and went to fetch my grandfather. He said, "Never mind. The razor stole in on her. Now the pain comes as a shock. She'll recover. What she's experiencing is only natural."

After a girl has been circumcised, her mother binds her with a length of clean cloth twisted into a rope and dipped in oil and iodine. She secures this to a belt tied around the child's waist. This is what my mother did, making me lie down with the large milking bowl between my legs for a time in order to prevent me from squeezing my legs together and causing the wound to heal over, in which case it would have to be slit open again.

On this first day I was in pain and wept a great deal. My mother wept with me and said, "Never mind, my darling, this is your day. It will pass." She boiled an egg for me and fed me grapes and dates to keep up my strength, saying all the while, "When you eat this you will be well." She also dissolved some sugar in water and gave it to me to drink, comforting me with her words, "Drink this, mama's little heart. It will relieve the stinging you feel and cool your wound." She went on this way until I got better, and then she stopped worrying over me.

On the second day of my circumcision, my mother prepared fresh bandages and took me down to the river to wash my wound. In treating this wound some girls respond to water and others to mud which has been ground fine and is applied in the form of a healing powder. The method chosen depends on where the child's afterbirth was disposed of after she came into the world. Daughters are most often like their mothers. If a mother's afterbirth was thrown into the river at the time of delivery then her circumcision wound will respond best to the healing power of water. If on the other hand, the afterbirth was buried in a mud brick wall, then the circumcision wound will best respond to the mud as a healing agent. Mothers will often change the position of the afterbirth if a child dies, hoping that by switching from mud to water or vice versa with the next child that she will give it a better chance for survival.

As my wound responded to Nile water, my mother took me down to the river on the second day of the operation and swabbed my wound with a chicken feather dipped into the water. She then told me to urinate standing up, allowing the urine to run freely over the wound. Urine cauterizes and is an excellent healing agent, even better than iodine. When we were done, we

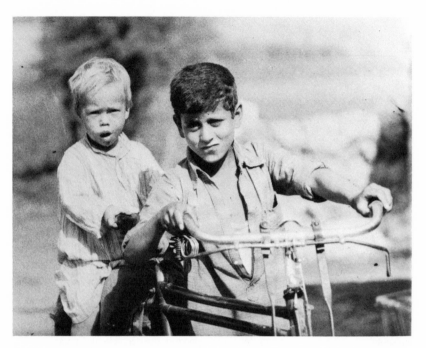

"Boys are more precious than girls in our countryside."—Om Naeema. Photograph by Asma el-Bakry.

walked home. I had to keep my legs well apart and was still in pain. The third day my mother did the same and bound me again with fresh bandages until the fifth day when my grandfather came to look at me and swabbed me with mercurochrome and declared that my wound was healed.

Recently a doctor was assigned to our village. He could circumcise and was supposed to perform the operation with scissors, snipping only a little part of the clitoris instead of taking out the whole "paper," as the midwife and the male nurse do and as it is the custom to do. But neither the families nor the girls themselves consented ever to go to him for the operation. Our village women rarely make use of the doctor for this or for childbirth. Only in cases of difficult labor do they accept his help, and even then they are put to shame for doing so. To be rushed to the doctor in case of a complicated delivery is considered a demonstration of weakness on the part of a woman. It is the midwife who must always assist at deliveries, charging one pound for each boy delivered and fifty piasters [about U.S. $1] for each female. The male nurse is never involved in childbirth but charges one pound for circum-

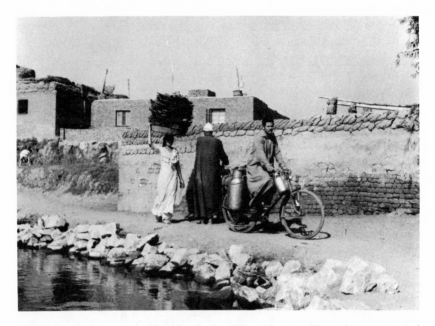

Milkman going home on his bicycle after his dawn deliveries. The girl is carrying fuel made of water buffalo and cow dung mixed with straw in her washbasin. Photograph by Asma el-Bakry.

cising girls and one pound fifty piasters for boys. The reason for the difference in fees is that boys are more precious than girls in our countryside, and therefore the reward expected for handling a boy is higher than that expected for females.

Because of this difference in the value of male and female children, a woman who has had many sons will try to hide the birth of a fifth or sixth son by saying she has given birth to a girl, thus averting the evil eye of ill wishers away from her newborn child. Often the boy's father will take him on the seventh day after his birth to Sayyed Badawi or Dessouki or wherever he can and circumcise him quietly without music or fanfare. This is, again, done to insure against the evil eye. For some reason, it is most often the poorest of families who have many children, and especially, many boys. Only their poverty saves them from the envy of others who see them as unfairly blessed in the number of their male offspring but otherwise unfortunate.

When my circumcision wound was healed and I was well again, my mother began to teach me housework. She said, "In no time you will marry and become a housewife, and so it is best now to stop going to the fields to work and to start learning to keep house properly. By the time I teach you what you need to know, young men will gather round asking for your hand in marriage, and it will be your responsibility to make one of them comfortable." So I began to learn to cook and bake, to grind wheat and corn, to milk the buffalo, and to keep the house clean, as well as make fuel for the mud brick oven out of a mixture of dung and straw. This training lasted two or three years.

My mother taught me by keeping me at her side as she worked. On baking days I would divide the dough for the bread into small balls which she would thin out and toss into the oven to make the round loaves we eat in the village. She would then save thirty or forty loaves for me to thin and toss into the oven for practice until I learned to do the job properly. She would take my hand to guide me and warn me never to fear the oven or the fire lest I remain afraid of them all my life. When she was satisfied with my performance as a housekeeper, she let me take over for her while she went to the fields to work alongside my brothers.

My day usually began at dawn. I was often up two hours before the rest of the family. First I milked the buffalo after washing my face and getting the milking bowl which was left face down at night on the mud brick oven. I would wipe it clean and sit down to milk. Next I fed the buffalo and collected the dung from beneath her and cleaned the stable. I would carry the dung home in a big wash basin which I balanced on my head. I took the dung to the roof of our house and mixing it with straw formed it into the flat cakes we use for fuel and then left it spread out to dry and harden in the sun.

I would then take a cake of soap and our water jug and go down to the river. I washed my hands and filled the water jug and walked home again. By the time I returned and had swept out the house and prepared milk and cheese and heated bread for breakfast, my brothers would be up. They would wash their faces and eat and leave for the fields, and I would continue my chores. If there were clothes to wash, I would wash them or take pots down to the river for a good scrubbing, and return to cook. If they needed my help in the fields, I would go with them.

My mother most often stayed home only on baking days. We would make the bread together. She would fire up the oven, and I would knead the dough. She would form it into balls and leave it to rise, and when each had risen, I would toss it in a quick circular motion over my hands and bake it while she kept the fire going. As each loaf only takes a few minutes to bake, you have to be on the spot and work rapidly. In preparation for baking day we would have ground the wheat and corn and stored it in baskets, ready to use.

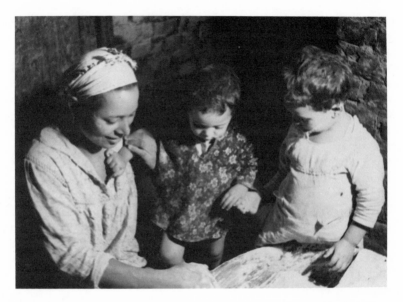

"My mother taught me by keeping me at her side as she worked."—Om Naeema. Photograph by Asma el-Bakry.

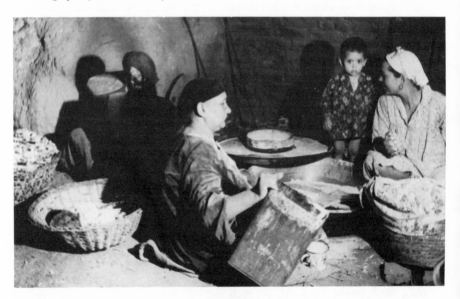

"It takes at least two people to bake, but if you are three, then one can knead, the other make balls of the dough then thin them on the wicker palette, and the third can take care of the oven."—Om Naeema. Photograph by Asma el-Bakry.

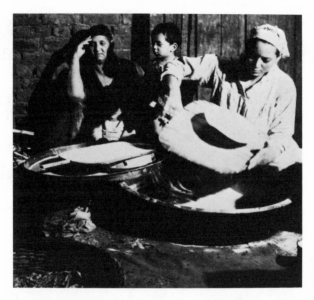

Thinning the bread dough on the wicker palette. Photograph by Asma el-Bakry.

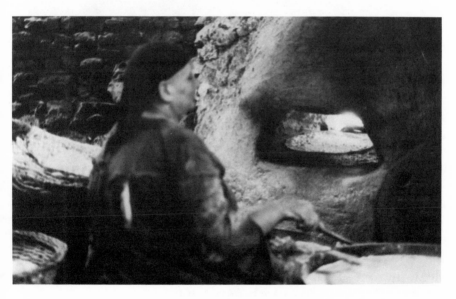

The mud brick oven with a thin loaf baking inside. Photograph by Asma el-Bakry.

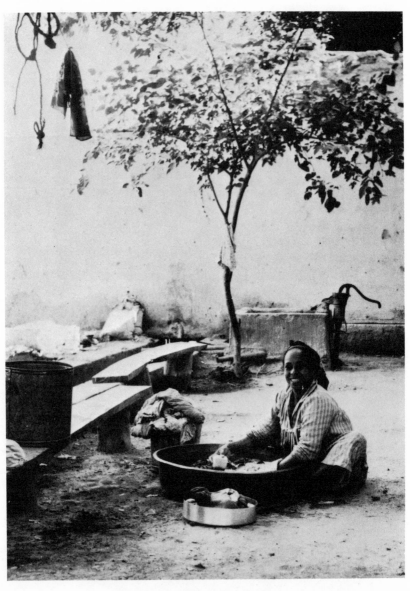

"My day usually began at dawn. If there were clothes to wash, I would wash them."—Om Naeema. Photograph by Asma el-Bakry.

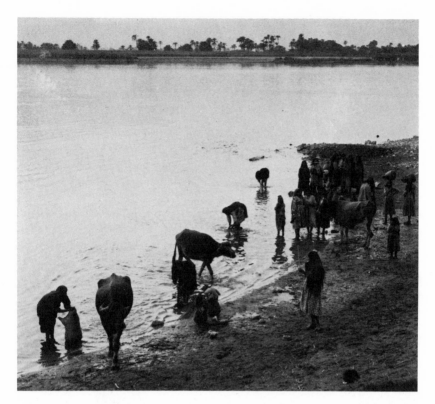

"Or I would take pots down to the river for a good scrubbing."—Om Naeema.
Photograph by Asma el-Bakry.

A day or so ahead of time we would take a ball of dough from a neighbor who
was baking and with it smear the inside of the milking bowl. We then put the
milking bowl face down on the oven, and on baking day we added warm
water to the mixture lining it to form the yeast we would knead into the big
batch of dough for making bread. This is yeast for corn bread, and this
homemade yeast allows the bread to last a long time. For wheat bread we
always bought yeast, but this made the bread spoil more quickly.

The time of my training as a housewife passed in this way, and when
I was a little more than fifteen years old, I was married off to my father's
maternal cousin who was then, as now, a fisherman on the Nile in Cairo. It so
happened that at the time when he came asking for my hand in marriage, I
had been spoken for by another young man who was not a relative.

My eldest brother had come to visit us from Tanta in order to give me away, and he was sitting at our local coffee house when Hamed's, my husband's brother walked in. He sat with my brother and said to him, "We want Aysha or Hamed." When the "big bone" our grandfather had died, the family had become less cohesive, and Hamed's brother felt that through this marriage, strong family bonds would be re-established. So my brother agreed, saying, "It would be a happy day for me to see your brother marry my sister and to see our family ties renewed and strengthened by this marriage." So it was agreed between them.

But my youngest brother was not pleased with this decision. He favored the first suitor because they worked together as farmers and were side by side every day. Hamed on the other hand lived far from the village on the river in Cairo and was out of touch with the land, having left his peasant roots when he was twelve or thirteen years old to earn his living as a fisherman. There was much discussion, but finally my older brother prevailed. He also had the support of our mother who said, "This boy is like a fifth son to me. He is brother to my children and the apple of my eye. I have already married off two daughters to outsiders, and this one will be the dearest and nearest to us because of the ties that bind us and the closeness of his father to us. His father and these children's father had cherished each other and would have approved of this further bond. So let it pass."

On the day of my wedding I was made ready in the usual way. My face and body were cleaned and depilated, and henna was applied to my hands. In our village we like to sign the marriage contract and consummate the marriage on the same day in order to insure that there will not be a change of heart on the part of the groom or his family. As it was, however, the mayor of the village had had a falling out with my brother-in-law's wife's people and had chosen the occasion of my wedding to antagonize the family. He had spoken to the judge who was to write out the marriage contract and complete the necessary papers and persuaded him to travel to a far off town on the very day of my wedding. So when we were ready to proceed, we discovered that he was gone, and I remained in a state of suspense, my hands bright orange with henna, for two days and two nights. I was shocked and confused by this incident, and everyone around me was at loose ends wondering what to do.

The mayor knew that my brother and other relatives had taken days off from their jobs to come to the village for the occasion, and he wantonly chose this time to settle an old grudge as he knew the consequences would cause the family much worry and discomfort. In his desire to further annoy them, he also mentioned that I had not reached the legal age for marriage and insisted that I be taken to the local doctor to have my age verified. I was in fact a little shy of the sixteen years necessary under the law for marriage. The family tried to get around this obstacle by taking another girl in my stead to a nearby village to see the doctor. The doctor examined her and gave the go-ahead and told her to sign the document stating her age with her thumb print. It turns out that thumb prints are not all the same, and this oversight got us into trouble.

The mayor soon got wind of what had happened and pointed an accusing finger at the doctor, saying he had falsified the documents. The result was that the doctor was angered by the incident and fined the girl who stood in my place six pounds and the groom ten pounds, all of which Hamed eventually had to pay from the money given us as wedding presents. The mayor, however, was not satisfied and wanted to take us to the local authorities. My maternal uncle who had come for the wedding and who was a brave and high tempered man intervened at that point, saying, "If my niece is dragged off anywhere, I will see to it that this village is knee deep in blood before the day is out." The mayor then realized that my uncle considered himself a lost man and would in fact kill him. My uncle, wanting to emphasize the point further, said, "I swear thrice by the name of the Prophet that if your footsteps lead you out of this village in search of further annoyance to us, that you shall never retrace them this way again nor ever cross the threshhold of your house after this day. I say this before all who are gathered here. So let what will come to pass come to pass, and do as you please with this poor child. What has she done to you that you should wish to disfigure her chances for happiness in this way?"

In the end the mayor explained himself to my uncle, and people patched up things between the families, and that same day my marriage was consummated. I was shaken by what had happened and afraid of what was to come. But I gave myself courage by repeating over and over again that nothing of what would take place now as far as marriage was concerned could be worse or more painful than the ritual circumcision I had experienced as a child. This thought gave me heart.

That same night we went through the customary public show of blood which proves to the groom and to all that the bride is a virgin. The midwife, my mother, and married female relatives were in the room with me for the defloration. Two lengths of clean white gauze shawls that are normally used for turbans were made ready for the ceremony. The groom wrapped one of them around his finger and entered me until he drew blood. When he was satisfied of my virginity, the midwife said to him, "Congratulations. Now go sit at the other end of the room while I do what remains to be done." She then inserted her finger into me several times, taking blood and spotting with it the two white shawls until they were adequately decorated. She then hiked them up on sticks, and they were carried out of the room for all to see, then taken in procession to the groom's house. This is called the ritual of exhibition.

After the ceremony the groom lay down with me, but it took about seven or eight days for me to get used to him. He was patient, but he wanted what he wanted. He had married at the same time as three or four other young men, and they sat together often at that time. I don't know what they talked about, but these conversations seemed to make him more intent on getting me used to intercourse. The first few days my body became swollen, and I felt as if the lower half of me were on fire. I sat in pans of hot water after sexual intercourse to relieve the pain, but by and by, after a time, I became hardened to the process and felt nothing.

Weddings in the village can be very big affairs. They are not only a source of entertainment but a time when people can come together. They often include not only the families of the bride and groom and the local villagers but others from neighboring villages and towns. The wedding in my day was set up in the street. Wooden benches were lined up for guests to sit on, and there were men and women's quarters. Guests bring gifts of money which are carefully recorded and kept track of in order to be returned in kind to the giver when one of his children is married off.

These occasions are also often used to settle grudges and long-standing feuds and can turn into blood baths. Weddings can be a time when revenge is taken, feuds begun or perpetuated, and problems among people stirred up because the general confusion, noise, and crowding serve as a cover for violence.

There are young men in the villages today who have gone to school and who have no respect for tradition and the ways of country folk. One of these might brazenly enter the women's quarters, for example, during a wedding and cast a roving eye on the pretty girls within.

The menfolk are constantly on the lookout for such behavior. If they see it taking place, they will fling themselves off the benches where they sit and confront the culprit and demand that he withdraw. If the offender agrees and goes off quietly, then all is well. If he objects or resists, then one of the men will say, "Why are you looking at the daughter of so and so? Have you no modesty? Are not the menfolk spectacle enough for your eyes?" The men will then locate the boy's father and sticks might be brandished and violent words exchanged. If the father apologizes and takes his son away, then there is no problem. If not, then animosities take root which could fester for years and retaliations take place later, perhaps under cover of another wedding.

This sort of flare up, however, has been common only in the last five or six years. It is the school students who are often at the bottom of it and who gather in clusters pretending to present their congratulations to the groom, when in fact they are intent on breaking rules of modesty and playing pranks. Sometimes, however, the offender will have a genuine grudge consuming his heart and will start a fight or act in a way which will help disfigure the happy occasion.

In a village near us one year, a wedding was in progress, and the drumming and singing and dancing were high. The father of the groom was at the center of all this activity when a shot rang out, and a bullet hit him square in the neck. He collapsed and died. In the village the shooting off of guns is an indication of joy and merriment. The groom was firing in the air to show his pleasure when one of the guests fired simultaneously intending to kill the groom's father and turned the wedding into a funeral.

In the meantime the dead man's wife had thrown herself on his body and was wailing and bathing in his blood saying, "It is my son who has done this evil deed. He has killed his father." The young man was stunned and answered, "Mother, what are you saying? Change your tune." But the woman persisted in pointing the accusing finger at her son. When the police arrived, the officer in charge said, "It is unlikely that a boy whose hands are just freshly covered with henna in celebration of his wedding day would turn such an occasion into a day of mourning."

This is just what the family was expecting him to say. The mother had accused her son in order to cover up the fact that she had seen who it was who had committed the murder. In this way the family would eliminate the interference of any outsider such as the police in the matter and take revenge with their own hands. They would show all possible courtesy to the murderer until he no longer suspected them of knowing what he had done and sometime later one of them would strike, very possibly at the wedding of this man's son. This is how things are done among our people.

There are many ways in which these feuds are begun, but one major source of violence is jealousy. People think, "How can your son walk around well dressed and well fed," for example, "and mine go hungry while yours mocks or insults him?" Or they might think, "How can your field be more resplendent and prosperous than mine?" The good fortune of one man causes ill feeling in another.

A young man might come asking to marry another's daughter, for example, and the parents will choose the richer of the two suitors. The poorer one will be vexed and say to himself, "If I had been richer or better, they would have chosen me." In his anger at being rejected, he might sneak into the field belonging to the girl's father and pull up the man's plants. He might poison the man's buffalo. Anything is possible. The fiancé of the bride would then intervene, now being a part of that family, and another feud will begin. That's the villagers for you.

In our village the crowds and processions have been forbidden in an

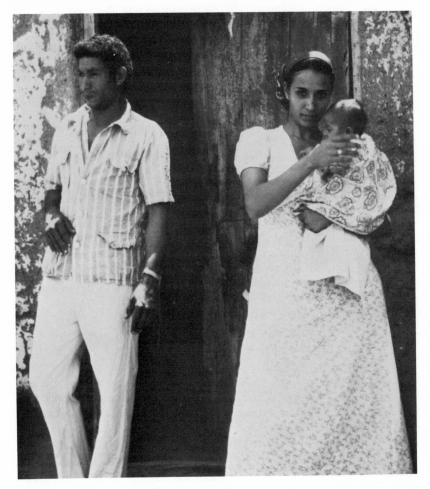

"A year or so after I was married, my first child was born. I gave birth without really knowing how I was giving birth."—Om Naeema. Photograph by Asma el-Bakry.

effort to stem this sort of violence. The writing of a marriage contract takes place in the morning with only the families gathered. They drink a glass of *sharbat* together in celebration, and all of those who are there are identifiable. No strangers take part in the weddings now as in the past. The boy and girl have their hands colored with henna in their own houses, and everything remains visible and under control.

A year or so after I was married, my first child was born. It was a boy, and I called him El-Bayoumi. I gave birth without really knowing how I was giving birth. Hamed was on the river at the time, and I was living in his family's house with his two brothers and their wives. We each had a room there. It was winter time, and there was a sheep who slept in the room with me at the time. One night I felt a knocking within me, and it seems that the womb was beginning to contract. Contractions with a male child are far gentler and quieter than those which come with a female child. We always know by the strength of the contractions and the sharpness of the knocking within our bodies whether we are giving birth to a boy or a girl.

My sister and stepsisters lived in the same village at that time. One of these had had six boys and a girl, and the others had had many children. They were all experienced in this matter. One of them came to me one day before my labor started and said, "Don't let the knocking within you catch you unawares. Be on your guard lest you start crying and wailing and shame us." Another one said, "Your stomach has dropped noticeably. Be careful when your pains come not to utter a sound lest the village start cackling and saying that the daughter of so and so has been giving birth for two days and call you a weakling and a good for nothing."

If a woman has a difficult labor, people will not spare her. They will annoy her with words and shame her. So when I felt my waters break and the pains come over me, I kept quiet and insisted to my sisters-in-law that it was nothing, just a little discomfort. But that night as I lay in my room, the child's head pushed out of me, and I cried out involuntarily. As I cried out my brother-in-law who was sleeping in the next room got up and came to the doorway of my room to see what was the matter. I cried, and the sheep bleated, and my brother-in-law ran to his wife and said, "Get up, you bitch, and go see what's becoming of the girl." So she came and found the child's head beneath me and the afterbirth hanging out. Her husband ran out into the night in his shirt to fetch the midwife, who was angry because she had not been called earlier. But my sister-in-law said to her, "When we saw her earlier, she stood there like a dolt and said nothing."

The midwife then cut the cord and sent for some old clothes to wrap the child in. We never buy clothes for a baby until it is born for fear that it might die. She then made me lie flat and pressed and massaged my stomach hard to get whatever blood remained in my body out. This she did by pressing against me with her knees. We do this in order to prevent ourselves from having protruding stomachs after childbirth. She then heated water and added a disinfectant to it and made me sit in a basin full of it. Then after a time she wrapped me snuggly and made *helba*, a herb tea, for me to drink and slept that night in the room with me.

On the third day she came back and swabbed the baby's eyes with a feather smeared with black *kohl* and traced over his eyelashes and eye brows with the black mixture so that they might grow thick and shapely. She then took a piece of butter and swished it around in his mouth so that he might never choke on his food. On the seventh day she returned and took the child's nipples in her hands and squeezed them to let out any milk that was stored up there. This we do in order that the child may never develop unpleasant body odor, and if as an adult he has to go without a bath for a time, his body would nevertheless remain sweet smelling. On the fortieth day she pounded an onion and mixed the juice with some fine salt and applied this to the baby's eyes and ears to keep them healthy and to insure that he would always see clearly and hear well. We also powder a baby in order to keep it from having diaper rash.

In the country a baby is bound up very tightly, leaving only an opening big enough for the mother to reach in and change his diaper. The diaper is made of old bits of cloth folded into a small square and inserted between the thighs. If you tossed one of our babies into the air, it would stay as stiff as a metal rod. This swaddling makes them tough. We leave the child's head uncovered and cover only the chest and midriff warmly as these are sensitive areas. If a child of ours survives its babyhood, he will be hard as nails and no cold will affect him or hot sun do him any harm.

In the countryside we always know whether a woman is carrying a boy or a girl by looking at her naked belly. If she is pregnant with a girl, her belly button will protrude and be very round and prominent, and her nipples will be dark, almost black. If she is pregnant with a boy, there will be something like a green stalk of wheat or a green hair running down the length of her belly, and her nipples will be as bright in color as red dates. Our people are well versed in this part of life which has to do with conception and birth, and their wisdom and knowledge runs very deep. It is the one thing in which they are clever. People rejoice at having children and do not like to practice birth control in the countryside.

After my first child I had a girl I called El-Sayyeda and then another I called Naeema, who is the only one surviving of my children. El-Bayoumi died before he was two months old. He was asleep near me when a woman entered the room and said to me, "How is it that this child is sleeping outside of the protective circle of a sieve even before he is seven days old." I didn't know about this custom, and when she said this to me, I began to worry and soon afterward he died.

He had begun to clench his fists, and his face had turned the color of mud, and it seems as though he had been given the evil eye. Hamed's maternal aunt came to see me one day and looking at the baby said, "This child has been pushed off the edge of our world. His little brothers from another world have formed a circle around him and are calling him away." Five hours later he died.

El-Sayyeda died after seven months. She had a lung infection, and nothing I did could save her. I have a relative who gave her injections but to no avail. When these children died, my heart was seared with pain and unhappiness. I lost my appetite for everything, and when I saw other women with their children perched on their shoulders, I wept and felt that indeed life had dealt me a harsh blow. For this reason, when Naeema was born, I carried her "in my teeth," that is she meant more to me than my life. I cared for her a well as I could. I nursed her for three seasons, and then people said to me, "Wean the child now so that you can conceive again while your breasts are still hot and active with the milk of this child."

So I weaned her, but I neither conceived nor ever got pregnant again. My period became erratic, and I went to see the doctors but with no result. Hamed went to have himself checked, which is humiliating for a man, and was told he had cysts in his genitals which would require an operation costing 30 pounds [about U.S. $50]. He managed to put together the money and have the operation but to no avail.

Here we are, with only one daughter to our name. When my period stopped, I felt bloated, as if I were in my tenth month of pregnancy. I am over forty now, and it is all but gone. My husband still has intercourse with me. A man can continue to beget children until he is walking with a stick in his hand for support, and we continued to hope that somehow we would be blessed. But we have not been, and if God had had more children in store for us, he would have given them to us long ago. I was pregnant three times and gave birth to three children. After that God gave me no more. I gave up trying and became resigned to my fate.

My childlessness after the birth of my third child may have been caused by a hex.

When a woman who has just given birth meets another who has just weaned her baby at the river's edge or runs across her on her way to the river, the one who has weaned her child will tell her mother, who'll say, "My child, you've just blocked this woman, and the milk in her breasts will dry up."

The mother will then milk one of her animals and take some of the milk and put it in a bottle. She'll take it to the mother of the woman who's just given birth. She'll say, "Have your daughter take this milk and smear it on her nipples and her stomach and insert a piece of cotton soaked with milk into her vagina. This will dispell the harm my daughter may have caused yours." This woman will then be indebted to the other for this act of good faith.

If a meeting like this takes place, and the new mother doesn't know who caused her milk to run dry, or if it happens to a new bride either by accident or because someone wished to harm her, she won't be able to dispell this hex and her misfortune will follow her wherever she goes. No doctor can help her.

If a hex is put on a childless woman in this way, this is what she has to do to dispell it. She must find another woman carrying a basin full of water used to wash a corpse before burial. Before that woman throws the water into the river, she'll ask her to fill a bottle with this water for her. The childless bride waits for the other woman by the river. She holds a bottle in her hand. She does this very quietly so as not to offend the family of the dead person and hides the bottle in her dress. She takes it home and swabs her breasts and belly with the water. With what's left over she rinses out her mouth. The hex is then dispelled. She becomes pregnant.

There are tombs in Baboor, a village in the delta, where the Prophet is said to have passed. If a woman cannot conceive, she may visit these tombs for three Fridays running. On the third Friday she performs her ablutions. She then takes a water jug she has drunk from for some time and throws it behind her and breaks it. By that time God will have had mercy on her. She'll become pregnant.

I was blocked, but I don't know who blocked me. It was surely one of my sisters-in-law, who walked in on me just after I'd given birth. One of them must have walked into the room where I'd just given birth carrying meat or clover seed. This is sure to stop you getting pregnant again. They would have done this on the sly. One would walk in on me perhaps with a piece of meat or some clover seed hidden inside her dress, against her breast, or else in her pocket. If she does this before seven days have passed after the birth of my child, she's sure to harm me.

You can dispell the clover seed hex this way. If I know, then my mother fetches some clover seed and gives it to me. Early in the morning just after dawn prayers, I take with me a woman I trust, and I walk out into the fields. I sow the clover seed over the seven ridges of a field. I then walk to the river with my friend. I put clover seed in my mouth, and immerse myself in the river. I blow the clover seed into the water, then I get up and walk home. I must speak to no one at that time. If someone talks to me or bids me good day, I let my companion answer for me. One must always take along another woman who's not menstruating for this reason. She mustn't be menstruating because she has to be "pure."

When you've done this, then likely as not the hex is broken.

If you've been struck with the meat hex, especially before a month has passed from the birth of your child, this is what you do. Before a month is out, you wait for the butcher to slaughter an animal. You run to his house and catch a little of the blood that spurts out of the animal as its head is cut off. You catch some blood in your cupped hand and drink it while it's still warm. You soak a piece of cotton with the animal's blood then insert it into your vagina as soon as you get home. You also swab your breasts and belly with a little of the blood. The hex is broken.

There is also the spell cast by someone walking in on you shortly after you've given birth, carrying barber's tools. To dispell this you run to the barber. You say to him, "Give me your whetstone." You put the stones in some water then rinse your mouth out with this water. The hex is broken.

Fear can also make you childless. When I went to live on the river, I used to see drowned people float by as I sat on our boat. My heart is weak. I took fright. This affected me.

I tried going to doctors to ask for help when I got desperate with wanting to have more children. Nothing helped. I then said to myself, "Is conception in the hands of doctors? It's in the hands of God." But people had said to me, "It doesn't hurt to give the Lord a little help." I tried, but it was all to no avail.

I tried other ways too. I went to those who know. I took my head scarf and my husband's turban to one of these in Giza. She took my scarf and looked at it and sniffed it. She said, "You need to have a black or a brown fowl slaughtered over your head. Let the blood drench you. This will break the spell which made you barren."

When I gave her my husband's turban, she said she wouldn't have anything to do with it. She said, "This man has no evil in him. He knows more than we do. I won't touch him." She smelled the turban and said, "He's a member of a religious order." In fact he is. I don't know how she knew by sniffing though.

I went to a number of other wise people. They gave me lots of remedies, including one like a pellet made with herbs to insert into my vagina. I would use it when I had my period. It drew a lot of moisture from my body and relieved cramps, but it didn't make me less barren. I then resigned myself. I said, "Dear God, if you saw fit to give me three children, and take back two of them, let your will be done."

My periods when they came lasted three days. It was just the same when I was a virgin and the same after I married.

When it didn't come five days or so after the fifteenth of each month, I'd feel hopeful. I'd think, "I'm pregnant." I'd feel overcome with nausea. I'd vomit for the first three months. Nothing came of it.

When Naeema was about three or four, my restlessness increased, and I wanted very badly to have more children. The other fisherwomen were giving birth every year, and I felt deprived and incomplete. Some of them got hold of my ear one day and began to whisper and say, "Why do you stay with this man? You know it is probably his fault that you are without more children." Their words began to work me over, and I thought to myself as I sat in our boat, "Why indeed do I stay with him? I could marry again and give myself a second chance at more children." Hamed was not aware of what I was thinking, but I had begun to be disagreeable and to treat him badly. I was hoping that by being contrary I would anger him and make him divorce me.

One day, sensing that I had changed, he said to me, "Do you want to have more children?" I answered sharply, "Of course. Do you think I don't?" So he looked at me and said, "This is God's will, Om Naeema. Neither you nor I have a hand in it. So how is it that when I address you plainly and forthrightly you take to turning your back on me? So I answered, "Who said I turn my back on you? Don't I work beside you and pull my weight?" But he did not let me finish and said, "This has nothing to do with anything. Conduct yourself gracefully from now on, and God help us get across this vale of tears in good faith."

When I did not answer, he said, "Didn't God give you the three children we first had? If he had something for you, he would have given it without the help of doctors or others. Do you think that I don't suffer and don't also want children? You now have a daughter who in time of illness or stress will care for you and comfort you. Who do I have? Will my daughter care for me when I am down? No. A girl is her mother's beloved. So be thankful, for if you persist in these ways you have adopted, you will bring nothing but heartache on yourself." He preached to me in this way but then added, "But if you still want me to divorce you, I will take you to the village and be done with it." So I answered, "How do I know what will become of me now? I have neither property or children to my name and nothing to fall back on. What if you should die?" So he said, "How do we know who will die first. Are these things in our hands, Om Naeema?" I remained unmoved.

No sooner had he said these thing to me than I began to feel ill. Three days after our talk I had a feeling of great heaviness and was baiting the hooks one morning as I always do, when I began to vomit a substance as dark as Coca Cola. Hamed said to me, "Shall I take you to the doctor?" I said, "No, take me to the Kasr el-Aini hospital." So he agreed but added, "Om Naeema, you have brought this on yourself by your cheating thoughts." I was quiet and began to feel guilty, and he said, "He who is not willing to abide by the judgments which God sees fit to mete out to him always loses. Health is far better than children or wealth. You have cheated yourself of it." I could say nothing.

At the hospital the doctor checked me and said, "You are not ill. I see no signs of anything wrong." So I answered, "Did you think I came here to play then, Doctor?" So he prescribed a bottle of some reddish white medicine and some pills for me to take. Thinking they would help, I took them all at once, but instead of making me better they made me more ill. I went to another hospital we call the Coca Cola hospital but could get no relief from the doctors there either.

Hamed belongs to a Muslim religious order. He has a paternal uncle who is a *Sheikh* and a wise man of standing in this religious order. His son is a policeman. One day I saw him coming down to our boat. Hamed was out selling our fish, and Naeema who was small then sat beside me in the boat waiting for her father to return. She looked up and said, "Here comes Gaber, the son of the *Sheikh*." I looked but was too ill to move. I said, "Is your father with you, Gaber?" And he answered, "My father is on his way here. Some people of his acquaintance waylaid him and insisted on offering him some refreshment just down the street. He will be here presently."

When the *Sheikh* came, he said to me, "Are you ill, Om Naeema?" I answered that I was, and he said to me, "The straight and narrow path is always the best one to follow, my child. You have strayed from it. You know that everything that happens to us is an act of God. Our fate is not in our own hands." He spoke in this way, in veiled terms, then said, "You know that marriages in our family are forever, and we neither divorce nor separate until death. So how is it that you have allowed yourself to be swayed by the talk and idle chatter of the womenfolk you come across?" Can't you see that it has done nothing but bring you illness and heartache? Look at the state you are in."

So I said, "O *Sheikh*, my mind is that of a woman. What can I do?" So he said to me, "Are you in great pain?" I answered, "Yes I am. Can you help me?" He answered, "No, stay that way a little longer." So I said, "I've been to the doctors, and they could do nothing for me." So he replied in anger, "Well, you just keep on going to doctors and see what they can do for you!" Hearing him speak this way, I wept. He looked at me and added, "God is merciful. I've told you to keep on the straight and narrow path. If God has something for you, he will give it. He does not serve gypsies and prostitutes. Remember that you are married to a God-fearing man who yearly invokes the help of the holy men and women of Islam saying, 'Praise be to Sayyeda Zeinab, and Praise be to Sayyedna el-Hussein, and Praise be to Sayyed Badawi,' and takes three days every year to go to each of their festivals. You should have thought of him and respected his feelings when the womenfolk and the devil began to play on your thoughts." With this he stopped.

At that point Hamed came back, and he embraced his uncle and offered him the appropriate courtesies. His uncle then said to him, "Don't worry. Her illness will pass." So I took heart and asked again, "Will you help me, Uncle?" And he answered, "No, I will not help you. You brought this on yourself." In this way he brought out the anger which was pent up inside of him.

I went to see the doctors again. One of them said to me, "Look here, Lady, you have been taking enough medicines to revive a camel if it was ill. Are you eating properly?" I said I was following a diet prescribed by him exactly. So he put his hand to my side and found that the place that hurt me was hot. He then said I probably had an inflammation of the kidneys and prescribed some more medicine. I took seven pounds worth of medicine but again to no avail. My side was like a burning coal, and I remained ill and in pain.

One day Hamed's uncle came back. He had in his hand a jar full of herbs carefully sifted together and a bottle of *hab el-baraka* oil. He had mixed together seven kinds of herbs, three pounds worth of each. I was lying in the boat when he came down and said, "Om Naeema, here is something for you. Take three spoonfuls full of this herb mixture in your hand at morning and night time and lick them up. Be careful not to mix them with water but follow them up with a spoonful of this oil. In no time you will be better." And in fact from that moment on the flame which was searing my side subsided, and I began to get well. It was as if my body had been covered with a sticky layer of honey which had suddenly been washed away leaving me feeling clean and light again.

Three days later he came back to check on me and said, laughing, "Are you better?" I answered, "Yes," so he said to me, "Now, either you stay with us in good faith, my woman, and from this time forward follow the path prescribed for you by God, or disappear from our midst like a glass of water drunk up in one draught." I looked at him and at my husband and said, "Hamed, I will never be contrary to you again. I shall never from this time forward go against your wishes or the will of God." So he answered quietly, "Whether you do or not is up to you. Take the road which best suits you. I have God above to watch over me and guide my steps. He made me as I am, and I submit to His will and will continue to jealously guard His feelings, keep His good name, and follow the teachings of Islam according to which He created me." I answered, "Come what may, I shall not leave you." And since that time, I have remained faithful to him. I feel that his goodness and his faithful adherence to the teachings of Islam are enough to sustain me.

A woman, if she speaks to a man who is not a relative, should always put it in her head to be more man than he is.

If I am in our fishing boat, and we are moored near a river steamer where there are men employed, I must be certain they will respect me or

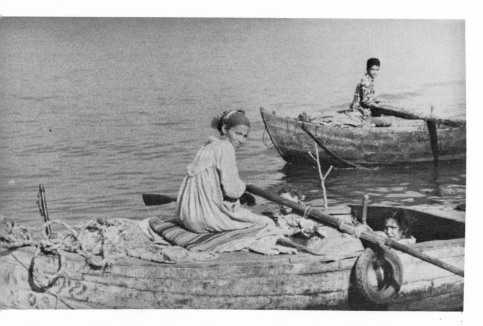

"A woman, if she speaks to a man who is not a relative, should always put it in her head to be more man than he is."—Om Naeema. Photograph by Asma el-Bakry.

make sure we move away from that spot. If one of these men should speak out of turn to me, I wouldn't say anything to my husband, because men have bad tempers and can be violent. We just move on.

If no one acts improperly to me when my husband is on shore selling fish or buying our supplies and I'm alone, then we consider this a safe place and remain there.

It is only courteous that if a man speaks to me, I answer. I must be on my guard at all times, though, and make sure that his intentions are honorable.

A man who is better off than we are may feel that he has a right to court the wife of a poorer man. He believes as all men do that a woman's head can be easily turned.

I trust in God. If such a man should come my way and tempt me away from my husband, he won't be able to do it. I will neither be impressed with his dress nor his wealth. He will use these to try and fulfill his desire. He would then trample me underfoot and persecute me.

My way of avoiding trouble is to be strong. I look such a person straight in the eye when I talk to him. I show him that my conscience is clear.

Living on the river is hazardous. I am not protected by the four walls of a room or the enclosure of a house. When my husband has to go ashore, I am alone and must fend for myself.

If a man passing by stops and looks down at me, I test his intentions. If they are good, then I have nothing to fear. If he's up to something and persists, I get my husband to move. If not, I'd have to choose between trying to hide from such a man, which is difficult as I am unable to leave our little boat, or to tell my husband. If I do that, the men would come to blows and a calamity would befall us.

This experience took place one time when I was still young and pretty and Naeema was a baby. I was sitting alone in the boat, nursing her, when the first mate from one of the big river steamers approached me. He said "O Lady, when you're sitting here as you are, what good is that to you? A fisherman's life is hard. It has neither security nor comfort. You're young, and you have only this small child at your breast, this bit of a daughter. Can this be reason enough to accept such an existence?"

So I said, testing him, "And where do you think I should go?" So he answered, "Try to get this man to divorce you and marry me instead. I would carry this child of yours in my eyes." So I said, "So you want me to leave my husband? And on what grounds?" So he said, "Because I'm better off than he is. I earn E£50 a month and can set you up in a comfortable room."

This man had sat on our boat and eaten bread and salt with my husband and drunk tea with us. I thought to myself, "This disloyal and ungrateful wretch has no right to talk this way. He's dishonorable and cunning."

I said to him, "Listen here, you can go to the devil or wherever you choose. Just stay away from me from this time forward. If you were surrounded by a farm on which a tree of every kind on earth grew and bore every variety of fruit, I wouldn't touch you because you're corrupt and underhanded. If my man fed me daily on a loaf of bread, that would appease my hunger. For me it's enough that my husband is a good Muslim and a man of good faith. I am content to keep my honor and that of my family intact even if life this way is hard. If you think that you can just reach out your hand and pluck me from where I sit here because you're richer than we are, you're mistaken. You're a dirty son of a bitch. Would you wish upon your womenfolk what you've just meted out to another man's daughter? Keep way from me."

This story is almost twenty years old, and until today when we pass near his ship, I turn away and neither of us speaks to him.

My husband knows nothing of this story. When he returned that

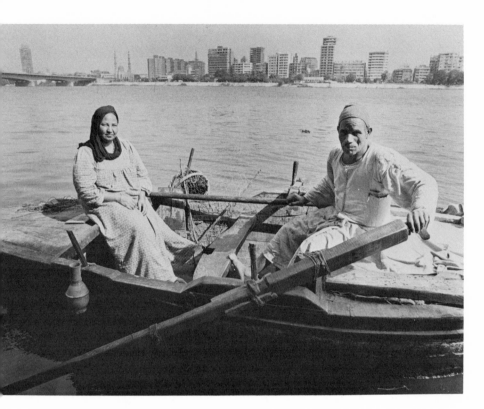

Fisherman and his wife on the Nile. Photograph by Jeanne Tifft.

day, he saw that I was upset. I told him we needed to move away. He wanted to know why, and I said it was because some children had thrown stones at me several times there.

God enlightens my husband because he is a good man. He agreed to move and of his own accord stopped speaking to the traitor. He doesn't even say "Good morning" to him now. He must have sensed the evil in him.

If I had told my husband the truth, then passions would have been stirred up. People would have come to blows. So I thought, "Why should I subject my husband to this and cause him to become violent and bring ruin in himself because of some unruly son of a bitch? Why should I take a chance on his spending the rest of his days in jail because of an unnecessary act of retaliation?"

My people and my husband's people would have had to be involved. They would eventually have laid the blame on me, no matter which way things turned out. They would have said, "So and so was ruined because another man dared look in the direction of his wife and covet her." His people would then be at war with me and persecute me, and my people would be ashamed of me. They would shout, "Go see, O woman, whom you favored above your husband and what you caused him to do." The other fisherfolk would then gossip and say, "No sooner had her husband gone ashore than this other man was found in her bed."

A woman has to be on her guard at all times. People will blame her no matter what happens or doesn't happen. There are men who will talk out of place just as there are dogs who bark. So let them talk and bark. A woman's business is to keep out of their way.

When Naeema was fourteen years old, she was engaged to be married. The bridegroom was not a relative. When my eldest sister heard of Naeema's engagement, she told her husband to come see us in the village to persuade us not to marry Naeema off to a stranger but to keep her for their middle son.

One night Hamed, Abu Naeema, was getting ready for the evening prayer when we heard the door of the house open and someone come in. In the country the houses have two doors. One outer door and one inner door leading directly to the house. Hamed then said, "Who can it be coming in this way unannounced? It cannot be a stranger. It must be one of your maternal uncles, Naeema." It was dusk, and we had the oven lit for warmth but we could not see very clearly.

Soon there was a tapping at the door of the courtyard, the *mandara*. We asked, "Who is it?" And he answered, "It is I, your brother-in-law from Cairo." So we were worried because of this unexpected visit of my sister's husband coming from Cairo at this hour. We feared bad news, and we said, "What news do you bring? Is anything wrong?" He answered, "All is well, don't worry." We asked him to come in, and he said, "I have come to make a request and God willing, it will not be denied." So Abu Naeema finished praying and then said to Naeema, "Heat some bread and prepare dinner for your aunt's husband." After he had eaten, my brother-in-law said, "I've come concerning Naeema. Had we not agreed that you would reserve Naeema as a bride for our son Mohammad? I now hear that she has become engaged to another."

So Hamed answered, "You wanted Naeema. But did you in fact name the son you wanted her for? You have six sons. Did you ever make it clear in any way that your intentions were serious or let it be known to those around you that you had in fact spoken for the daughter of so and so?"

So my brother-in-law answered, "Well, you know that we don't go looking for our brides in the streets and collect them like bits of scrap from unknown sources. Our daughter-in-law must be the daughter of our loved ones in order to become the wife of the dearest among our children." Hamed did not answer, and my brother-in-law continued, "I have come with high hopes that we would become further related by this marriage of Naeema to Mohammad. You will not disappoint me and turn me away with a negative answer." So Hamed answered that his brother was staying with us at this time and that he would consult him first.

At that point one of my brothers came in and said to my brother-in-law, "Good evening. What brings you here at this time Sayyed?" So my sister's husband answered, "I've come to ask for Naeema in marriage for my son Mohammad." My brother said, "You want Naeema for Mohammad?" Sayyed said, "Yes, and I consider it done." My brother was vexed by this answer. He wanted to discuss the matter and know just what Sayyed's intentions really were and why he had suddenly appeared out of nowhere with this proposal of marriage. So he said to him, "You say it's done. But when do you plan to have a wedding, and what are the conditions you propose?"

Sayyed answered in a rough way and insulted my brother as if he had no right to interfere in the matter. Of course, as the girl's uncle, he had a right to give his opinion. Sayyed answered, "You're rough spoken and ill bred. Don't you see that the matter is settled? What causes have you to take umbrage. Don't you know that we have formed a cooperative to collect money and intend to do all that is necessary so the wedding can take place in six months? By that time the girl will be of age, and we can consummate the marriage."

When my brother felt the sting of my brother-in-law's insult, he stood up and did not answer him. Hamed answered neither of them, and because he did not wish to make up his mind about Naeema just then, he kept quiet. It was then that his brother walked in and hearing what had passed between the two men decided the matter by saying, "Look here, it is not as if Sayyed were a stranger trying to buy us out. After all, the girl is our girl, and the boy is one of our sons. When you have made preparations, Sayyed, then come and take the bride for your son. On our side we shall do our duty, and her father will see to her needs. After all, no marriage has taken place yet, and it is acceptable for this engagement to be broken in favor of a marriage from within the family." So they left it at that.

When the matter had been settled verbally, Sayyed insisted that a gift of gold be given to the bride as a firm sign of their good intentions and to firm up the engagement. My husband suggested that the money that would go into gold should be given to the couple to use in some more practical way, but

Sayyed answered, "No. The gold is an essential part of the agreement. We want to make sure that when people look at us, they see that we have attached this bride to our son with an appropriate gift according to the traditional custom of our people."

So the gold was purchased, and it consisted of an 18 karat gold bracelet for Naeema and two wedding bands for the bride and the groom. Hamed on his side bought a gold ring for the groom for twenty pounds [about U.S. $35].

It is customary among our people at the time of the engagement for the bride's parents to offer the groom's family a quantity of fowl and poultry. But as we had none, Hamed said, "We are neither going to give them chickens nor ducks. We don't raise any poultry living on the river most of the time. We shall buy the groom a ring to wear on his finger with the money which we would have spent on these."

When all of the purchases had been made and the gifts exchanged, we gave a big feast in celebration. At that time Naeema's paternal uncle said, "Now we should write the marriage contract." Sayyed replied, "The time is not right since the bride is not yet of age. She is shy eight months of the legal age for marriage." So Hamed answered, "All right, let it be. Let fate decide how things will turn out."

The engagement took place, and no sooner had we concluded it than Naeema's aunt, my sister and the mother of the groom, began to quarrel with me and to argue over the gifts which had been given and whose responsibility it was to offer what and prepare this and that for the couple. She said that the ring we gave was too meager in return for what they had given, and we began to bicker about the bracelet this and the ring that, and when we got up the following morning, Hamed said to Naeema, "Take off the short dress you are now wearing. You will not marry this man. Although fate brought him our way, it seems that he and his family are all talk and no action, and I don't believe that our future is to be linked to theirs. You will not marry Mohammad, I feel quite sure of that." And so our daughter, after being engaged, remained in this state for three years. She became more and more despondent because the bridegroom's family would neither let her go nor make a firm commitment in her direction.

The quarrel I had with my sister also created a gulf between us that would not be bridged. Naeema remained in her father's house in the village, and we had to be in the river in Cairo to earn our living.

As time went on the bridegroom inquired less and less after his bride. One day we heard that they had announced that the engagement was off without so much as a word or an explanation. It is possible that in the three years that Naeema stayed engaged to Mohammad, the family thought they could do better for their son. We were still poor fisherfolk, while they were getting richer and better as time went on. They had moved from the village to the district of Boulac in Cairo. They probably felt that we were beneath them and so decided to let our daughter go. This did not prevent them from coming to the village at feast time. All eight members of the family would appear on our doorstep and stay in the house, eating and drinking and in the end would ask us to provide them with all manner of country delicacies to take home with them. They also insisted during those three years that we turn over to them whatever we earned from the fish we caught. Hamed did not agree to that.

Before they broke off the engagement, my sister's husband arrived one day and called my name from the street above. I looked up from the boat where I was sitting. I was baiting the hooks, and I answered him. He said to me, "Om Naeema, are you not going to prepare a few things for your daughter to begin housekeeping with? We are planning for the wedding to take place at the big feast." So I said, "Of course. All of the beautiful things necessary will be prepared for Naeema." He then said, "Yes, I know the things that you mean. But what I had in mind were a few couches or a bed or cupboard. This sort of thing is what I meant." So I replied, "Didn't you agree to provide the bedroom set when we discussed the conditions of the marriage? And didn't you agree that we would clothe her and provide the girl with whatever personal effects were needed and throw in some gold jewelry? In any case, we shall provide her with whatever God gives us the strength and means to provide her with." Sayyed replied, "It is your sister who asked me to come and tell you these things." He looked at Hamed, but Hamed sat there not uttering a word. He neither said "yes" nor said "no," nor this is good nor bad. My brother-in-law felt the weight of Hamed's silence and turning to him said, "Well, Uncle, in any case we intend to marry these children come the next feast." Hamed then looked at him and said, "You intend to marry them come the big feast? Well, I see no reason to object. May God give you strength."

After this conversation we began to prepare our daughter in earnest. When she needed this or that, we bought it for her until one day my eldest brother came to visit from Tanta and seeing our preparations said, "Did the groom's family rent a room for the couple yet?" Hamed said that they had not. So my brother looked at him and said, "Then there will be no wedding, and this man Sayyed is just not serious. These children cannot marry before there is a place for them to live." At that time Sayyed's eldest son came, and my brother quizzed him, saying, "Did your father in fact say to you that they would marry your brother at the time of the big feast?" So the young man answered, "I have heard nothing." So my brother said, "Is this some sort of a joke then?" The boy answered, "No, but let me go see what my father has to say about the matter, and I will return and clarify this situation for you."

When the boy spoke to his father, the father is supposed to have said, "Is marriage something one demands or comes to claim?" When the boy said that we were anxious because a long period of time had passed since the bride was first spoken for, Sayyed is said to have answered, "What if I said to her father that we would have the wedding at feast time? A bride can remain engaged for seven and ten years. It's only been three years today. What are three years in a lifetime?"

So the son reported the father's words to us, and then Hamed went to see Sayyed himself. The groom's father said again what he had said to his son, and the two men fell heatedly on each other and quarrelled. When this happened, we all drew apart, and the father of the groom would come to our boat and say, "There will be no wedding. We no longer wish to marry from among you." They took to treating us with disrespect, and little by little they foresook our girl. Although people said to my sister, "Isn't it a shame, Om Ali, that you should bind a girl like this for three years and a girl who is an only child at that, and then treat her in this way?" My sister answered, "That's just how it is. Let it be."

When we tried once more to remind them of their promise, they said, "Is marriage the sort of thing one comes to claim?" In our anger we would say, "Of course it is something which can be claimed. Do you think that you can just 'mortgage of a show of blood' [the consummation of the marriage] for three years in this way and then all at once wash your hands of any responsibility? You have given neither financial support in these three years, nor let our girl go to seek her fortune elsewhere. She could have found a solution to her life through another door all of this time."

But the groom's father remained inflexible and persisted in saying that a bride could be kept for ten years. They were not ready, they insisted, on starting their son off on married life quite yet. It was not long after this that a messenger came from Sayyed to say that they wanted nothing more to do with us.

One night during Ramadan when we had eaten our last meal of the day before the next day's fast, we moored our boat in a sheltered place and went to bed for the night. We slept. Soon I was aware of Hamed moving around and getting ready for the dawn prayer. Then I had a vision. Someone was waking me up. Someone was calling my name in my dreams, and he called my name three times and lifted up my head and shook me. He spoke to me, saying, "Get up and go see for yourself, see with your own eyes what is happening in Boulac. So that you may see who it is who is standing in your daughter's way and wishing to harm her." It was a man who appeared before me but not an ordinary human being such as we see every day. Three times he beckoned to me, and I woke up.

It was early and still gray and hazy out, as the day had not yet uncovered itself. I got up and sat in the belly of our boat as Hamed said his prayers. He then finished, and I said to him, "Let's not work today. I'm going to go to Boulac." So he asked, "Why?" and I said, "By God, someone came to me in my sleep and said such and such. I want to go see who is the ill wisher who stands in the way of our daughter's happiness."

So I got ready and went to the bus station near Cairo University, and I inquired of a lady standing there, "Which bus do I take for Boulac?" She answered, "It's the one I am taking. I will tell you where to get off." When we came to my destination, she said. "Here it is, soul of your mother." Once in Boulac I knew the way to my sister's house.

When I got to the door of my sister's house, I was met by one of the tenants, who said to me, "Are you Om Naeema?" I said, "Yes," and she said, "Your sister and her family are going to go and trick you and your husband as he sits in his boat on the river and take from him the engagement present they gave your daughter. They are going to forsake the girl altogether." So I asked, "And who told you this? How do you know?" She answered, "They have sat up the whole night eating and talking, and my niece and her husband were with them. They gave and took and talked much and planned this evil against you. I heard them. They plan to go to your husband and say that if he is not willing to meet their demands to furnish the house for the couple, then they want their gold bracelet back."

I thanked the neighbor who had enlightened me and then went to knock at my sister's door. Something held back my hand. I tried over and over, but my hand refused to respond. So I left and as I stood on the stairs, I could see them. They were dressed and ready to leave. They were on their way to find us. I wanted to hide and find my way back to my husband before they got there.

I walked out and reached a little garden spot not far off. All of a sudden I felt as if a chain had descended upon me from an unknown place. It began to wind itself around my legs and kept me from moving. I could not take another step, and so I sat down where I was.

I couldn't move, and as I sat there, I saw my sister and her people coming in my direction. The bridegroom then saw me and cried, "Isn't that my aunt?" and his mother looked and saw me and exclaimed, "O black day, it's my sister!" When they were directly in front of me, the chain which had riveted me to the ground suddenly fell away, and I spoke. I said to them, "I was standing at your door and heard what you said. Are you not afraid of God's judgment? Are you not ashamed to be plotting and scheming at this holy time which comes but once a year? Do you realize the serious consequences of your meddling? You are interfering in the life of a woman, yet you claim to be good Muslims and to read the Koran! Do you think that because you are blessed with male children that you can do violence in this way to a powerless girl and one who is an only child?"

The words gushed out of me. I said to my sister before she could reply, "I swear by the God who made us and by this holy month of Ramadan in which you have contrived to harm me and my husband through our only daughter, that this deed will not pass over you or your husband without being repaid with pain and sorrow. You are people who can depend on a regular income, and you live content within four walls. I depend on God's will, and my living is bound up in my husband's footsteps. It is God who has willed it so. The outcome of this affair I leave in his hands."

They said nothing but got ready to go. They wanted me to come with them in a taxi, but I swore never to be in the same car with them. When I got back to the boat, I found Hamed sitting there. My arrival coincided with theirs. He looked at me first. He noticed I was unhappy, then he greeted them. I said to him, "Don't greet them. They're out to cheat you." So he answered, "I know everything, but there are certain civilities which are their due and which I must perform regardless of what they have said or done." Abd el Megeed, my niece's husband, then said to Hamed, "O Uncle, I shall be coming to call on you and will tell you what has happened." Hamed answered, "Whether you come or not is of no consequence. Do what you please, and may God be your witness."

Throughout all of this the bridegroom seemed surprised. It seems that the family had hidden their intentions from him. He had been led into thinking that the troubles and objections to the marriage had come from me. So he said to his mother, "Have you been scheming and plotting to get everyone to turn against everyone else and get me caught in the middle?"

It seems they had told him that I had not been satisfied with the initial conditions of the marriage contract and that I had said, "I don't have eight or nine girls to throw away. You must pay a decent dowry for the bride." So the bridegroom is supposed to have said, "You mean she wants us to pay for all of the preparations?" My niece then answered, "It must be that Om Naeema is trying to discourage us because she has her sights on someone else, otherwise they would be more accommodating now. Who can he be?"

It was all lies, and in fact what had happened was that they had moved up in the world and we were still modest fisherfolk, and they no longer really wanted to be attached to us by this marriage. They had been indulging in double talk. This had soured the spirits of all those assembled.

After abandoning Naeema, my sister married her son off to someone else, and I cast a spell on him, hoping that he would find no peace and that his life and that of his family would be a series of misfortunes.

I went to one of those who know and had the wiseman draw

Mohammad as a devil and write a spell against him on seven lemon leaves. I burned one of these every night for seven nights, and whenever I did so, he would become crazed and would come running looking for us on the river so we could break the spell and he could find some relief. He would run in the streets and over the bridges looking for us, and he was wild and didn't know what had taken hold of him. He would cry out, "Where is my aunt? Where is her husband? I must see them." His family would race after him, and we could see them sometimes, and they would be desperate and shouting, "The boy has gone mad." He answered them, saying, "You have done this to me. You are at fault. You antagonized my aunt and her husband, and now her ill will is tormenting me." His mother would wring her hands but could do nothing.

I also wrote a spell that would prevent his wife from ever conceiving from him. And in fact he has remained "chained." She is childless until now and will stay that way. He will not be able to give his face to any creature in this world.

When a distant relative heard that Naeema's marriage had not been consummated and that we had broken up with my sister's son, he came to our village and said he wanted Naeema for his son. I said her father was not here and had sworn never to marry his daughter to any relative again. So this man, Abdallah, answered, "Well, I'm not a very close relative!" So the negotiations began again.

When Abdallah went to find Abu Naeema to propose his son, Salem, for Naeema, her father answered, "I'm sick of relatives. They have done nothing but stop my daughter's progress toward happiness. I don't want to think of marrying her now. She has only been out of this mess two months. Let her be until she recovers from the shock."

So Abdallah answered, "I'm neither like Sayyed, your brother-in-law, nor like anyone else. The engagement could take place this month and the marriage immediately after it at feast time." But my husband kept them waiting for four months despite their insistence.

In the end they spoke to an irrigation engineer under whom Hamed was working. He was collecting water hyacinths from the Nile on our boat. Abdallah asked him to intervene on their behalf. So one day this engineer called Hamed, "Tie up your boat and come up. I'd like a word with you." So he came, and the engineer said, "These people have been after you for months. Why are you so set against them?" Hamed answered, "Well, Sir, my daughter was engaged to her cousin, and it didn't work, so now I have a complex when it comes to relatives, and she is embittered and doesn't wish to marry again."

But the engineer insisted, saying, "These people are serious, coming and going to visit you here on the river and in the village. Give them a chance." So Hamed said, "The folks from that village are reputed not to be very serious or responsible, and as she is an only child, I hesitate to marry her to someone who would take her away from home and might not treat her well. There are three kilometers between our villages. How would I get to see her this way? She would neither have aunts nor uncles there to look in on her, and she'd feel isolated." The engineer then answered, "As the groom is now in the army, he would probably rent a room in town for her, and she could be close to you in Cairo."

My husband was perplexed and so asked the engineer's sincere opinion on the matter. "My opinion is marry her." So Hamed said, "Well, let it be." The engineer then wanted to be sure that Hamed would not change his mind when he left him. He asked him to swear he would not change his mind. So Hamed said, "I have only one word, and I have given it."

As there were forty days left before the feast, we decided to wait and do the engagement at feast time and to write the marriage contract then.

When this was decided, Hamed went to see his brother who lives in Mounira, another district in Cairo, to inform him of what had passed and to consult him. His brother said, "Well, why not?" These things are all a matter of fate anyway."

So they gave her a dowry, and we made her ready for marriage and set her up nicely and all was well. The two families had bought each other's good will with this agreement and were acting in good faith. Everything was fine. There were no problems. The bridegroom was decent toward us, and he liked his bride and she liked him. So the wedding took place. The groom's brother was also married at the same time, and thus the family killed two birds with one stone.

The night of the wedding the drum came and took Naeema away to her husband's people, and they gave her a nice wedding party, and we did what we could, and everyone was happy.

She had barely been married forty days when it became clear that her father- and mother-in-law and the bridegroom and his sisters could not stand her. Her presence was hateful to them. Suddenly they could not stand the sight of her. They turned against her and left her no peace. So the girl grew puzzled by this sudden change and grew more and more unhappy. She asked them, "Can you tell me what I've done, Uncle? Can you tell me what displeases you in me?" They would answer, "We don't know." It was as if a spark had caught them unaware and set them all on fire, fixing in their hearts the desire to humiliate and hurt Naeema. The girl fell ill. We were in Cairo at the time and could do nothing to help her.

One day she went into her bedroom to get away from the cruel words that were being said to her. She shut the door behind her. Her husband had been stationed away from the village and was gone at the time. It was dusk, just five minutes before the evening prayer. She was lying on her bed and fell asleep.

Then she saw before her an apparition. Someone was shaking her to make her wake up and was calling her name. So she answered, and the man in the dream said, "Get up, I've come to tell you to walk out and retrieve the bundle which has been working magic against you and striking hate in the hearts of those around you. Step out over the threshold of the house and walk toward the river." But she fell asleep again. Again the calling woke her up. She was a sad captive. She shook herself and got up finally and went out as she had been told.

There is a sandy beach by the river. She walked along it. Suddenly her foot sank in a soft place. She reached down and felt a lump beneath her foot. She picked it up and found it be a bundle, knotted at the top. She opened it and found inside the bundle writing on small scraps of paper, a snippet of her underwear, bits of her hair and, generally, things that belonged to her. So she took these and threw them into the river and walked home.

The next day her in-laws were at peace with her. She herself felt weight lift from her shoulders, and what was ailing her fell away, leaving her well.

Her in-laws knocked on her bedroom door the next morning and invited her to join them for breakfast, which they had not done before. Her sister-in-law, that is the wife of her husband's brother, then looked puzzled at their change of heart toward her. She walked in on her and said, "Naeema, Naeema." So Naeema answered, "Yes, Rasmiyya, what is it?" The sister-in-law then said, "Did you come upon the little bundle I had buried just beyond the threshold of our house?" So Naeema answered, "What bundle? There was no bundle, but I uncovered your evil works against me." They then began to quarrel.

Rasmiyya, who was then about forty years old, had married this brother late. She had one daughter from the marriage who was about two years old and no sons. She saw Naeema as a threat since she was young and might produce sons. Naeema might upstage her.

This was the second time an evil spell had been cast on the poor girl. She has been unlucky.

When we first came to live on the river, we saw a woman one day sitting naked on the shore. She was a *Sheikha,* a wise woman. My husband averted his eyes. He rowed away from the place where she was. He didn't want to embarrass her. The men on the Nile taxi looked brazenly at her nakedness though. They taunted her. She was as bare as the day her mother bore her, and she was very beautiful. She was an older woman, tall, broad, with a golden complexion and a rose on each check. Her eyes were large and green. Her beauty, when later she wrapped a green turban around her head and over her forehead, was forbidding.

When the Nile taxi men looked at her, she shouted, "What are you looking at you sons of bitches?" So I looked in her direction, and she addressed me. She said, "Are you looking at me? Are you looking at me, you unfortunate wretch?" My daughter was then with us, lying down in the belly of the boat. She was hidden. The *Sheikha* called to her, although she couldn't see her. She said, "Get up, you only child, you unfortunate one. They've oppressed you and worked evil spells on you. Your bridegroom will never return to you. He's gone far from you."

I asked, "Who did this?" She answered, "Those who live in Tanta and Cairo. Your blood relatives have worked evil on you. They've made your daughter's belly swell up so that she looks pregnant before she's married. They did this to shame you."

I asked the *Sheikha* to help us. She recommended I buy some herbs, *hargal* and *halfet barr* at the spice market. She said, "Brew these, and let her drink them first thing in the morning. This'll bring down the swelling. It'll purge her of the spell cast on her."

I did as I was told. When my daughter drank, a huge lizard with four legs, as black as mud, came sliding out of her rectum. She was relieved. But she wasn't pregnant. Her breasts were flabby and soft, not swollen and ripe like a pregnant woman's are.

The *Sheikha* wanted to help us because she knew my husband was a pious Muslim. She'd sat there waiting for us. We didn't know her and haven't seen her since.

Rasmiyya, Naeema's sister-in-law, continued to antagonize her and scheme against her until Naeema felt completely beaten and came to find us. She said the family locked her up and beat her and deprived her of food. They wanted to get rid of her and take her furniture.

Her father gave her a little money to spend on food if she felt a need to, and neighbors, seeing her plight, invited her to eat with them, saying, "We are like father and mother to you." But she was always too proud to accept. When she complained to her husband, he answered, "They are acting this way under my orders, and if you don't like it, too bad for you. You haven't seen anything yet."

When her father saw how shrunken and thin she had become, he told me to go stay in our own village where I would be closer and keep an eye on her. He had a helper on the river then, a boy of ten whom he paid a pound a month to assist him with rowing and baiting the hooks.

When Naeema was desperate at that time, she could at least reach me. She would come to the village to be near me. I would feed her and comfort her. But when she returned to her husband's village, her in-laws abused her even more. They would say, "You and your mother spend all your time talking and setting your hearts against us. Your mother spoils you and tells you to go against our wishes. She encourages you to be lazy." Naeema would answer them, saying, "Everything you have ever asked of me I've done." But they would not let her be, and she continued to be miserable.

As time passed her clothes became worn and shabby. She needed something to cover her decently. She said to her in-laws, "Aren't you going to get me a new dress?" That is their responsibility. They answered, "No, we don't clothe anyone."

So she came to her father and told him. He bought a couple of pieces of material to be made up into dresses for her. She took them to the seamstress in her husband's village. After she had given her the materials, the family all ganged up on her and beat and abused her and chased her out of the house. The seamstress took their side. Naeema then, terrified, came to us in the village, leaving the material for her dresses behind. We found out that the groom's mother had had it made up into pajamas for him. He wore these, and Naeema went in rags.

She got two more dresses from us but said that she could not go back to her in-laws anymore. "They harm me at every turn, and as long as my husband takes the side of his father and mother, he will never show me any good will." Her father agreed, saying, "You have not experienced a day of happiness in this marriage it's true. You've seen nothing but trouble, my child."

My husband then decided the matter had to be resolved in a court of law. He made a complaint to the local authorities because withholding food from a woman is cause for divorce. He wanted at least to retrieve her furniture.

This is what happened. Hamed and Naeema's father-in-law went before a police officer, and Hamed lodged a formal complaint. The father-in-law denied that they had Naeema's furniture or that they had abused her. The police officer then said to him, "You had better mind what you say!" The man insisted, saying, "My son and his bride plotted together and carried the furniture away in the dead of night without my knowledge."

The officer then said, "But I have before me here the inventory of this girl's furniture and a signature from you as witness and guarantor for its safety. How can it have been taken without your knowledge?" So the man said, "I am a sailor on the Nile, and I don't sleep at home." The officer said, "You mean there is no one at all at home except the girl and her husband?" He said, "No, her mother-in-law is there, but she goes to bed at sunset." So the officer said, "You mean she brought a cart and took her furniture without making a sound? Or did she perhaps carry it on her back?" So the man said, "It's just as I've said."

The officer then told the father-in-law to wait outside. After a while he called him in and said, "Old man, if we could console your daughter-in-law and return her to you, would you care for her properly and do your duty by her?" He said, "Yes," so the officer asked, "And if you care for her well, what is she going to sleep on when she returns to you?" So the man answered, "On her own bed." The officer said, "Where is that bed?" The man answered, "We have it." So the officer said, "You have her furniture?" So he had to confess. The officer took the words from the man's mouth and wrote them down without comment.

In the end he said, "Well, why don't you turn over the furniture to us?" Then the father-in-law began to deny having it all over again. So the officer said, "Step outside. You're under arrest."

He put him in jail for nine days and told Naeema's father, "We want the boy, Naeema's husband, wherever he may be. When you find him, stop him, and turn him over to us." So Hamed agreed.

The groom's village is north of us. One day we received a message through the grapevine telling us, "Your son-in-law has been in his village three days. His people are hiding him, and he leaves tomorrow." So his wife went after him, caught him, and turned him over to the authorities.

Here is how she did it. Misery has its inroads and can sometimes give its victims a lucidity that others who are content do not have. Naeema got up the morning after we received the message concerning her husband, and as we were sitting down to breakfast, she said to her father when he returned from dawn prayers at the mosque, "Father, I saw my husband and my father-in-law in a dream last night. They were riding bicycles one after the other. So I pounced on my husband and collared him, and he cried out, saying, 'Leave me be. We have a death in the family, and I must attend the funeral.' But I said to him, 'Leave you? Never. I have caught you and your father, and I'll never let you go until you return my furniture and my belongings to me.'"

Her father listened to her recounting of the dream and chuckled. I said to her, "What is this business of bicycles in dreams." She answered, "How should I know? But I think I'll go to market today and see what I can see." So her father agreed to let her go. She said, "Father, you must stay put in case I need to send for you." So he agreed.

She got ready then and went to the bus stop just north of us, and as she came close to it, she saw her husband standing on the bus, leaning on the window nearest the driver. So she boarded the bus. She stood there and said nothing to him. The bus conductor came and called for tickets. She bought one to the market village for two piasters and waited.

The bus started up, and the conductor said to her, "Move to the back, my lady." So she answered, "By God, my good man, I have received orders to stand in this place as I have a piece of unfinished business to attend to. Is there any objection to my standing here?" He said, "No, none."

So she came up to her husband and tapped him three times on the shoulder and spoke to him sarcastically. He said, "What do you want?" She answered, "There are orders out that you should get off the bus with me and come to the police station. Do you have any objections?" He said, "Me go down with you after you have put my father in jail? By God, woman, I'll have you running up and down the 'seven roads' before you know what hit you!"

This means that he'll neither acquiesce to her wishes, nor return her things to her, nor let her go. It means he'll give her a hard time. It means he'll confuse her so much that she won't know whether she's coming or going.

He said, "If you want me, then send notice to the army camp where I'm stationed. I'm in the army now." So Naeema cursed him and the army and cried, "Did the army instruct you take the children of others and run them up and down the 'seven roads' and make them desperate?"

They quarreled, and finally she said to the driver, who is from our village and a relative, "To the police station, Ahmad, and stop there!" So he went. She grabbed her husband by the collar and said to him, "You'll go down whatever you say. You'll agree to do as I say whether it takes courtesy or violence to make you do it. Take your choice." He still refused to go with her, so she said to the driver, "Take us right to the police precinct and let us off there, Ahmad. I said I wouldn't let you go, and I won't until you return my belongings to me, you greedy bastard, son of greedy bastards."

As she said this, two plainclothes policemen knowing her case boarded the bus as well as an inspector of government cooperative stores in the area. They arrested her husband and ordered him to hand over his identity card, saying, "So you think you're going to walk this child up and down the 'seven roads' until she's dizzy? Are you going to come with us or not?" So he answered, "I'll come with you, your Honor." So the policeman said, "Where is her furniture?" He answered, "In my father's house." So he said, "Then why does your father deny it?" So the boy said, "What does my father have to do with all of this?" The officer said, "He said you had taken the furniture, and we have a document he signed at the time of the marriage to guarantee its safety and to insure that if disagreement occurred between you and your wife, it would be returned to her."

Naeema's furniture includes a bed, a wardrobe, a pair of wooden couches, a night table, another table, a dresser, many copper utensils, pots and pans, two mattresses, two comforters, two pillows, and all of the bedding and linen for the couches.

This man wanted to get hold of all of this and leave us helpless. How could we ever have enough money to give her all that again? Without it she would never marry again. She had left some gold jewelry which they also wanted to lay their hands on. Although the father stubbornly insisted he had none of these things, the son confessed.

Some good people from the village who had been on the bus with Naeema gave her some money and told her to take it and get a cart and carry home her furniture. She answered that her father was in the village and would help. She telephoned him from a public booth. There is also a telephone at the corner of our street. Her father had gone to pay the electric bill nearby, and so someone brought us the message. The messenger came to our house and said to me, "Tell your husband to come with a donkey cart to take away Naeema's furniture. Your daughter caught her husband, and he is now under arrest."

So her father went and fetched the girl's uncles, that is my brothers, and they went. They found her waiting for them. They brought her home, and the next day took a donkey cart and armed with an order to release the furniture, they went to the boy's village and brought back everything.

The boy's father then got out on bail for E£20, and I don't know what they plan to do to him.

That's what the marriage of girl children entails. I keep saying, "God, you have given her to me as an only child. Must you disfigure her chances for happiness in this manner and leave us without a moment's peace on account of this child?"

We have asked Naeema's husband to divorce her or support her. He will do neither. We have sued him in the court, but he fails to appear on the court dates set. Nothing can be done in his absence. His only answer to our plight is this, "I will neither divorce nor support her. Let her stew in her own juices." His family tried to bring her back. She did go back last spring, but again they treated her badly. She returned to us in the dead of night this last time, beaten and miserable. It's no use.

She has since stayed with us on the river from time to time, but she has to return to the village for fear that her in-laws might break into our house and burn or destroy her furniture. She needs this furniture if she is to marry again, once she is rid of her husband.

What can we do? Can we question the will of God? Her husband still comes around and says to her, "Supposing I shatter your nerves, my girl, and you die of grief? Who can claim your things? They'll be mine. You neither have a brother nor a sister to inherit from you."

Her husband means to confuse her and make her miserable. "Do you have a brother?" he asks her. "You don't. Supposing you were to give birth to a child. Do you think that child would have an uncle? It wouldn't," and in this way he torments her. He sets her mind in turmoil and troubles her thoughts. She becomes ill with too much thinking. She feels alone in the world, and this makes her shrink into herself.

Now she only says, "I'll never marry again. I'll stay alone, fasting and praying. I've seen all I want to of marriage. I want nothing more to do with men."

Her father will let her be. But of course people talk and prod her, especially women, saying, "Your husband will marry a second wife, Naeema." "He doesn't ask after you." "Your husband has left you stranded, Naeema, like a bump on a log." These words hurt and worry her.

Words are without substance, but they work on one's health and well being. She would have done anything to please her in-laws. They had her do work she was not used to. She cut grass and walked in fields she was not familiar with.

She said to us, "You married me to this man. I would have gone with him and begged at his side if he had been a beggar and not put my father to shame by an act of disobedience, but they didn't give me a chance."

So Naeema stays in the village. We are on the river fishing and worrying about her. The way things are in our countryside, if one person is loving, ten are full of hate.

We would like our daughter to be divorced from this man. We would like her to marry someone who will look after her and care for her. We can only do what we can. The rest is in the hands of God, and everything in this world, in the end, is a matter of destiny.

KHUL-KHAAL

was composed in 10-point VIP Goudy Old Style and leaded two points,
by Utica Typesetting Company, Inc.,
with display type in Foundry Legend by J. M. Bundscho, Inc.;
printed by sheet-fed offset on 55-pound acid-free Glatfelter Antique Cream,
Smythe-sewn and bound over boards in Joanna Arrestox B,
also adhesive bound with 10-point Carolina covers,
by Maple-Vail Book Manufacturing Group, Inc.;
and published by

SYRACUSE UNIVERSITY PRESS

SYRACUSE, NEW YORK 13210

HQ 1793 .A87 1982

74439

Atiya, Nayra.

Khul-khaal, five Egyptian
women tell their stories

74439 ✓

CABRINI COLLEGE LIBRARY

KING OF PRUSSIA RD.

RADNOR, PA 19087

DEMCO